Excelling in Sport Psychology

Written for graduate students and early professionals who are conducting applied sport psychology work for the first time, *Excelling in Sport Psychology* is a guide for planning, preparing, and executing this work. Each chapter addresses a critical component of the internship experience, such as selecting a site for an internship, preparing to begin the work, evaluating the completed work, and marketing oneself throughout one's early career. The diverse experiences of the various authors provide a range of viewpoints for trainees to consider and apply to their growth as sport psychology or mental skills professionals. The text is written in a practical manner, with suggestions and questions that will drive this personal and professional growth. Each chapter also includes a personal account from a current student or recent graduate about their experience in that area.

This book will appeal to students in academic sport psychology programs seeking additional support and guidance about the internship process, as well as post-graduates who did not have an internship component to their program. Supervisors will benefit from reading the book as it highlights diverse ways to work with trainees. Drawn from the experience of the applied Sport Psychology Department at John F. Kennedy University, which has helped students set up internships, have successful experiences, and attain jobs for over 25 years, this book can provide a model for training programs approaching the challenges of fieldwork.

Alison Pope-Rhodius received her Ph.D. from Liverpool John Moores University. She is a Professor, the Chair of the Sport Psychology Department, and a Faculty Fellow at John F. Kennedy University. Alison is a certified consultant with the Association for Applied Sport Psychology (CC-AASP) and has guided many trainees and their supervisors during applied work. She is also the host of the *Wee Chats with Brilliant People* podcast.

Sara Robinson received her M.A. in Sport Psychology from John F. Kennedy University in 2006 and has worked as a practitioner in applied sport psychology since then. She has taught Performance Enhancement courses and supervised students at JFKU since 2009.

Sean J. Fitzpatrick received his Ph.D. from West Virginia University in 2012; since that time he has held academic appointments at John F. Kennedy University and Marian University. He has supervised students in a diverse range of internship settings.

Excelling in Sport Psychology

Planning, Preparing, and
Executing Applied Work

Edited by Alison Pope-Rhodius,
Sara Robinson, and Sean J. Fitzpatrick

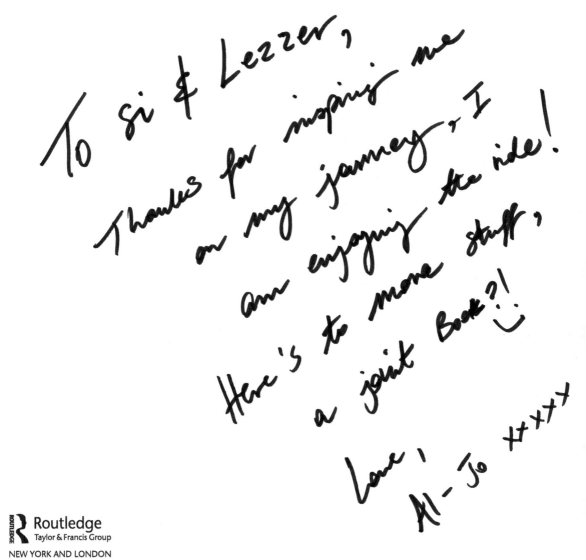

Jan. 2018.

To Si & Lezzer,
Thanks for inspiring me
on my journey, I
am enjoying the ride!
Here's to more stuff,
a joint Book?! :)

love,
Al-Jo xxxx

Routledge
Taylor & Francis Group

NEW YORK AND LONDON

First published 2018
by Routledge
711 Third Avenue, New York, NY 10017

and by Routledge
2 Park Square, Milton Park, Abingdon, Oxon, OX14 4RN

Routledge is an imprint of the Taylor & Francis Group, an informa business

Library of Congress Cataloging-in-Publication Data
Names: Pope-Rhodius, Alison, editor.
Title: Excelling in Sport Psychology: planning, preparing, and executing
applied work / edited by Alison Pope-Rhodius, Sara Robinson, and
Sean J. Fitzpatrick.
Description: New York: Routledge, 2018. | Includes bibliographical
references and index.
Identifiers: LCCN 2017022161 | ISBN 9781138193482 (hardback):
alk. paper) | ISBN 9781138193499 (paperback): alk. paper) |
ISBN 9780203729649 (ebook)
Subjects: LCSH: Sports—Psychological aspects. | Psychology, Applied.
Classification: LCC GV706.4 .E92 2018 | DDC 796.01/9—dc23
LC record available at https://lccn.loc.gov/2017022161

ISBN: 978-1-138-19348-2 (hbk)
ISBN: 978-1-138-19349-9 (pbk)
ISBN: 978-0-203-72964-9 (ebk)

Typeset in Sabon
by Keystroke, Neville Lodge, Tettenhall, Wolverhampton

We dedicate this book to the students and trainees in sport psychology. Without you, there would be no need for a book of this kind. Specifically, thank you to *our* students, interns, and colleagues throughout the years who have helped create a strong training program at John F. Kennedy University (JFKU). This book is also dedicated to our peers in the field, many of whom have contributed chapters to this text.

Contents

Foreword

Gail Solt, M.A., was the Chair of the Sport Psychology Department for 25 years, and it was through her urging, drive, and dedication that the Master's Program was created out of a specialization in Clinical Psychology. Her interest in the field stemmed from her own experiences as a parent of a talented athlete. During her time in the position as Chair of the department, she focused on developing a strong academic program that set a foundation for effective applied work with athletes and performers.

What do you do with a family that has a strong interest in sports and has two young, growing athletes? How do you ensure that you're being the best sport parent you can be for them? It was during the 1980s that I had been thinking about and researching these questions. My children were in every athletic endeavor they could find the time to participate in. I found myself considering a myriad of questions: What should I do to improve my interactions with my young athletes? How could I effectively communicate with them before and after games? Probably even more importantly, how should I behave during their games?

These thoughts and questions stemmed from my interest in sport and from trying to be a good sport parent. I was surprised to learn there was a professional field that focused on many of these same topics, although I had never heard of the field of sport psychology until I discovered John F. Kennedy University! I lived near the campus and learned that they offered a Master's in Clinical Psychology with a specialization in Sport Psychology; I thought this might be the avenue to pursue in order to answer questions on how to be the best support possible for my young athletes. What I found at JFKU was so much more than that; I found what became a 25-year career.

I soon enrolled in the Clinical Psychology Program at JFKU so I could pursue my Sport Psychology Specialization. I was mentored by Dr. Ron Levinson and Dr. Keith McConnell, who were psychologists with a strong knowledge of and interest in sports. Under their leadership I became enmeshed in the world of sport psychology. The teaching model of the Clinical Psychology Program, with its focus on internships, greatly influenced my belief that the best way to develop future professionals is to have them doing hands-on, supervised work.

It became very clear to me that interest in the field of sport psychology was increasing and after I finished my clinical degree I felt JFKU could expand its offerings. With the help of many other faculty members, I designed the Sport Psychology Master's Degree, which started in 1990. Just as with the Clinical Psychology Program, the internships became the heart of the training experience within the curriculum. This was very important to me because I felt we had an obligation to the students (to provide professional training) as well as to their clients (to provide professional services).

Prior to my work at JFKU, as a young adult and mother, I spent many hours volunteering in my community. Based on my experience in volunteer work, I looked for a way that our students could not only become professionals in the sport psychology field, but could also serve those in need within the community. Thus, LEAP (Life Enhancement through Athletic Participation) was established. Students, working through LEAP, completed their first internship with incarcerated youth, a practice that continues to this day. At the site, the interns spend a week teaching sport psychology/mental training skills to the young men. The skills, which are taught with an initial goal to successfully complete a high ropes course, serve as valuable life skills that can be utilized in and out of the facility. The students at JFKU are well trained and well educated. But what makes the students so special is that, through experiences like these, they come to realize that the more they give, the more they receive.

The Sport Psychology Department at JFKU is thriving as well as expanding. I feel honored to have been part of such an outstanding program and I am so proud of the work that our students have done and will do in the future. I believe that this text well help future generations of trainees as they begin their applied experiences.

Gail Solt, M.A.
Founding Chair of the Sport Psychology Department at JFKU

Preface

This book has been in the works for several years. Gail Solt, the founder of the original Master's Program at JFKU, wanted to produce a resource to help guide interns and supervisors based on the wealth of knowledge we have accumulated at JFKU. As editors, we wanted to share various insights about *how* to do effective work in sport psychology as a trainee or early professional. The opportunity came a few years ago and the three of us have been working on it ever since.

When we first started to work on the idea for this book, we noticed that there was a glaring need in the applied sport psychology/mental skills training literature for a resource that guides trainees and supervisors through the process of applied work. As supervisors, classroom instructors (online and on-site), and former trainees ourselves, we know how impactful the first applied experiences are. We have observed many students who have excelled, and many who have struggled (often it is the students in this second group that end up being the most successful professionals because they push boundaries!). During these first experiences, habits are created and trainees begin to develop their framework for what they believe applied sport psychology is and how they want to contribute to the field.

At JFKU we have been guiding students through the process of doing applied sport psychology work through internships for over 25 years. We aim to provide (and help find) a diverse range of experiences; we require that they complete four supervised internships to receive their M.A. Degree. During these internships they work with both an individual and a group supervisor and receive a minimum of three hours of supervision per week. From these experiences, we have developed best practices that we want to share, so that others entering internships can learn from the thousands of students who went before them. Those who have been integral in developing these best practices and processes for being successful in applied work have contributed to this text as authors, and most also continue to supervise our students. These contributors are also either current or past practitioners in the field of applied sport psychology and bring a wealth of knowledge to this book. As editors, our vision was to share the experiences and ideas from numerous sources to help students and early professionals get the most out of their early applied sport psychology work.

How to Use This Book

This book is written for both those in training via academic programs and early professionals looking to do post-degree training. The material is written for a broad audience as we realize that educational and training experiences of individuals within the field of sport psychology are incredibly diverse. This resource is written from a non-clinical perspective given our own training, but does include extra information when clinical issues may be pertinent, including chapters from licensed clinicians in our department.

This book is written in a developmentally linear fashion; we begin with chapters most relevant to the timing prior to starting your internship. Next come chapters that address what happens during your internship, and the final chapters address topics that are important as you wrap up your work and transition from trainee to professional. Some readers may find it beneficial to move chapter to chapter as they progress through their internship. Others might want to pick it up and read a chapter or two that seem especially relevant for their needs and experiences. Though the book is written with trainees primarily in mind, supervisors should also find the book useful as a companion to their supervision sessions and some chapters have specific sections devoted to notes directed toward supervisors.

You'll find introductions of each author at the beginning of each chapter, rather than in one list at the beginning or end of the book. Each biography highlights the author's training, how they're linked to JFKU, what they're doing now, and how to contact them. We did this to help you understand who they are and to give you context to their work. Each chapter also includes a short piece written by a current trainee or recent graduate of JFKU. We hope that you find the experiences of these individuals helpful to further contextualize the chapter's information within the internship setting. All of the chapters end with questions to ponder and tasks to consider. We added these to stimulate reflective practice and encourage you to take the time to complete at least one or two before you move onto the next section or into applying the ideas. Reflective practice is a deliberate and conscious means of learning from one's experiences. It is a focus of the internship experiences at JFKU, and is a habit that we hope you develop and utilize often.

A Few Comments on Terminology

The term *internship* is used throughout the book to refer to applied work in the field of sport psychology and mental skills training, working under another individual who is taking responsibility for that applied work. We realize that different terms may be used dependent on the program, country within which the trainee is working, professional associations' preferred terms, etc.; however, we are using *internship* to refer to all training experiences in applied sport psychology to simplify the information shared about this type of experience. The individual taking responsibility for the trainee's work is referred to as the supervisor. The internship may involve being trained as part of an academic curriculum or via an independent supervisor, and the work the trainee is doing is typically offered for free. We will be using *trainee* and *intern* to denote someone who is working in an academic program and/or someone receiving supervision. Some chapters may also refer to the supervisee, which would be the *trainee* or *intern* in that particular situation. Our emphasis in this book is based on what we teach at JFKU in the Sport Psychology Department and is therefore focused on sport, but doesn't preclude any other performance domains and many of the principles (especially for training in the field) will transfer across into other arenas.

As most of the authors are based in the U.S., we have assumed American-centric processes and procedures in sport psychology and will discuss many of the guidelines given by the Association for Applied Sport Psychology (AASP), though much of the information will be applicable in other countries as well. If you are based elsewhere in the world, please consult your country's laws and guidelines that pertain to the work of someone in sport psychology/mental skills training. If, however, your country does not have rules and regulations in this field, we would still highly recommend you seek training and support in the form of supervision or mentorship from qualified professionals, as described in this book. If you're not already in a training program for applied sport psychology, we suggest you begin; even if you already have a doctorate in psychology, you will still need sport psychology-specific academic coursework and supervised applied experiences. We do not intend for this book to be a substitute for supervision and mentoring, and even though we are immensely proud of what we have produced, it is no substitute for the guidance offered by a quality trained supervisor.

We are glad that you have decided to use this book on your journey to become an effective practitioner in applied sport psychology and mental skills training. Good luck! Be brilliant, and be well!

Alison, Sara, and Sean

Acknowledgments

Thank you to the authors who shared their knowledge and experience throughout this book. Thank you also for putting up with our seemingly endless edits and requests for "just one more . . .". We also want to thank Gail Solt for writing the foreword and, more importantly, for developing the Sport Psychology Department at JFKU. It was her vision and hard work that laid the groundwork for this book. A hearty thank you to the students and recent graduates who added trainee perspectives to each chapter; your experiences provide authentic views of being a trainee that we could not replicate ourselves. To the publishing team at Taylor and Francis, especially Georgette, we are indebted for your hard work and your support throughout the writing process, you truly are the best in the business. We greatly appreciate the time of Stephanie Buck for her help with the book proposal and the huge help of Bryanna Bruger and Anna Shakal for their help with organizing, editing, and indexing. Without their help there would have been a lot of tears! Lastly, our thanks go to Dan, "Danny Hoops," Ourian, Akasia J-Riggins, and the athletes at College Preparatory School in Oakland for assisting with creating our cover image, and to Karen De Jager for the fantastic photo for the cover.

Alison: A particular thank you to my husband, Virgil, who is my "Rhodius rock" and helps me steer through murky waters when times are tough. He still keeps me laughing after more than 28 years together, which will help us when we're old and wizened! Thanks also to my peer support group, the CCSP (California Center for Sport Performance) for helping me be accountable and inspiring me to live large! Finally, a big thank you to my co-editors, and for being such fun team players; I have enjoyed your company greatly along the way and it simply wouldn't have happened without you.

Sara: Thank you to the three gentlemen in my life who made it possible to get this book done. B, E, and N, I love you. To Alison and Sean, I am proud that we made this happen, and glad that this is the team that did it.

Sean: Thank you to Alison for bringing me onto the JFKU team years ago, and to Sara for being my reliable lunch companion and hijinks co-conspirator (you're also the best acronym creator west of the Mississippi!). Lastly, to the Skype-meeting-interrupter-extraordinaire, Carl, for always reminding me that a walk is a great way to clear your mind.

Contributors

Brian Alexander, Athlete Mental Skills Coach, San Diego, CA, USA

Michelle Bartlett, West Texas A&M University, Canyon, TX, USA

Brad Baumgardner, The Mental Component, Olympia, WA, USA

Brian Baxter, Sport Psychology Institute Northwest, Portland, OR, USA

Megan Byrd, John F. Kennedy University, Pleasant Hill, CA, USA

Hillary Cauthen, Texas State University, San Marcos, TX, USA

Carrie Jackson Cheadle, Carrie Cheadle Mental Skills Training, Petaluma, CA, USA

Michelle Cleere, Dr. Michelle Cleere, Oakland, CA, USA

Andre Demian, Momentum Performance Consulting, Marin County, CA, USA

Perri Ford, Bell Lap Mental Performance Coaching, Calgary, Canada

C.A. Gajus-Ramsay, C.A. Ramsay Marriage & Family Therapy, Inc., CA, USA

Tyson Holt, Pittsburgh Pirates, Pittsburgh, PA, USA

Michael Howard, Performance Coach, Corvallis, OR, USA

Elizabeth I.R. Hunter, Mental Skills Consultant, Walnut Creek, CA, USA

Spencer Ingels, West Virginia University, Morgantown, WV, USA

Katie Irwin, Mental Training with Katie Irwin, Union, WA, USA

Meg Kimball-Hodges, Assessment and Peak Performance, Evergreen, CO, USA

Fernando Lopez, John F. Kennedy University, Pleasant Hill, CA, USA

Trey McCalla, ASCEND Excelerate Performance, CA, USA

Noelle Menendez, HigherEchelon, Inc., United States Army Contractor, Joint Base Lewis-McChord, WA, USA

Deborah Munch, Deborah Munch Consulting, Concord, CA, USA

Sean-Kelley Quinn, Moawad Consulting Group, Scottsdale, AZ, USA

Daniery Rosario, Leadership Public Schools Richmond, Oakland, CA, USA

Amber M. Shipherd, Texas A&M University—Kingsville; Next Level Mind Consulting, TX, USA

Rebecca Smith, Complete Performance Coaching, Petaluma, CA, USA

Victoria Tomlinson, John F. Kennedy University, Pleasant Hill, CA, USA

Alexsandra Walton, Peak 5 Consulting, Oakland, CA, USA

Michael-Thomas Wilson, Evolving Concepts, Santa Barbara, CA, USA

Zane Winslade, FlowSport Performance Coaching, Mount Maunganui, New Zealand

Special Thanks to our Trainee Contributors

Dafna Aaronson
Ava Blennerhassett
Tammara Bode
James Branham
Elisa Chapman
Julian Coffman
Richard Iacino
Lindsay Jones
Nicholas Kalustian
Fernando Llamoca
Joy Marquez
Tommy Muir
Martin Rasumoff
Philip Schmitz
Derek Swartout-Mosher
Damon Valentino
Joey Velez

Abbreviations

AASP	Association for Applied Sport Psychology
APA	American Psychological Association
BASES	British Association for Sport and Exercise Sciences
BPS	British Psychological Society
CC-AASP	Certified Consultant through the Association for Applied Sport Psychology
ISSP	International Society of Sport Psychology
JFKU	John F. Kennedy University

1 Pursuing Applied Work

Are You Ready?

Alison Pope-Rhodius, Sara Robinson,
and Sean J. Fitzpatrick

The decision of whether someone is ready to begin doing applied work in sport psychology is a critical step that cannot be overlooked in the process of the training experience. Trainees must be prepared; they need to have taken the necessary coursework, gained the core competencies required, and, most importantly, feel confident that they are ready to take the next step in their development. Beginning this process too early may lead a trainee to doubt their potential, while waiting too long may hinder a trainee's development. Through self-reflection, as well as conversations with supervisors and other trusted individuals, trainees can ensure that they are ready to begin "doing" the work.

This chapter will help readers make this crucial decision about readiness to begin by providing information on when, in an individual's development, an internship should be considered. Additionally, this chapter will aid trainees in their decision-making process by providing several issues and questions to consider, such as how much coursework the student has taken and the timing of the internship in relationship to other training demands.

Background Information on the Authors

The first author of this chapter, **Alison Pope-Rhodius**, is the Chair of the Sport Psychology Department at JFKU. Having done all her formal training in the UK (Ph.D. from Liverpool John Moores University), she was first accredited for applied work with BASES in 1996 and has since become a CC-AASP. She teaches a foundational course at JFKU called Sport Psychology A and the more advanced Sport Psychology B class, and regularly supervises M.A. interns and post-Master's and doctoral trainees. She has worked as a non-clinical practitioner for over two decades, has a small private practice that specializes in elite individual performers, and is the host of the podcast "Wee Chats with Brilliant People." She can be contacted at arhodius@jfku.edu.

The second author, **Sara Robinson**, received her Master's Degree in Sport Psychology from JFKU in 2006. She has taught Performance Enhancement courses in the program and supervised students since 2009. Additionally, for several years she was responsible for setting up internships for the program's LEAP (Life Enhancement through Athletic Participation) Project, which supports underserved youth. In this position, she worked directly with coaches and interns developing and supporting applied internships from beginning to end. She has worked as a practitioner in applied sport psychology for the last ten years. Sara can be contacted at srobinson@jfku.edu.

Sean J. Fitzpatrick was trained at West Virginia University (WVU). At WVU Sean received his Bachelor's, Master's, and Doctorate in Sport and Exercise Psychology as well as an additional Master's in Community Counseling. Sean's work at JFKU focused on research methods, assessment of learning, and supervision of interns working within a wide range of sports. He is currently an Assistant Professor and Department Chair of Exercise and Sport Science at Marian University in Fond du Lac, WI. He has worked with a variety of athletes and exercisers across various sporting domains. Sean can be reached at sjfitzpatrick02@marianuniversity.edu.

First things first, congratulations! The decision to begin an internship in applied sport psychology is exciting for trainees to consider. In our experience, trainees often report that their first applied experience is the most influential in regard to their growth as future professionals. This is not surprising as internships have been identified as a critical component of applied sport psychology training (Owton, Bond, & Tod, 2014; Tammen, 2000; Watson, Zizzi, Etzel, & Lubker, 2004; Wylleman, Harwood, Albe, Reints, & de Caluwé, 2009). Whether you are searching for your own internship or working with your academic program or professional organization to secure a site, it is critical that you begin your internship only when you are ready. Deciding when that moment is can be difficult.

For many trainees, the choice of when to begin an internship is decided for them. When a certain milestone is reached, be it coursework or other indicators, internships can begin. Even if the decision about timing is made for you, spend time reflecting on whether or not you are prepared to begin your internship so that you can enter the experience with confidence. There are a number of factors to consider when tackling the decision to begin an internship, which we will discuss in more detail. Starting an internship before you're ready, or starting an internship too late, can have potentially negative consequences.

Beginning an internship too early, before you are ready, can lead to a loss in confidence, as well as unnecessary stress from facing challenges that you are not yet equipped to handle. Let's imagine an intern in this scenario. Pat has taken a few sport psychology courses, and was also a former athlete. An opportunity to work with a local youth soccer team as a mental skills intern becomes available, which Pat pursues and then secures. During Pat's first presentation with the team, the athletes are not engaged and Pat struggles to find an effective way to deliver the information. Over time this pattern continues, and Pat's lack of group management skills, as well as an inability to synthesize and deliver various sport psychology concepts, leads the coach of the team to ask Pat to present to the team less and less. As Pat's time with the team decreases, so does Pat's confidence. Pat's initial impression of applied work in the field is poor, and Pat believes that she is missing some *it* factor that is needed to be successful as a mental skills coach. Trainees' internship opportunities are where their future professional identities begin to develop (Foltz et al., 2015), and experiences like Pat's can lead to a premature negative judgment regarding one's potential in the field.

There are also potential ethical issues with starting an internship too soon. Without possessing the foundation needed, interns may end up doing more harm than good. A core characteristic of someone who is unprepared is an inability to realize what they do not yet know (Robinson, 1974). This ignorance can lead an intern to not consider the negative consequences of certain actions. Mental skills are taught incorrectly, identifiable emotional triggers with clients are overlooked, and/or fundamental ethical principles such as dual roles are not considered, all of which can have negative consequences for the athlete.

As Pat's case highlights, starting an internship without possessing certain competencies is worrisome. However, on the other end of the spectrum, waiting too long hinders development as well. Delaying internships can prolong the time it takes for a trainee to become a professional as this training experience needs to be completed prior to the beginning of a career in the field. Additionally, the accumulation of other training experiences prior to supervised applied work can falsely cement assumptions about working with athletes. It can be difficult to overcome the angst that may occur when a trainee realizes that prior beliefs based on their training were incorrect. Therefore, trainees who have waited too long for an internship may develop a less flexible approach to their work. Despite these potential concerns with starting internships too late, many trainees may find themselves hesitant to label themselves as ready for an internship.

At the heart of many ethical codes is a commitment to practice only when one possesses the competencies necessary. For potential interns, the calculation of whether or not one is competent can be paralyzing. There are always more classes to take, more observations of professionals to be done, or more journal articles to read. If you wait until you know *everything*, or feel 100% confident, then you will never begin an internship! Most graduate students have a strong desire to be effective in their work, and the thought of making mistakes with athletes can be a hard pill to swallow. It is only natural to be anxious ahead of your first internship (Tod, 2007), but if you have prepared correctly (and with appropriate guidance) you will find few other training experiences that are as impactful as your first. Most students find their internship experiences to be satisfying (Fitzpatrick, Monda, & Butters Wooding, 2016), and ensuring that you are ready for the internship is step number one to getting the most out of this valuable training component.

When to Begin an Internship

What are the elements to have in place before you start your applied work in the field? There is no legal protection around the terms *sport* or *mental skills* in the U.S., thus anyone who has a license to practice psychology could, in theory, also practice *sport* psychology. However, ethically this would not be appropriate and is not something we could recommend. In addition, just taking introductory courses in this area does not qualify you to practice. After all we do not want you to start doing applied work just having read about the importance of being mentally strong or how to relax before you play! Lastly, even someone who has been an athlete and who has experienced the mental demands of sport themselves is still not ready to begin working with athletes without adequate training. Examples of individuals without training in sport psychology who are *not* ready to work with athletes and coaches are:

- Weekend Warriors or recreational athletes/exercisers
- Experienced high-level athletes
- Athletes who may have experienced working with a sport psychologist or mental skills trainer
- Personal trainers and other professionals who have experience working with athletes
- Individuals with education in and training in psychology who do not have specific training in sport psychology

The individuals in each of these groups may very well possess experiences that will aid their eventual applied sport psychology work, but they all still lack the knowledge and skills needed to ethically and skillfully practice in the field. Knowledge of particular sport environments will often help you be a better practitioner, but will not replace learning about the work in academic courses or the guidance you will receive during supervision.

Thus, to *be ready* for starting applied work in sport psychology, what elements do you need to have considered and have in place? You need to consider whether you have the necessary knowledge, skills, beliefs, values, attitudes, and supervised experiences in order to start. Various certifying/accrediting associations, e.g. AASP, have knowledge areas within which you need to have passed specified coursework, gained various supervised experiences, and (eventually) pass a certification exam to practice in the field. At JFKU, we have seven Program Learning Outcomes (PLOs) that, when viewed as a collection, describe the work of a competent sport psychology professional. The PLOs are what are expected of students by the *end* of the Master's Degree and are assessed at different levels at various points during the students' time in the program. While other great training programs exist, we believe ours gives a strong foundation to train individuals for practicing in the field as a mental skills coach. JFKU's Sport Psychology PLOs are as follows:

- Performance Enhancement Skills—The students will be able to describe, explain, synthesize, and apply performance enhancement techniques with individual performers and teams.
- Theory—The students will be able to describe, explain, synthesize, and apply theoretical perspectives from sport psychology and related fields.
- Assessment—Students will be able to describe, explain, synthesize, and apply various assessment tools in a continuous and evolving process to create effective action plans. Students will be able to screen clinical issues.
- Counseling Psychology Skills—The students will be able to identify, describe, and explain how to use counseling psychology skills to develop a working relationship with the client. Students will be able to identify, describe, explain, and apply how the self impacts the client–consultant relationship.
- Multicultural Competence—The students will be able to identify sources of bias within themselves, integrate concepts, and adapt their skills to work with a diverse range of populations.
- Ethics and Professionalism—The students will be able to identify, explain, synthesize, and critically analyze ethical principles in a professional and culturally appropriate manner. Students will be able to utilize decision-making principles and explain choices made relating to ethical situations.
- Evidence-Based Practice—The students will be able summarize and critique research in the field of sport psychology. Students will assess and apply both established and current research findings to their applied work.

These PLOs cover what we believe are the required foundations for working in the field. You may find it helpful to assess yourself on these seven areas and consider how to seek additional training experience in the domains in which you think have deficits. Having a conversation with a faculty member or potential supervisor about the needed skills and abilities within these areas can also help to illuminate areas where growth is needed prior to beginning your internship.

In addition to growing your knowledge, skills, and abilities, your attitude to what lies ahead and how you conduct yourself in applied settings will be crucial in terms of if you are successful in the field. When you have a high task focus (Nicholls, 1984) or, as Dweck (2016) suggested, a growth mindset, you believe that your success comes from effort and that you hold your fate in your own hands. Feeling a sense of autonomy and (hopefully) feeling competent can also enable you to feel more motivated (Ryan & Deci, 2000).

In addition, not believing that you are perfect will also be helpful along this journey. You are going to hear critique and feedback from your professors, supervisors, peers, and clients, so being open to hearing this without being devastated by it can be very helpful, to say the least.

Self-reflection is an important element in all applied work, especially when starting out (it is also integral to the framework of this book). Reflective practice is "an intentional process that enhances self-awareness and understanding through thinking about applicable 'events'" (Rhodius & Huntley, 2014, p. 91; also see Chapter 5 of this book for more information on reflective practice). By doing periodic and consistent systematic reflective exercises, you can learn to realize what your own beliefs, values, and assumptions are around many aspects of the world (not just sport psychology). Reflective practice should begin before you start the work. Then, once you are consulting, you should use a consistent method of reflecting on your own thoughts, feelings, and actions.

Before starting an internship, you will not (by definition) have much (if any) supervised experience in sport psychology under your belt. However, a good training program will have guided you in various activities such as mock consulting experiences, presentations in class, role plays, and shadowing more experienced students/consultants doing applied work, all of which test and develop your knowledge and skills. If you can, try to practice your skills in environments where you will get quality feedback from someone who can guide you (ideally a CC-AASP supervisor or equivalent), as this will help give you a sense of when to begin your first applied internship.

As we discussed at the beginning of the chapter, coming to the decision that you are ready for an internship can be difficult and is one that should be approached deliberately. Work with your peers, faculty, and/or supervisors to gain their input. You may also find it useful to utilize a decision-making model to ensure that you are carefully evaluating your readiness (see Cottone & Claus, 2000, for a review of ethical decision-making models).

Improving Your Readiness

If your training program tells you that you are ready and you have taken the coursework, practiced, researched, and prepared, and all signs are pointing to you being ready, but still *you* don't feel ready—what then?

Firstly, know that this lack of confidence is common. Then, take the time to reflect on the areas you are most comfortable and least comfortable with. Additionally, consider asking others, such as peers or faculty you have worked with about your readiness in the weaker areas. Then, take the time to address those gaps. If there are core competencies that you have not met and do not understand, then more education is likely necessary. For example, if you live in a geographical area where the majority of the population is of a different cultural background and socioeconomic status than you, a diversity/multicultural class would be prudent (it would anyway as training in diversity is essential and now required for some certifications, e.g. AASP, and is an important element of being a competent practitioner, but even more so if this is one of your personal areas of weakness). If you are uncertain of how to choose educationally sound and research-based techniques to help clients, then you would likely want to take a course that addresses research and theory.

When your education has left you feeling uncertain about your skills, as discussed above, take the time to practice more such as role playing with your peers or friends, or practice your presentations and sessions through imagery. Reading can also be a great additional step to bolster your knowledge, although it is a less formal way of keeping up with your education. Continuing education is also important and covered later in this book (Chapter 17). When you feel educationally sound but still uncertain, you may want to consider solutions such as observing other professionals; this is not so that you can copy what they do, but rather to get ideas for how you may want to approach the work and learn vicariously. If you cannot observe a local professional, consider reaching out to an applied practitioner for an informational interview: learn about their work, how they approach securing and retaining clients, and how they first began in the field. If you have developed a relationship with a professional and are unable to see them live and in action, you might want to ask if they can record some of their work for you to see.

For some of the students we have worked with, they lack confidence not only in their sport psychology knowledge and skills (as these are often new concepts) but also in their inter-personal skills. Areas such as speaking confidently in front of others, being comfortable sitting with a client in a one-on-one situation, or reaching out to people they do not know to secure work can all be areas of concern. Areas such as these may not have been addressed directly nor taught within your program. Strong interpersonal skills likely help in this type of profession but these may not be your strengths yet. Examples of interpersonal skills include, but are not limited to:

- Being able to build rapport well
- Helping others feel comfortable quickly
- Ability to sit in silence with someone
- Presenting to large groups
- Empathizing with others
- Ability to be confident without turning others off
- "Reading the room" you are in and being able to adjust

Lubker, Visek, Geer, and Watson (2008) found that a sport psychology practitioner who is friendly, approachable, trustworthy, and can maintain confidentiality is one who can be effective in this line of work.

If the above skills are areas you have apprehensions about, take the time to find ways to work on these skills, such as joining Toastmasters International, an organization that helps individuals become more effective public speakers and offers groups in 135 countries worldwide. Information can be found at www.toastmasters.org. You may also want to consider attending some type of therapeutic or mental skills training sessions as a client to gain a deeper understanding of a client's experience. Or, you can write out a potential script for what you might say when you call an internship site and practice out loud or in front of family and friends.

Some students may feel that they are ready to begin an internship but their training program says that they are not; in this case, schedule a meeting with the decision makers and take a calm approach to learning more about their expectations, what you can do to meet these expectations, and how the program might be able to support you along the way. Find out what specifically you need to show to them in order to be ready and follow up in the manner that they ask you to. If you are unclear or uncertain in any way, ask for more information.

If you or your training program/supervisor have a number of concerns about you beginning your applied experience and these concerns are not easily addressed, it may ultimately be an indication that this work is not for you. Applied sport psychology work is not for everyone; this is okay and it is important to consider if you have what it takes to serve your clients well and be content doing this work. It may be one of the toughest decisions you have to make to determine if this work is for you, but it serves you well to consider this before you fully complete a degree, program, or applied experience. Perhaps your personality will hold you back or does not allow you to connect well with individuals.

Maybe you are an extreme introvert and speaking with others causes severe anxiety. While you may be able to address these areas of your personality or skill set, you may also be better suited for other work. Keep in mind, however, that sometimes you do need to discover if you can do this work by actually going out there and doing it. If, during or after an applied experience, you still feel that this work is not for you, then it is time to look at this further. Supervisors and training programs may also realize that certain students or supervisees are not a strong fit for applied work and may need to have hard discussions with their trainees. For individuals who are passionate about the field, but perhaps not well-suited for applied work, you may want to consider other career options within the field of sport psychology such as research, teaching, and writing.

Conclusion

When you make the decision to begin an internship, and you work to select a site, it is normal to have some doubt, and with time your confidence will grow (Owton et al., 2014; Rønnestad & Skovholt; 2003). Remember that it is not uncommon to have worries, concerns, and a lack of confidence as you begin your work. Keep in mind that you can continue to prepare yourself through further study, practice, and preparation as you get closer to the starting point of your applied experience. Know that you are not alone in these feelings, and that a strong peer support network and supervisor can assist you with working through the feelings and challenges that come with this new, exciting component of your training. The rest of this book will guide you through various aspects to consider and decisions you need to make along your journey toward becoming a trainee in the field and eventually a competent practitioner in sport psychology.

A Trainee's Perspective on Pursuing Applied Work

Elisa Chapman, M.A., M.B.A., student at JFKU 2014–2017

Elisa's goal is to live and work in the North Lake Tahoe/Reno area of California as a Sport and Performance Mentality Coach. Her career pursuits include: establishing a private consulting practice, working on-staff or contracted by a ski and snowboard club, the Reno 1868 United Soccer League, and/or Sierra Nevada College NAIA athletic program. She would also like to be a part-time, adjunct university instructor. Elisa can be contacted at echapman@email.jfku.edu.

I was nervous to start my first solo internship. I had done a group internship with other students first, but we had our supervisor about 20 feet away at all times. Stepping out on my own was exciting, but it was also sobering to think these athletes would be putting their trust in me alone. While the internship provided training for me, I understood that it was real life for the athletes I was providing services to. Therefore, I felt pressure regarding the importance of providing high-quality, professional work.

Additionally, the opportunity I had before me included a few athletes competing at junior world and senior world level competitions. I thought this may be too far of a reach for my first solo applied experience, as I wanted to provide ethical services and operate within my scope of knowledge. Instead of making my own judgment on this, I called the Fieldwork Director (FD) at JFKU to hear his thoughts on the opportunity. He was positive about my readiness for it and advised that I move forward. From his encouragement, I chose to trust my training and proceed with this internship. Making the most of your education prior to starting as a trainee is fundamental to being ready. This way, even if you are nervous, cognitively you know you have done everything in your ability to prepare. If your advisor says you can do it, you can trust in this. However, had the FD told me he thought it was too much to take on at that point, I was ready to shift directions. I wanted to be in a situation where I was set up for success, for both my own sake and the sake of the clients, because this is where everyone can best grow. Therefore, I was willing to take the advice of an experienced professional and implement what the FD thought that looked like for me.

Being ready to accept feedback is essential when you start applied experiences. The fact that I understood I had limitations to my knowledge base actually helped me be more effective in the work. It allowed me to be humble and drove me to prepare to the best of my ability. It also increased my willingness to be vulnerable with my supervisor. Instead of holding back information that might highlight areas of incompetency, I was willing to be forthright and share scenarios where I thought I may have messed up. This proved helpful because at times my individual supervisor would complement me for something that I thought I did wrong. At other times my supervisor provided feedback on how I could fix what had happened, or approach a similar situation differently in the future. Either way, I was able to learn and grow.

In addition to being transparent with my supervisor and preparing to the best of my ability, I also knew I needed to have the room in my life to allow for this internship to happen. I began my internship at the end of fall quarter. I did not take any fall classes, and when I started my internship on the first of December, I was working only part time. This way, I set myself up so the internship was my sole focus. I had seven weeks at my site under my belt before winter quarter classes commenced. This allowed more time to learn about the sports I was working with. I also had time to engage in additional research to increase my knowledge of performance enhancement skills. This way, I was able to apply more evidence-based practice with the athletes. In turn, the athletes increased their buy-in to the process and implementation of the work.

I understand that setting aside time in this way for an internship may be a luxury for some, and others may not find this approach necessary. For me, these conditions allowed the best opportunity to grow as an applied practitioner. Knowing what will create this environment for yourself is an important aspect of being ready for and maximizing an internship experience. In doing so, I provided a strong enough product that each of the three sports I worked with asked if I would be able to return in the future for paid work.

Reflective Questions and Activities for You to Consider Before You Proceed

- What does a competent trainee look like to you?
- Complete a self-evaluation to decide if you're ready. You can use the PLOs identified in this chapter or work with your training program or supervisor/mentor to determine the appropriate components. Consider using a reflective journal (Knowles, Gilbourne, Cropley, & Dugdill, 2014) or a performance profile (see Weston, 2016, for a review) to help you.
- Share your self-evaluation with someone you trust and get their feedback on critical areas. How well does their assessment match up with yours?
- How do you plan to improve the areas where work is needed?

References

Cottone, R. R., & Claus, R. E. (2000). Ethical decision-making models: A review of the literature. *Journal of Counseling and Development, 78*, 275–283.

Dweck, C. S. (2016). *Mindset: The New Psychology of Success*. New York, NY: Ballantine Books.

Fitzpatrick, S. J., Monda, S. J., & Butters Wooding, C. (2016). Great expectations: Career planning and training experience of graduate students in sport and exercise psychology. *Journal of Applied Sport Psychology, 28*, 14–27. doi:10.1080/10413200.2015.1052891

Foltz, B. D., Fisher, A. R., Denton, L. K., Campbell, W. L., Speight, Q. L., Steinfeldt, J., & Latorre, C. (2015). Applied sport psychology supervision experience: A qualitative analysis. *Journal of Applied Sport Psychology, 27*, 449–463. doi:10.1080/10413200.2015.1043162

Knowles, Z., Gilbourne, D., Cropley, B., & Dugdill, L. (Eds.). (2014). *Reflective Practice in the Sport and Exercise Sciences: Contemporary Issues*. New York, NY: Routledge.

Lubker, J., Visek, A., Geer, J., & Watson II, J. C. (2008). Characteristics of an effective sport psychology consultant: Perspectives from athletes and consultants. *Journal of Sport Behavior, 31*, 147–165.

Nicholls, J. (1984). Concepts of ability and achievement motivation. In C. Ames & R. Ames (Eds.), *Research on Motivation in Education: Student Motivation* (pp. 39–73). New York, NY: Academic Press.

Owton, H., Bond, K., & Tod, D. (2014). "It's my dream to work with Olympic athletes": Neophyte sport psychologists' expectations and initial experiences regarding service delivery. *Journal of Applied Sport Psychology, 26*, 241–255. doi:10.1080/10413200.2013.847509

Rhodius, A., & Huntley, E. (2014). Facilitating reflective practice in graduate trainees and early career practitioners. In Z. Knowles, D. Gilbourne, B. Cropley, & L. Dugdill (Eds.), *Reflective Practice in the Sport and Exercise Sciences: Contemporary Issues* (pp. 91–100). New York, NY: Routledge.

Robinson, W. L. (1974). Conscious competency—The mark of a competent instructor. *Personnel Journal, 53*, 538–539.

Rønnestad, M., & Skovholt, T. (2003). The journey of the counsellor and therapist: Research findings and perspectives on professional development. *Journal of Career Development, 30*, 5–44.

Ryan, R. M., & Deci, E. L. (2000). Self-determination theory and the facilitation of intrinsic motivation, social development, and well-being. *American Psychologist, 55*, 68–78.

Tammen, V. V. (2000). First internship experiences—Or, what I did on holiday. In M. B. Andersen (Ed.), *Doing Sport Psychology* (pp. 181–192). Champaign, IL: Human Kinetics.

Tod, D. (2007). The long and winding road: Professional development in sport psychology. *The Sport Psychologist, 81*, 94–108.

Watson II, J. C., Zizzi, S. J., Etzel, E. F., & Lubker, J. R. (2004). Applied sport psychology supervision: A survey of students and professionals. *The Sport Psychologist, 18*, 415–429.

Weston, N. J. V. (2016). The application and impact of performance profiling in sport. In A. Lane (Ed.), *Sport and Exercise Psychology* (2nd ed.). (pp. 250–275). New York, NY: Routledge.

Wylleman, P., Harwood, C. G., Albe, A. M., Reints, A., & de Caluwé, D. (2009). A perspective on education and professional development in applied sport psychology. *Psychology of Sport and Exercise, 10*, 435–446. doi:10.1016/j.psychsport.2009.03.008

2 Securing an Internship Site

Where in the World Are You Going?

Deborah Munch and Andre Demian

Choosing a site for applied work is one of the most important decisions a trainee will make. There are many considerations and steps involved in determining and then contacting appropriate sites. Though some trainees will be placed at a site by their academic program, this chapter will provide relevant information about making initial contact with a site regardless of whether it has been assigned or not. When choosing a site, trainees are encouraged to consider factors such as type of sport (individual vs. team), gender, and age of clients, as well as looking beyond sport for potential internship sites (e.g. other performance domains such as music and business).

Even when an individual has determined an ideal site, he or she must then approach the site, which can be a daunting process. Understanding who to contact at the site and how to "pitch yourself" confidently and professionally are necessary steps. Trainees must be able to communicate about the role that he or she will take, including scope of practice and boundaries of the work. Additionally, knowing what questions to ask of the site contact, what topics to address in these initial conversations, and learning about any necessary business items such as clearances and background checks are critical to begin work.

Background Information on the Authors

Deborah Munch received her Master's Degree in Sport Psychology from JFKU. Post-graduation, she worked as the Life Enhancement through Athletic Participation (LEAP) Coordinator for the Sport Psychology Department. LEAP is a program that runs on donations and grants and focuses on helping underserved youth. In the position, she coordinated and oversaw the first-year internships for students. She worked to develop and maintain relationships with local camps and organizations and fostered connections with schools who work with underserved youth. Deborah's role increased the number of internship sites available through the JFKU Sport Psychology Department. Currently, she teaches an introductory sport psychology course at Dominican University in San Rafael, California in addition to working as a mental skills consultant with athletes. Deborah can be reached at dmunchconsulting@gmail.com.

Andre Demian is a mental skills professional who works with athletes, teams, coaches, and organizations on performance-related mental skills. As a director of fieldwork for JFKU, Andre's responsibilities have included placing interns at sites, working directly with fieldwork sites throughout the world, monitoring student progress, mentoring students, and providing meta-supervision of adjunct faculty supervisors. Andre's educational background includes a Master of Arts Degree in Sport Psychology from JFKU as well as a Master of Arts Degree in Educational

Leadership from The University of San Francisco. Andre's professional experience includes working in a variety of school environments and professional roles, coaching high school lacrosse and basketball, middle school teaching and leadership, and consulting with athletes in golf, tennis, volleyball, and soccer. Andre can be contacted at ademian@jfku.edu and through his website (www.buildmoremo.com).

The prospect of actually *doing* the work in applied sport psychology can be exhilarating, nerve-racking, and complex for you to navigate. As you prepare for an internship, there are initial steps and considerations that will help to create a valuable internship experience. The information covered in this chapter is derived from the authors' experiences working within the Sport Psychology Department at JFKU. Each author experienced fieldwork as a student, and then as a professional in the fieldwork program. JFKU has created a structure to help trainees identify, negotiate, and secure placement with a site which may include but is not limited to a team, club, school, and non-sport setting. The overall goal of the Sport Psychology Department is to help develop and support effective sport psychology professionals. Students are given substantial support during the internship process to identify, communicate with, and then secure internship placement. Our hope is that by presenting our collective experience in the form of guidelines and useful tips in this chapter, trainees seeking to secure an internship or applied experience in the field of sport psychology will be supported in their efforts.

Regardless of whether an initial internship site has been chosen for you or if you will be largely responsible for working to secure an internship, the information provided is intended to serve as a roadmap to identify, contact, and secure your internship. As Palmer (2009) suggests, most successful endeavors are guided by a deliberate process that includes a period that he refers to as "the work before the work" ("The Woodcarver", Palmer, 2009, CD 2, track 3). This chapter will help guide you in the work that must be done before you can begin the work of your internship.

What You Need to Do Prior to Contacting a Site

Prior to approaching a site, you are encouraged to spend time thinking about the type of sport or performance setting(s) you would like to work in. Having a clear vision about a specific site, population, or performance setting can direct your focus and effort in securing an internship.

Who Do You Want to Work With?

You may have a clear sense of the work you aspire to do both in an internship and in a professional setting, or you may have yet to narrow in on your ideal population. Regardless of how clear you are in your aspirations, as you begin to envision your internship experience, try to define the end goals of both your internship and your education. Considering where you would like to be long-term can serve as a directional tool in identifying an internship site. Answer the following questions to help create this direction:

- What do you want to do with your degree?
- What population or demographic do you eventually want to work with?
- If you have already begun your professional career, who do you hope to be working with several years from now?

Knowing what you want to get out of your educational experience or within your career will help you more clearly decide on what population or demographic you want to work with now. For example, you may be interested in using mental skills training to help injured athletes on their road to recovery and return to play. If this is the case, you would likely want to seek out sites that provide access to athletes who are in the injury recovery process, such as physical therapy centers or athletic departments with rehabilitation programs.

Having a specific population you aspire to work with upon graduating, or in your early career, can help direct your efforts to secure an internship; however, it is not a requirement. In fact, many trainees do not have clarity on their professional plans or goals, and only through the process of completing internships do they find the setting or site that inspires them. You are encouraged to consider the numerous populations who may be served by a mental skills training professional, as you might be surprised by how enjoyable the work is in a setting that you were not as familiar with or did not first consider. Additionally, not all populations are aware of the potential value of mental skills training, so you may be connecting with sites who do not have experience with someone in the field. Don't shy away from these opportunities, and be aware that sites vary widely; openness to and support for working with you will also vary.

If you are uncertain about the type of population you would like to work with or are an early professional, consider a site with access to demographically diverse populations. This can provide unique opportunities for professional growth and skill development. For example, you may want to seek out a site that allows you to work with different age groups to see how you enjoy working with younger and older populations. A YMCA (Young Men's Christian Association) or club tennis program is an example of an internship site that may give you access to both youth and adult programs. In choosing a site that allows for work with a variety of individuals, you may leave the experience having more clarity on who you would like to work with.

As the field of sport psychology expands, and performance psychology becomes a viable field for mental skills consultants, you have the opportunity to work in non-sport-related areas as well such as music, theater, and business. Many professionals in these areas may have never considered how sport psychology can assist them. When you reach out to a non-sport location, be ready to educate the main contact at the site and be prepared to provide examples of how sport psychology has benefited clients in that setting in the past, as well as what your work would look like.

Who Are You Best Suited to Work With?

An additional step in working to determine internship sites to pursue is to examine your individual strengths. First, consider your own educational experience. Do you have any degrees or certificates that demonstrate knowledge and expertise in a particular sport-related discipline? If you are in the earlier stages of your sport psychology or academic program, perhaps working with youth is a suitable starting point, rather than working with elite athletes. Ideally, you will have some mentorship in determining your strengths and weaknesses as they relate to choosing appropriate sites and clientele. Educational programs, supervisors, or mentors can assist you to be clear on the applicable skills you offer as an unpaid trainee.

If the internship site you are considering is a sport where you have prior playing or coaching experience, you will want to think about how your background may influence your consulting. There may be potential advantages to working with a sport you are familiar with as you will understand the communication norms and rules, as well as the culture of the sport and team dynamics. However, despite some of these advantages, sometimes a background in the sport leads to offering coaching tips and strategies or making assumptions about the client's experiences. It is vital to understand your own tendencies and biases going into an internship when you have experience with that sport. If you do secure an internship within a sport you played or are very familiar with, prior to beginning, explore ways to either leverage the advantages or recognize potential biases. As a regular habit of professional practice, it is valuable to reflect on the experiences you have had as an athlete, coach, or spectator to examine how your past experiences may influence your consulting. Reflection and awareness of these topics are good practice regardless of if you are working with a sport you have experience with or not (for more on how to best utilize reflective practice, see Chapter 5). Discussions of past experiences and potential impact should take place with one's supervisor prior to beginning as well as throughout the internship.

You Have Your List of Potential Sites. Now What?

Once you have identified potential populations and sites you want to work with, as well as examined personal strengths and challenges related to working with these potential sites, there are a few more considerations to make before contacting those sites. Below is a list of site qualities to evaluate when considering your list. Each of these factors can have a profound impact on your experience and your effective development as an intern and a professional. You are encouraged to consider each potential site regarding this list to determine which sites would allow you a rich experience, and therefore which you want to contact and in what order. Keep in mind that these are points to consider (along with support from a training program or mentor) in determining how you prioritize these factors into your own needs for growth and development. You will likely need to contact more than one site to secure a final internship, as we will discuss coming up, and these considerations can help you prioritize your initial list of sites. Keep in mind that you will not have all the answers about these topics prior to talking to the coach or contact; these are ideas to consider yourself and to potentially discuss with someone at the site.

Team Size

Some teams, such as football, track and field, or swimming have large rosters, making it less of a challenge to find clients to work with. Large teams provide a variety of formats to do work with clients including small group sessions, large group workshops, and individual one-on-one consultations. In larger team settings, once you explain your role and what services you may provide, athletes can then contact you directly to set up meetings. You may find that when an athlete makes contact with you directly, s/he may be more motivated to attend sessions and find value in the work of the mental skills field.

Other types of teams, such as gymnastics or tennis, may have smaller rosters, which give you fewer opportunities to work directly with clients through individual consultation sessions. This smaller team size may make it more of a challenge to obtain your needed number of contact hours. Obtaining your required hours with a small team is certainly not impossible as we have worked with many interns who have had very successful experiences with smaller teams. However, working with a smaller team is a point you need to be aware of and consider, especially if you may not be as comfortable pursing clients and initiating contact for meetings. In smaller teams, you may be able to work with all the athletes, especially if the coach requires that all athletes work with you. The coach's *buy-in* to the mental skills trainings will impact your work, so keep this in mind as you have discussions with potential sites. The positive side of an arrangement where meetings with you are required is that you will get to work consistently with all members of the team. Those who may not have taken advantage of the opportunity to work with you if it was voluntary may eventually open up to the idea of sport psychology and find benefit through the work when it is required. On the negative side, some athletes can see the consulting sessions as just one more thing they have to do and may not be completely invested in the sessions or intentionally avoid scheduled meetings even if they are *required* to attend.

If you do decide to work with a small team or client base, and your program allows you some flexibility in how you reach your contact hours, consider the following tips to increase your contact time with clients:

- Can you work with another level or gender of the sport team simultaneously? For example, adding a junior varsity or frosh/sophomore's team to the varsity team you are working with.
- Is it possible to do workshops for parents of the athletes?
- Can you work with the coaches? Be sure to consider the ethical implications of this relationship. For example, if you are working with both coaches and athletes, how might you communicate information received from athletes to coaches or from coaches about athletes?
- In addition to one-on-one sessions, can you do small group sessions (e.g. 2–4 athletes together, or work with the captains)?
- Can you conduct any sessions using an electronic form of communication when the athletes travel (e.g. Skype or Google Hangouts)? Be sure to consider how you will maintain confidentiality when conducting the sessions, and check for any state or country guidelines regarding remote consultation.

Site Proximity to Where You Live and Work

An internship site that is near your home, or where you spend the majority of your time, should be prioritized. This is because if you choose a location close to you, you do not have to spend a lot of time or money to travel to practices, sessions, or home competitions. This convenience will allow you easier access to the team and likely help you avoid burnout from traveling back and forth often. Remember that you will likely be spending several days a week at the site. We have heard from numerous trainees that they prefer sites that are conveniently located and don't require extensive travel. However, with an internship that is close in proximity to your residence, keep in mind that you have a higher chance of running into athletes/clients outside of your internship when you are *off the clock*. You will want to plan ahead how you will (or won't) address the clients in a public setting.

If the site is far from your residence or where you spend most of your time, you will want to assess the cost of travel and time on your schedule and budget. Time spent traveling to and from your internship site is time spent away from school, studies, family, rest, and self-care. Even if a site requires more travel, you might still want to pursue it; we have had students complete very rewarding internships that required commuting on a regular basis. This may be the case if you want to work with an upper-division collegiate team or if you live in a small town or area that doesn't have many sport teams.

Timing and Length of Internship

Some sites will be very flexible with when you begin your internship. For example, a fitness club is open year-round and typically is void of competitive seasons so you can probably start at any time of the year. An internship in a business setting may also fall under this flexible framework. Other internship opportunities have teams that have very specific timing for their training and competitive season, and this timing will need to be considered as you pursue a site. For example, you will need to connect with a site well before the start of their season in order to complete the steps needed to secure the site and prepare. You will also want to examine how the sport season fits into your own *seasons* of life in terms of school, family commitments, and even vacation plans to see if there are any major conflicts. If there are some unavoidable schedule conflicts, a proactive approach of talking with the coach or leader about the dates and alternative options at the onset of your internship is always best practice. Additionally, you will want to run these absences by your academic program to make sure they also approve of the time off.

The length of the internship is also a point to consider. Ideally, you are with the team from just prior to the start of their pre-season through the time they finish the season. Think about your required academic obligations as well as your own personal goals regarding how long you will work with the team. If the sport team has a lengthy season, e.g. over six months, how will this impact your academic course load and projected graduation date? Stratta (2004) notes that, in regard to the length of an internship, some students declined internships of a year or longer because they were too lengthy and would delay completion of goals such as graduating by a certain date. While this may be the choice you make, to decline a lengthy internship, also consider the benefit of being involved with a team for an extended period and how that may positively benefit you. Some students choose to extend their time in school in order to finish the season with a particular team, ultimately delaying their graduation date. Regardless of what you decide, be very clear on the timing and length of the season before you commit to an internship.

Demographic and Cultural Composition

Depending on how many internships you will do, consider the different ways that you can diversify your experience. As you map out your internship experiences, think about how you can add diversity into your site options. Try to create a varied and rich experience regardless of if you have one internship experience or many. For example, if you have multiple internships, you can work with a variety of sports; basketball or volleyball will differ from individual sports like tennis or swimming. Gender is another consideration, as you can work with a male population, female population, transgender, or co-ed population. Even age is a factor to consider. Youth sport has different challenges because these athletes present different physical, social, and emotional characteristics as compared to high school, collegiate, or adult athletes. Each of these types of populations will provide you with a unique experience. If you only have one experience as a trainee, look for a site where there is a great deal of diversity, for example a high school team where you can work with the freshmen and the seniors, or a tennis club where you can work with youth and adults as well as recreational players and those who are more competitive.

If the potential site involves youth (children under 18 years of age), you will need to check with the head of the program and the site to ensure any additional requirements are fulfilled. Some youth sites may require a consent form signed by both the youth and their parent/guardian, and often a background check including fingerprinting and a tuberculosis (TB) test are also required to begin work.

Level of Coaches' Buy-In

There are significant advantages to interning at a site where the coach/manager/leader supports the work you do. Ideally, the coach refers athletes to see you and reinforces techniques taught to the team. For example, if you lead a goal-setting workshop with the team, the coach has the ability to refer to goals at various times during practices and competitions. This helps to reinforce the lessons and direct attention to how to accomplish them. A coach or leader who has *bought in* to sport psychology sees value in the work you do. If, in the planning stages of the internship, your main site contact and/or coach does not seem supportive of you or your work, you will likely want to consider a different site as you may well run into challenges within this setting.

Time You Are Allowed with the Team

While you may be very available to work with your team, you might find that they have limitations on how much time they can spend with you. For example, the National Collegiate Athletic Association (NCAA) in the U.S. requires collegiate teams to adhere to certain rules and regulations. Included in these rules is that coaches are allowed to see their team, or have their athletes involved in athletic functions, up to a set number of hours each week. If the athletes spend more than the allotted hours, this would result in an NCAA violation. If you are planning on working with a collegiate team or one that has a governing body, it is strongly recommended to talk with the coach to gain awareness of current rules and regulations regarding practice hours. With awareness of these regulations, you will want to determine if and how this governs your work with an individual athlete and/or the team. Even if there are not governing body rules, your coach or athletic program may have program-specific guidelines for how much time the team spends in sport-related activities. Be clear on this before you begin your work. You might want to talk to other practitioners in our field who work with NCAA teams and find out how they successfully work within these regulations.

Location(s) Available to Conduct Individual and Team Meetings

As you are in the planning stages with a site, you should discuss meeting locations that are available to you. You should determine if the site provides adequate space for individual and/or team meetings. Team meetings are often fairly flexible in terms of location; for example, you could meet in the gym, a classroom, or even out on the field, but be sure the space provides adequate room for the whole team. You may consider both indoor and outdoor options to handle weather changes. Will you be able to meet with individuals at the site or need to arrange for an off-site meeting location? Think about the privacy of the meeting location as well as convenience for the athlete. Many high school students do not have their driver's license and therefore an on-site location would be preferable. Although finding an ideal meeting space is not always possible, you must put in the effort to consider suitable locations. If there is not an appropriate meeting space to be found, consider how you can meet with clients at an alternative site, such as a coffee shop, and if this is a feasible plan for both you and the client.

Opportunities for Observation of Athletes in the Performance Setting

Observation of your athletes in their performance setting is a key element of any internship. This time allows you to understand individual and team dynamics and norms as well as develop rapport with the players and coaches. Being present at the team's practices and competitions shows that you are committed and available, and helps to further build the relationship with your clients. Ideally, you would be at as many practices and competitions as possible and you will want to find a site that allows for ample observation time at both.

Check with your school or certification program to see what observation hours are required. Make sure that your personal schedule allows you to observe during the times the team is together, as it may be difficult as a trainee to juggle work, a job, and a full-time internship. For example, if the swim team practices at 7 a.m. and you are at work or in school in the morning, you will not be able to attend many practice sessions. Attending both home and away competitions is also beneficial to your work and your relationship with the athletes. It is in these observation moments that you may also find opportunity for check-ins, rapport-building, and time for brief consultations. In non-traditional sport psychology internship settings, such as a business environment, ask about opportunities to observe business presentations, conference calls, etc.

The initial meeting in the planning stage is an appropriate time to talk with the coach or team manager about the importance of observation so that they can support these different layers of the internship. If you determine you cannot observe the majority of practices and competitions, you should look for an internship site that better fits your schedule so that you can benefit from observation experiences.

Team Travel

Teams are constantly on the move and some teams have intense travel schedules that take them to far away venues. Before you commit to a site, be clear on how often the team travels as well as how often you will be able to travel to away games. Even if you are willing to travel, there are additional considerations such as: Is the coach okay with you accompanying the team? Will the team pay for you to travel with them? Will you be able to travel with them or do you need to go on your own? Consider the financial expenses of the internship and if you can incur these additional costs. You will also want to consider your own schedule with school, work, and general rest time to determine how travel with the team may or may not fit in.

The above points should be considered in order to prioritize potential sites or determine where you would like to focus your efforts in making contact with sites.

Tips on Contacting a Site

Once you have created and prioritized your list of sites using the above ideas, you are ready to begin making contact with the coach, team manager, or other program gatekeeper. If you have personal connections to those sites, consider gathering contact information and making contact through personal networking. A friend or professional contact that you have worked with in the past can provide ease of entry to possible sites.

If you do not know someone at the site, and nor does anyone in your network, you will need to identify and contact a site leader. For example, if you have identified a sport team at a local high school, contact the coach of the team as well as the Athletic Director. Obtaining a coach's approval of your internship is often the first step. Typically, an approval from the appropriate school officials (e.g. Athletic Director, Principal, etc.) or team manager will need to be obtained as well but you will likely want to start with the coach.

In this initial contact, explain to the site contact that you are seeking an internship as part of your academic program or early professional experience. Share the time frame you're looking at, or the minimum time requirement of your academic program, and that you would be grateful for an opportunity to work with their team or organization during this time. Providing the site contact a clear picture of the types of services you intend to provide, as well as giving a sense of how you would be of value to the community, will likely help secure an internship placement. Information regarding services can be shared over the phone or via email if you are having trouble getting in touch with the individual in person. When calling your identified site contact, it can be helpful to write out a script of what you want to say and the important topics you want to cover. If you are able to offer your internship as a free service, be sure to mention this early in your conversation as it is a great selling point. Practice your pitch out loud so that you feel comfortable with your talking points. The phone may help you set up a face-to-face meeting with the coach to talk in more detail about the parameters of the internship and answer any questions for both you and the coach.

When initiating an introduction with a coach, manager, or leader at the internship site via an introductory email, include: relevant qualifications to work in the field of sport psychology (degree completions or degrees in process), background information about the internship process and requirements (e.g. how much time you will ideally spend with the team), and your contact information. The objective of this initial email is to pique the interest of the coach or team manager so that they follow up and contact you for more information. Additionally, it is a good idea to plan a follow-up phone call to confirm they received your email, answer questions, and aim to set up a face-to-face meeting. Be sure to read as much as you can on the organization or team so that you have an understanding of their mission and how they work. A team or organization values trainees who have the appropriate skills to perform the necessary tasks and have an understanding of that organization (Stier, 2002).

If the coach or contact seems uncertain or hesitant, you may not want to give up just yet. As a student at JFKU, I (Deborah) knew I wanted to intern with distance runners. I pursued a local, small, private college that had a cross-country team. In the initial cold call to pitch my services to the coach, I could sense he was unsure of how this would fit into the athletes' busy schedules. He was concerned about the time commitments of his athletes and the impact the additional time for mental skills meetings might have on their school and athletic experience. Rather than give up, I proposed the idea of presenting my services to the team, along with potential benefits of working with me, in order to determine their level of interest. The coach ultimately presented the idea to the team and learned they were open to working with me. I went on to have a very fulfilling internship experience. This story helps to illustrate that you may not want to take initial hesitation as a final answer that an internship won't work out (the same may be true of securing new clients once you are qualified).

Keep in mind you will likely want to make initial contact with multiple sites. Reaching out to pursue various options is a vital first step in the process of securing an internship. Some sites will not respond to you, or in the follow-up conversations you may learn that the site is not an ideal fit or will not meet your internship needs. A common mistake of new trainees is to contact only one school or site they want to work with and then ending up having trouble meeting program or training deadlines if the site does not work out. Ultimately, if a site ends up backing out at the last minute or becomes unresponsive beyond the initial contact, you already have other options.

Following Up with the Site Contact

Chances are, you won't make contact with someone at the site on the first attempt, so you will likely need to follow up. Understand that athletic personnel are busy with many responsibilities and may not prioritize your internship needs, especially if they are unclear about how you can assist the team. Be sure to account for delays in response time in your own timeline of a placement. You may need to be persistent in following up with them. Although difficulty in communication can be extremely frustrating, especially when it impacts your potential program deadlines, you must be able to remain professional when communicating with a coach. Respectful persistence and follow through is often appreciated and may lead to an internship placement.

If you have reached out to the coach through multiple channels on numerous occasions, you may want to rethink working at this site. As we have noted, the coach's buy-in to the program will have a big impact on the success of your experience. Difficulty reaching the coach or getting the coach to respond to phone calls or emails may be a red flag for the future working relationship. Work with your program supervisors to help you discern the difference when weighing the option to persist and pursue or to abandon and move on.

The Initial Meeting with a Prospective Site

An in-person meeting allows the coach or team manager to meet you, learn about the work you do, and receive answers to questions s/he may have. In addition, a face-to-face meeting allows you to meet the coach or team manager and learn their style of leadership, gauge their organizational skills, and determine if this is a person and team you would like to work with. The initial meeting is an opportunity to explain the role and value that you will offer to clients and the site.

Topics to cover in your initial meeting with the coach or team manager include what falls within and outside of your scope of practice, confidentiality and when you will breach it, and any questions the coach may have. Be sure to accurately describe the services you will be performing to assure the coach you are not providing any coaching on physical skills or drills, or strategic coaching tips. The initial meeting is also a good time to learn about the team's schedule and season dates if you could not find that information online. If your graduate school or program has a contract that sites need to sign, you may want to bring this to the initial meeting as well.

Sport psychology is a growing field, however, there are still many coaches who have misconceptions about what a sport psychology trainee can and will be able to do, and what your work will actually look like. Clients often confuse clinical psychology with the sport psychology specialty (Cremades & Tashman, 2014), so you may encounter some coaches who think you are able to deal with clinical issues such as depression, anxiety disorders, or eating disorders. The initial meeting is an optimal time to address what is in and out of your scope of practice. Expect that you may find yourself in multiple situations both prior to and during your internships where you will need to give definition to the scope and nature of your consulting role with coaches, clients, and even parents.

Any initial conversations with the coach should outline the working relationship with the athletes. For example, let the coach know that all sessions are confidential, with the exception of a breach of confidentiality should concerns about harm to self or harm to others be present. If there are client issues that manifest and are determined to be beyond your scope of practice, you need to be prepared to provide a referral to an appropriate resource. Often coaches struggle with the nature of what constitutes athlete rights and confidentiality protections. Educating the coach about the value of allowing an athlete to feel safe within the consulting relationship and to more deeply explore the athlete's experiences should provide a basic understanding of the purpose of confidentiality. Explain to the coach that the athlete can talk about the content of the sessions if they wish, but you, the trainee, will maintain confidentiality. You should also share your informed consent agreement with the coach, especially if the clients are under 18 and parents/guardians will be signing. If you will be using audio or video recording for sessions, you will need to explain why the sessions will be recorded, who will be listening to them, and how you will keep the recordings safe and confidential. An additional point about confidentiality is that you need to be aware of and abide by your program's and state/country's confidentiality standards. Also, keep in mind that some sites (such as schools) may have specific protocols and procedures about what confidentiality means as it relates to making referrals, so you will want to discuss the school's expectations regarding counseling and referrals during initial meetings.

The initial meeting is also a good time to talk about your title, or what you will be calling yourself during the internship. Examples of titles suitable for trainees at the internship level may include mental skills intern or mental skills trainee. It is important to include either intern or trainee in your title so that everyone knows you are not yet a professional. The term psychologist and psychology are protected terms in the U.S. and are often not allowed in titles without proper credentials and licenses. If you wanted to use a title such as sport psychology intern, be sure to check with your state or country's guidelines to be clear on proper usage. Even after having this conversation about what your title will be, you will more than likely be called a sport psychologist by a coach, athlete, or other member of the team at some point. When this happens, be prepared to politely correct the person and use it as an opportunity to educate them about what you do and how the sport psychology field is structured.

You will also want to be clear on administrative personnel who may have jurisdiction over the approval process. For example, an enthusiastic high school coach who says "yes!" to you joining his/her team may be only one of several people in the approval process. Inquiring what additional steps may exist to obtain final approval at the site can often be overlooked. Keep in mind that the coach may not know all of the steps that will have to happen to fully approve you for the site. If you miss certain steps, such as visiting the Athletic Director and/or the Principal of the school for approval, this may delay your start with a team. Additionally, many sites have paperwork and processes similar to what employees go through in the hiring process and you may be required to work with Human Resource personnel for additional steps and approvals. Don't lose hope if you have to go through multiple steps for approval; start early so that you have plenty of time for whatever is needed to be ready to start at the site if you decide to move forward.

Next Steps After You Meet with a Coach or Site

After your initial meeting, review the pros and cons of the site. If it feels like it will be a good fit for both you and the team, then it is time to move forward with any paperwork from your training program (e.g. a contract) or specific site requirements (e.g. liability release forms, background checks, etc.). If the site does not have any official paperwork, or you are not a part of an academic program, you may consider working with your supervisor or mentor to create a contract for the site or team. This contract can help to ensure everyone is aware of and understands the type of work that will be conducted, as well as the time frame and each party's responsibilities. From there, you can continue to move forward with any paperwork and next steps required by your program, supervisor or site, and prepare to start your internship (see Chapter 7 of this book for more information on how to prepare). If you have been in contact with other sites, be sure to send a professional follow up thanking them for their time and informing them that you have secured a location for your applied experience.

If you do not feel that the site will be a good match, you can revisit the list of potential sites you have created, choose another site to contact, and follow the steps noted above. Remember how much time and investment is involved in the actual internship experience, so don't rush into a placement without thinking it through or taking the proper steps for approval. Additionally, even when you have been diligent about locating a site that meets your educational needs and is with clients who will benefit from your services, there are occasionally unanticipated circumstances that can cause an internship to fall through. Sometimes plans change or teams back out at the last minute. For example, an internship can fall through at the last minute when the coach gives you approval, but the Principal does not accept the parameters of work and will not authorize you to work at the school. Or, there may be a coaching change before the start of the season and the new coach decides they do not have the necessary time to allocate to mental skills training. This is where the list of potential internship sites will prove useful; reach out to another site to begin the initial planning process. If you are in an educational program, be sure to stay in communication with your supervisor and/or the person who oversees fieldwork regarding any issues or delays with approvals, or if it is looking like your site may back out.

While there are many steps you'll need to take to secure a placement for your applied sport psychology experience as a trainee, these steps also set a strong foundation for a professional job search, which will be covered in more detail in Chapter 14. One final note is to consider how you can organize yourself during this process and keep track of details such as who you have contacted, when you need to follow up, and what additional information or steps might you need to take. Creating organizational and professional habits as a trainee will likely help you when you step into the professional world.

Lastly, trainees must gain familiarity with the program and/or supervisor's expectations regarding the work that you do. Being clear about what you will be responsible for in terms of documentation, hourly requirements, and communication and relationship parameters with a supervisor are foundational to an internship. The program is largely responsible for educating a trainee about these pre-placement expectations and supervision will be discussed in more detail in Chapter 6. Academic programs and supervisors are encouraged to hold orientations and provide materials such an internship handbook where trainees can review and reference the expectations and requirements.

Conclusion

As there is much planning and preparation that goes into securing an internship placement, you are encouraged to start thinking about this critical piece of your training sooner rather than later. If you are in an academic program, check in with your fieldwork director (or similar person) to find out their recommendation for when to begin the planning based on your academics and when you will have completed the appropriate courses. If you are working to secure an internship on your own, then now is a good time to start reflecting on the sites you may want to contact. Remember that securing an internship is a process, and one that prepares you for the nature of the work of this profession, so you are encouraged to approach the task in a professional, organized, and positive manner.

A Trainee's Perspective on Securing an Internship Site

Fernando Llamoca, M.A., M.B.A., student at JFKU 2013–2015

Fernando's goal is to use his sport psychology knowledge with business organizations to help with the training and development of employees. He would also like to have his own private sport psychology practice and to work with runners. He is currently employed as a Master Resilience Trainer–Performance Expert (MRT–PE) through the Armed Forces Services Corporation (AFSC). In the position, he assists soldiers and their families to increase mental strength and readiness. Fernando can be reached at fllamoca@email. jfku.edu.

When researching graduate programs, I paid attention to the number of internships required within each and the different types of applied experiences offered by each program I considered. The variety and quantity of required internships at JFKU was one of the main reasons I decided to pursue my degree there. After a year of coursework, my first two internships were provided through the program; I could essentially sign up for the opportunities available to me that the program secured. For the third and fourth internships, to gain experience in finding work, I chose to pursue sites that the school did not have existing relationships with.

The process of finding a site did not start just a few weeks before the internship began; it started well before that (sometimes months before) as the process involved networking, outreach, and reconnecting with old contacts. All of this needed to happen long before the expected start date to determine, approach, and then confirm an appropriate site. Going from being given a site to having to set up my own was scary task at first. Fortunately, my peers were going through this process as well and we could provide each other with support and advice on how to go about it.

Through guidance from the program, I learned a process for securing an internship site. I first began with introspection to determine what sports I would like to work with. It helped to create a list of sports that interested me and then ask myself why I wanted to work with these athletes. I needed to consider how this experience would help my growth as a student who wanted to become a professional. The main sport I wanted to work in was soccer, wrestling coming in second, and cross country third. Once I had my top three, I further researched what teams were around my area, what levels they competed at, and the seasons each played in. Once those teams and sports were identified I would locate the appropriate contact person at the site.

During this time, I also worked on my email *sales pitch*: who I am, how my services could help the team, and what they could gain from this free service. I looked to professors and peers for feedback; they suggested points that worked for them, helped me clarify my thoughts, and supported me to create the final product.

I then emailed the coaches and Athletic Directors of the teams I wanted to work with. I got a variety of responses: some expressed interest as to what I could provide their team, which was exciting; others would say no thank you, which felt harsh at first; and others would not even respond, which was upsetting. I learned the importance of following up with sites and I also realized it's important to become comfortable with rejection and not take it personally. Fortunately, through the program we are taught skills that help with resilience and how to cope when such situations arise. Our mental skills stretch beyond the classroom and sport to help us work through our own life's obstacles to become the best interns, consultants, and people we can be. The process of securing an internship certainly helped prepare me for seeking out sites for employment after I received my degree.

Reflective Questions and Activities for You to Consider Before You Proceed

- What type of sites come to mind that would be a good fit for you based on your education, experience, and career goals?
- What specific timeframe factors will you need to consider to prepare, locate, and secure a potential placement?
- What are three experiences or outcomes that you hope to gain through your training placement?
- How might you be challenged in the process of finding, contacting, and securing a placement? How will you prepare to overcome these challenges?

References

Cremades, J. G., & Tashman, L. S. (2014). *Becoming a sport, exercise, and performance psychology professional: A global perspective.* New York: Psychology Press.

Palmer, P. J. (Speaker). (2009). *An undivided life* [Audiobook CD]. Boulder, CO: Sounds True.

Stier, W. (2002). Sports management internships: From theory to practice. *Strategies, 15*(4), 7–9.

Stratta, T. (2004). The needs and concerns of students during the Sport Management Internship Experience. *Journal of Physical Education, Recreation & Dance, 75*(2), 25–29.

3 Finding a Supervisor

How Can You Create the Right Match?

Victoria Tomlinson and Brian Alexander

Connecting with the right supervisor can create a harmonious experience for both supervisee and supervisor, as well as for the supervisee's clients. Some trainees are in the fortunate position of having their internship supervisor assigned to them via their academic program (however, they don't then have the experience of finding a supervisor), while many trainees have to find their own supervisor. This chapter will address trainees' potential concerns, such as how to find a supervisor, what credentials, training and level of experience should be considered as appropriate, what fees might be included in the service, and what questions to ask a potential supervisor. The supervisor can also be a resource for the trainee in terms of helping secure the clients/team/site, so the timing of contacting a supervisor needs to be considered. Addressing pertinent issues ahead of the supervisory process will help the trainee get the most out of the experience of locating and then working with a supervisor.

Background Information on the Authors

Victoria Tomlinson is an Associate Professor and Co-Fieldwork Director at JFKU. She is a CC-AASP and meta-supervisor within the JFKU fieldwork team, and she supervises trainees within the graduate program. Originally from the UK, she has predominantly worked within the applied field of sport psychology as a BPS Chartered Psychologist in the UK (non-clinical practitioner) and also BASES accredited practitioner. With over a decade of experience, her training and practice has chiefly been within European soccer and GB archery, working as a part of a collaborative multidisciplinary team (coaches, sport scientists, and medical practitioners) with particular reference to psychological well-being, youth development, and coaching practice. Victoria can be reached at vtomlinson@jfku.edu.

Brian Alexander received his Master's Degree in Sport Psychology from JFKU and is a CC-AASP. Post-graduation he has worked in a supervisory and consultant role for coaches and parents at the youth, high school, collegiate, and professional levels of sport. He also supervises sport psychology graduate students as an adjunct faculty member of JFKU. His private applied work has led to experience in a variety of sports, but most notably in the sport of water polo where, after competing for Team USA as an Olympic alternate, he has become the official athlete mental skills coach for the USA Water Polo Olympic Development Program. To learn more about his private practice visit www.athletementalskillscoach.com. He can be reached at balexander@jfku.edu.

The Supervision Process: Why Is It Important?

Supervision is essential for trainees in the field of applied sport psychology. It is also a mandatory requirement to attain certification throughout professional associations (e.g. AASP (who prefer the term mentoring), BPS, BASES) and organizations that seek to promote and provide quality services as a result of their professional certification program (professional conduct, code of ethics, and responsibilities). However, the "mandatory" requirements differ from one association to another and from one country to another. There is no uniform *one-size-fits-all* approach to the supervision process (Dosil, 2006; Dosil & Rivera, 2014).

Supervision plays a crucial role in the training process to guide and facilitate learning and development, and to increase confidence and competency of new trainees entering the field. Andersen (1994) advises that supervision is designed to "help the supervisee emerge from the process wiser and better equipped to handle future problems. Allowing supervisees to self-explore, self-critique, and self-evolve can only benefit their growth as professionals" (p. 161). Consequently, the role of supervision can be invaluable to the learning experience of trainees and competency in their application of knowledge.

The requirements of supervision are continuously growing within the field of sport psychology, as the value and importance of supervision has been recognized as an integral part of the process in the education and development of trainees. Recently, Hutter, Oldenhof-Veldman, and Oudejans (2015) called for more in-depth knowledge about learning, professional development, and excellence within the field of sport psychology, stating that the bar is continuously raised as professionalization in sports continues. As a result, higher demands are being placed on sport psychology professionals within the field.

Within the Sport Psychology Department at JFKU, the role and purpose of supervision is designed to meet the needs of trainees, both on-site and online. Please note that our interns are also required to do group supervision every week they are doing applied work; however, the focus of this chapter is about finding someone for individual supervision (see Chapter 6 of this book for more about our group supervision). The trainees meet with their clients in-person, however (outside the mandatory two-week residential component of the M.A. program in northern California), supervision can happen in-person or remotely depending upon the location where the trainee, and supervisor, are based.

The JFKU supervision model is provided to guide and support trainees (and supervisors) through their fieldwork experiences, in order to facilitate their learning and development, and to enhance their knowledge, understanding, and application of skills to competently work with clients. Additionally, JFKU trainees are typically assigned a different supervisor for each internship. This allows the trainees to be exposed to different supervisors and their unique supervisory styles that may facilitate and challenge the trainees to further develop their professional knowledge, understanding, and skills. For example, it was suggested by Andersen (2012) that professional growth with clients could be limited if the trainee is exposed to only one model of supervision. Andersen (2012) purported that "models of supervision come in a variety of flavors" (p. 727) and proposed that choosing a supervisor with a different theoretical orientation than your own may further expand your professional development and areas of competence.

Although JFKU trainees are in the fortunate position of having their internship supervisor assigned to them, outside of this program there are many trainees who face the task of finding their own supervisor. Attempting to find your own supervisor and deciding how to go about doing so can bring many questions into consideration. In this chapter, we will discuss how to conduct informational interviews with sport psychology professionals in hopes of finding the right match. This strategy will not only expand your professional network with viable contacts, but it will also help you find potential supervisors to fulfill future needs.

Supervision Structure: Creating the Right Match

Conceptualizing the right match between a supervisor and supervisee becomes the most important first step to ensuring a successful supervision experience. The ultimate goal of supervision is to provide the highest level of service and delivery of performance enhancement and counseling services for the clients (Barney, Andersen, & Riggs, 1996) of the sport psychology trainee. There are a number of models of supervision which are commonly followed by professionals who are AASP-certified consultants. Supervision models commonly utilized in sport psychology include the phenomenological model based on the work of Rogers (1956), the behavioral models of Boyd (1978) and Delaney (1972), and Stoltenberg's (1981) developmental model (Andersen & Williams-Rice, 1996; Bernard & Goodyear, 2009; Foltz et al., 2015; Van Raalte & Andersen, 2000). Other existing models of supervision include Hart's (1982) three-stage model of developmental supervision, Teitelbaum's (1990) supertransference, and Bernard's (1997) discrimination model (Rhodius & Park, 2014). The basic tenets of these models can be used by the sport psychology trainee to craft an ideal vision of what they are seeking in a supervision relationship.

It is recommended that, before recruiting the services of a supervisor, you should identify an ideal structure of supervision that you would like to experience. There are specific qualities in a supervisor that have been discovered to be most effective for the supervision experience and those will be addressed later in this chapter, but this first step requires more of an outcome-based focus that will stretch the competence and confidence of the aspiring trainee. Supervision should provide the less experienced with guidance, mentorship, and a forum in which to discuss personal or professional issues and struggles encountered during client contact (Barney et al., 1996; Hart, 1982). At JFKU, the structure of supervision is built on evaluating students' knowledge, skills and competencies around specific Program Learning Outcomes (PLOs; see Chapter 1 for the full list). To *create the right match*, the sport psychology trainee could include the following learning outcomes, adapted below for fieldwork from the PLOs of the program, as an ideal structure for supervision and a comprehensive applied experience:

- *Application/Intervention* of performance enhancement techniques with clients in the moment of need to be administered accurately and effectively.
- *Theory* in sport psychology to be understood and applied accurately and effectively.
- *Assessment strategies* to be understood and applied in a continuous and evolving process to create effective action plans.
- *Counseling skills* to be used effectively to develop working relationships with clients and also to build awareness of how the self impacts working relationships.
- *Multicultural competencies* to be understood and addressed appropriately in order to work with a diverse range of populations.
- *Ethics and professionalism* to be followed and upheld in a professional manner in compliance with governing bodies such as AASP.
- *Evidence-based practices* to summarize and critique research in the field of sport psychology, to assess and apply both established and current research findings to applied work.

Trainees can use the PLOs as a framework to discuss and assess their knowledge, skills, and competencies, and to identify strengths and areas for improvement. For example, you could identify your strengths and areas for improvement using a self-rating scale (from 1 to 5). This could then be a useful discussion point to have with a potential supervisor, and to find out about their strengths in these areas.

Aspiring to achieve the highest level of competence in sport psychology service delivery may not always be an attainable short-term goal as a trainee given personal, life, and university time demands, but it should be the ultimate long-term aim. However, a remedial approach to adhering to fundamental requirements in the supervision experience should always be expected based on the demands of a program's or governing body's ethical code. The nature of sport psychology requires that supervisory practice be flexible and cater to the divergent needs of supervisees (Barney et al., 1996). Thus the trainee's supervision structure should also cover multiple modalities of delivery including face-to-face and virtual meetings that are flexible with the changes in schedules of both the supervisor and trainee. The trainee should include in their ideal supervision structure technological requirements that would serve their needs when virtual supervision is needed with the right supervisor.

Additionally, as a sport psychology trainee, you need to assess your reasons for seeking supervision. The most common reasons for supervision are driven by the desire of the trainee to fulfill mentored experience hours for certification. However, some may be seeking to expand their competence levels. Other times, academic requirements demand a specified number of hours of applied experience in order to fulfill the requirements of the program for graduation. For example, JFKU requires each M.A. student to complete four internships, with each requiring a minimum number of hours of combined direct and indirect supervised experience. Certifications through sport psychology organizations require their own unique numbers of hours of supervised/mentored experience. For the trainee aspiring to achieve certification through AASP, it is important to include the number of hours needed in your ideal supervision/mentoring structure so that you can then determine if the supervisor/mentor candidates can meet those needs. Overall, care must be taken so that both parties recognize their roles in the new relationship and that these roles are in the service of fulfilling the supervisory needs of the trainee (Barney et al., 1996).

Items to consider for an ideal supervision structure before starting the search to *create the right match* include:

- Supervisor credentials
- Frequency of meetings
- Meeting structure (e.g. time, topics, pre-work needed, etc.)
- Modality available (phone, internet, location, technology needs)
- Experience with trainee clients
- Connection and similarities between supervisor and trainee
- Competency needs of trainee and areas of expertise of supervisor
- Fees and other demands of supervisor

Finding Your Own Supervisor

Finding your own supervisor can be a daunting prospect when considering how to effectively navigate through this process in an attempt to *create the right match*. Although there is not a handbook to guide you through this process (until now!), the steps you take to finding your own supervisor may ultimately shape your supervision experience. Whether you are a sport psychology trainee in a university program (on-site/online) or a post-graduate, it is important that you conduct your own research to explore the options available to you, and to complete a needs analysis of what you feel is a best fit for your needs.

If you intend to work toward AASP certification, then your supervisor will generally need to be a CC-AASP. A good place to start would be the AASP website, where you can search for and find certified consultants. If your preference is to meet with your supervisor in person, then you could use the AASP search engine to identify certified consultants in your area or close by. Otherwise, if distance is not an essential requirement, and you know that you are able to video the work you are conducting (with permission and consent), then a distance supervisory relationship is a viable option to ensure that you are able to meet AASP requirements for direct supervision hours. However, if you do not intend to become AASP certified then you are not mandated to find an AASP-certified consultant, and other options are available to you. For example, consultants and practitioners that are willing to supervise can be found within different environments, such as universities, clubs, teams, and private practice.

If you are not seeking AASP certification but are seeking supervision in another country, then different options and/or requirements may apply. This will also depend on the country's professionally accredited associations, organizations, and/or governing bodies, and their requirements for certification. It is important to consider and research the different associations, organizations, and/or governing bodies that offer a certification pathway, as this may dictate the type of supervision you undertake, and inevitably the type of work you are qualified to conduct. It is also more than likely that you would need to find a supervisor who is certified by that association. Most associations provide a list of certified supervisors who can be contacted via their webpage.

When you have identified your interest in potential contacts for supervision, it is then crucial to consider what information you would like to know that will help to better inform your decision on finding the right supervisor and creating the right match. Informational interviews play a key role during this stage of the process, as this can provide a platform for you to find out more about the supervisor, with background to their credentials and experience, and an insight into the way they work and their supervision style (see Box 3.1). This is also an opportunity for you to outline your needs and expectations of the supervision process. For example, what are your expectations of the supervisor within the supervision process? This is an important question to address in the initial stages when attempting to create the right match, particularly if the trainee is relying on their supervisor to provide access to clients and supervised experience opportunities to meet their required hours, as this may be a difficult expectation to guarantee and/or meet (Eubank & Hudson, 2013).

Box 3.1   Example: The Informational Interview

The following example questions will demonstrate what a sport psychology trainee could ask and the sequence in which the conversation may develop during informational interviews. This is by no means an exact script; however, it is meant to offer examples that prompt the development of trainees who are looking to find a supervisor to *create the right match*. Some of these questions may also be useful for someone for whom their supervisor has been assigned to them.

- What credentials have you earned?
- What governing bodies are you a member of?
- What types of athletes have you worked with in your practice?
- What sports do you have experience playing?
- What is your philosophy of practice in your own work?

- Have you supervised other sport psychology trainees?
- What expectations do you have of the trainees you supervise?
- What are some of the biggest challenges you have found with supervision?
- What is your ultimate goal with the trainees you supervise?
- How often and when do you typically meet with those you supervise?
- What do you expect in terms of time commitment for supervision from the trainee?
- Are you available to meet via telephone and video conference?
- What do you charge for supervision?
- Do you offer a sliding scale?
- Does your practice insurance cover my work or will I need insurance for myself as well?

Often, utilizing an internet search engine and/or a search engine housed within the official website of a professional association and/or organization that connects you with certified consultants can allow trainees to seek out supervisor professionals that may fulfill their specific needs, and can provide valuable insight prior to the informational interview. In addition, it is also worthy to note that, for trainees who are assigned a supervisor, it may be equally helpful to address such questions during your initial meeting.

Identifying Supervisor Qualities

Once the search has begun and active informational interviews with potential supervisors are underway, you should put your counseling skills to the test to assess each candidate. Foltz et al. (2015) found that skills and qualities needed from a supervisor by a trainee should be (a) a clearly articulated model of supervision, (b) the development of trust, (c) the ability to collaborate, (d) establishing boundaries and roles, (e) experience operating within sport environments, and (f) experience working with performance and mental health issues. Although this list is not a comprehensive representation of every need, it should be considered when developing the list of questions to ask the candidate supervisor. Supervisors need to demonstrate that they are non-judgmental of the current abilities of the trainee, that they allow the trainee to build their competence within desired learning outcomes, and that they are collaborative in nature during the learning journey.

No consensus has emerged as to what constitutes an *experienced* sport psychology professional or what is adequate training in sport psychology supervision (Barney et al., 1996). A potential supervisor candidate who has earned a certified consultant credential from AASP should be a competent professional. CC-AASP does not guarantee, however, that they have the experience and knowledge that makes them a great supervisor. The assumption that experience equals competence is also questionable (Andersen, 1994), so the potential supervisor should still be learning how to be effective through continuing education opportunities, even though they may have supervised many trainees before. In fact, a survey of professionals providing applied sport psychology supervision reported that more than 75% had received little to no training on how to provide supervision (Watson II, Zizzi, Etzel, & Lubker, 2004). However, it is beneficial to receive supervision from a faculty member of a university who collaborates with other supervisors. This element adds an aspect of professional peer evaluation of the supervisor.

The Sport Psychology Department at JFKU provides training for supervisors to address expectations, competencies, and protocol. Supervisors at JFKU also receive a training manual for additional support and guidance, along with meta-supervision. In meta-supervision practices at JFKU, quarterly supervisor meetings are held for shared learning and reflection purposes—in particular, to learn and reflect on recent and/or current supervision experiences, in an attempt to share, discuss, and collaborate on methods of best practice and changes for improvement.

Supervisors who practice self-awareness through reflection and other skills should have an ability to preview potential multicultural competency challenges, cultural differences, and multiple relationships and roles that would signify any ethical dilemmas with their supervisees. Those qualities will need to be determined by the trainee and a values match between the two parties will most likely also need to be assessed, either formally or informally.

You should also consider the potential supervisor candidate's philosophy of practice, their expectations in supervision, and their supervision process demands. Cropley, Hanton, Miles, and Niven (2010) specifically address the need for trainees and practitioners to engage in reflective practices. Seeking validation during informational interviews of potential supervisors that they practice the skills in their own work which match those identified in the trainee's supervision model help you identify the right person that meets your needs.

Negotiating Fees and Structure

When it comes to negotiating fees and structure, certain supervisors may have a specific fee already determined as part of their supervision structure and services. However, there may also be some supervisors who invite/offer the flexibility to negotiate fees and structure depending on the type of supervision required. This is an important stage of the process in finding a supervisor, and cannot be overlooked when working toward creating the right match and reaching a contract of agreement.

There are many factors to consider when negotiating fees and structure:

- *When, where and how often would you like supervision?* Availability and scheduling of supervision sessions. Consider preference of meeting in-person, virtual or hybrid supervision meetings, and the optimal meeting frequency.
- *What are the fees? What does this include?* Cost range of example supervision (per meeting or package) and what is offered.
- *Will there be communication between meetings?* Expectations between meetings, communication, and contact availability.
- *What do you need from the supervisor, and what can they offer?* The scope of the work may include securing clients/team/site, so consider the timing of contacting a supervisor depending on the sport and season. Also consider the need for and structure of direct and indirect supervision, facility use, resources, etc.
- *How can the supervisor support your growth? What are your goals?* Commitment to the process, creating the opportunity to learn, practice, and develop new skills (e.g. reflective practice).

Depending on the supervision contract, there may also be the opportunity for the supervisee to shadow or observe their supervisor in the consultant role, creating another platform for learning. As previously highlighted by Andersen (1994), supervisors "are in a position to model what may become lifelong patterns of professional behavior" (p. 153); therefore, the opportunity to shadow or observe your supervisor in action can be a valuable piece of the learning experience. In a similar vein, Tod, Andersen, and Marchant (2009) mention that, in reference to counseling psychologists, trainee sport psychologists prefer to learn from their supervisors and follow by example, particularly when developing ways to apply interventions with clients. This may be an important form of support to consider within the supervision contract, creating further opportunity to learn and develop through observation.

Conclusion

Taking the time to address pertinent issues is an essential part of the process in finding a supervisor and creating the right match, even for trainees that are assigned a supervisor. The supervisor can be a helpful resource for the trainee, and from our experience of the supervision process (both having previously been the trainee and now in the role of supervisor), *creating the right match* and connecting with the right supervisor can be invaluable to the supervisory relationship and learning experience. Overall, not only can the supervision experience shape the trainee, and ultimately the consultant they choose to become, but both the trainee and the supervisor can learn, develop, and evolve from the supervision experience.

Top Tips for Finding the Right Supervisor for You

- Create an ideal structure of supervision before contacting potential candidates
- Identify a needs analysis of what would be a best fit
- Determine short-term and long-term goals for supervision aligned with desired learning outcomes from supervision (reference the JFKU Sport Psychology PLOs as an example)
- Identify supervisor qualities that would *create the right match* for you
- Utilize the certified consultant search tools on the Association for Applied Sport Psychology website (www.appliedsportpsych.com)
- Schedule informational interviews with potential supervisor candidates
- Prepare for informational interviews with a list of questions to ask
- Ask for a weekly meeting schedule that fits educational program, certification, or personal needs
- Agree on fees and structure of the supervision relationship before starting

A Trainee's Perspective on Finding a Supervisor and Creating the Right Match

Derek Swartout-Mosher, M.A., student at JFKU 2014–2016

Derek's goals are to enter the field and build his own practice as well as pursue a career in professional sports. His interests are in golf and baseball, and he is looking forward to jump-starting his career in the summer with a professional baseball organization. He can be contacted at derek.swartoutmosher@gmail.com.

I remember the work I did with my individual supervisor during my first internship, which at JFKU is an intensive two-week-long summer experience. As a beginning trainee it was daunting enough to test my skills for the first time with real people and situations, let alone to be evaluated by someone else. What I found was that, if I utilized the skills I had learned throughout my training with JFKU to get to know my supervisor, I could establish the trust and confidence in myself to be vulnerable enough to learn.

Creating the right match was key to the success I experienced during the supervision process. I found that preparing for the initial conversations with my supervisors using the developmental model by Andersen and Williams-Rice (1996), as suggested by Tomlinson and Alexander, allowed for clarity in my vision of expectations. It was a goal of mine to get to know as much as possible about my supervisor's model of supervision, as they were going to play a crucial role in guiding me to understand my philosophy of practice.

Sport psychology has always been a huge passion of mine. I've read countless books and research articles, watched videos, and attended conferences, but nothing compares to the trusted interaction with an established professional in the field. Knowing the goal of the supervision process is to facilitate learning and development, I knew I had to open myself up to this process. This was a huge step in my growth as a young professional in the field of sport psychology. Every meeting I had with a supervisor became an opportunity to learn. What I enjoyed most was learning from the applied experiences of my mentors. Experiential learning often cannot be found in a book; rather, it is a part of the journey. Through the experiences shared by my supervisors I was able to relate to my own process and discover a newfound confidence in my ability to practice sport psychology.

Creating the right match comes with its challenges as well. At JFKU, I was assigned a different supervisor for all four internships. Having a different supervisor brought new perspectives and new learning, and required more openness to the process of supervision. It required flexibility with scheduling and the mode of communication from both the supervisor and myself. With each new experience, I gained more knowledge about what I needed to continue my growth; listening to stories from the supervisors' applied experiences in the field was instrumental.

Reflective Questions and Activities for You to Consider Before You Proceed

- What credible databases or reference websites are available to start your search for a supervisor?
- Who do you know who could introduce you to a potential supervisor candidate?
- What types of information should you research that would help you determine the type of supervision you need?
- What is the main purpose of supervision and what should be the ultimate focus?
- What are the qualities and values that create a valuable supervision experience?
- What questions would you ask potential supervisor candidates during informational interviews? (Hint: Refer to your ideal supervision structure to create a written list.)

Brainstorm aspects of an ideal supervision structure that addresses your needs. Include how often you would like to meet, the modality of meetings, the structure of the supervision, the number of hours you need, the supervisor's qualifications, the fees involved, and the qualities a supervisor would need to *create the right match*.

References

Andersen, M. B. (1994). Ethical considerations in the supervision of applied sport psychology graduate students. *Journal of Applied Sport Psychology, 6*, 152–167.

Andersen, M. B. (2012). Supervision and mindfulness in sport and performance psychology. In S. M. Murphy (Ed.), *The Oxford Handbook of Sport and Performance Psychology* (pp. 725–737). New York, NY: Oxford University Press.

Andersen, M. B., & Williams-Rice, B. T. (1996). Supervision in the education and training of sport psychology service providers. *The Sport Psychologist, 10*, 278–290.

Barney, S. T., Andersen, M. B., & Riggs C. A. (1996). Supervision in sport psychology: Some recommendations for practicum training. *Journal of Applied Sport Psychology, 8*, 200–217.

Bernard, J. M. (1997). The discrimination model. In C. E. Watkins, Jr. (Ed.), *Handbook of psychotherapy supervision* (pp. 311–327). New York, NY: John Wiley.

Bernard, J. M., & Goodyear, R. K. (2009). *Fundamentals of clinical supervision* (4th ed.). Upper Saddle River, NJ: Pearson.

Boyd, J. D. (1978). *Counselor supervision: Approaches, preparation, and practices.* Muncie, IN: Accelerated Development.

Cropley, B., Hanton, S., Miles, A., & Niven, A. (2010). Exploring the relationship between effective and reflective practice in applied sport psychology. *The Sport Psychologist, 24*, 521–541.

Delaney, D. J. (1972). A behavioral model for the practicum supervision of counselor candidates. *Counselor Education and Supervision, 12*, 46–50.

Dosil, J. (2006). Applied sport psychology: A new perspective. In J. Dosil (Ed.), *The sport psychologist's handbook: A guide for sport specific performance enhancement* (pp. 3–18). Chichester, UK: Wiley.

Dosil, J., & Rivera, S. (2014). The seasoned supervisor: Challenges, models and lessons learned. In J. G. Cremades & L. S. Tashman (Eds.), *Becoming a sport, exercise, and performance psychology professional: A global perspective* (pp. 339–346). New York, NY: Routledge.

Eubank, M., & Hudson, J. (2013). The future of professional training for professional competence. *Sport & Exercise Psychology Review, 9*, 61–65.

Foltz, B. D., Fisher, A. R., Denton, L. K., Campbell, W. L., Speight, Q. L., Steinfeldt, J., & Latorre, C. (2015). Applied sport psychology supervision experience: A qualitative analysis. *Journal of Applied Sport Psychology, 27*, 449–463.

Hart, G. M. (1982). *The process of clinical supervision.* Baltimore, MD: University Park Press.

Hutter, R. I., Oldenhof-Veldman, T., & Oudejans, R. R. D. (2015). What trainee sport psychologists want to learn in supervision. *Psychology of Sport and Exercise, 16*, 101–109.

Rhodius, A., & Park, M. (2014). Who's supervising the supervisor? A case study of meta-supervision. In J. G. Cremades & L. S. Tashman (Eds.), *Global practices and training in applied sport, exercise and performance psychology* (pp. 322–329). New York, NY: Routledge.

Rogers, C. R. (1956). *Training individuals to engage in the therapeutic process.* Washington, DC: American Psychological Association.

Teitelbaum, S. H. (1990). Supertransference: The role of the supervisor's blindspots. *Psychoanalytic Psychology, 7*(2), 243–258.

Tod, D., Andersen, M. B., & Marchant, D. B. (2009). A longitudinal examination of neophyte applied sport psychologists' development. *Journal of Applied Sport Psychology, 21*(Suppl. 1), S1–S16.

Van Raalte, J. L., & Andersen, M. B. (2000). Supervision I: From models to doing. In M. B. Andersen (Ed.), *Doing sport psychology* (pp. 153–165). Champaign, IL: Human Kinetics.

Watson II, J. C., Zizzi, S. J., Etzel, E. F., & Lubker, J. R. (2004). Applied sport psychology supervision: A survey of students and professionals. *The Sport Psychologist, 18*, 415–429.

4 Acknowledging Biases

How Can Who You Are Affect What You See?

Michelle Bartlett and Zane Winslade

Prior to beginning to work in applied settings it is important to unpack one's own feelings, biases, assumptions, and concerns. Without adequate self-awareness, trainees run the risk of coming to premature, biased conclusions and assumptions about their clients. Each trainee brings their own unique experiences with them when they meet with clients. By developing more self-awareness, trainees will be able to critically examine their beliefs and assumptions, and approach their work with an open mind and without preconceived judgment. This chapter aims to help you examine yourself and how who you are can impact your session, and enhance your knowledge on how you can best work with any client that differs from you.

Background Information on the Authors

Michelle Bartlett has a Master's Degree in Community Counseling and a Master's Degree in Sport and Exercise Psychology, as well as a Doctoral Degree in Sport and Exercise Psychology, all from West Virginia University. She also has a Bachelor's Degree in both Biology and Psychology from Syracuse University. Michelle is a Certified Consultant of AASP (#543). She is currently an Associate Professor in Sports and Exercise Sciences at West Texas A&M University, teaching various graduate and undergraduate sport and exercise psychology courses. In addition, she provides a valuable service to the profession by supervising future mental skills consultants through the Master's Program at JFKU. Most of her sport psychology consulting work is with collegiate athletes and in the exercise psychology realm as the director of her university's wellness program. She can be reached at MBartlett@ jfku.edu.

   Zane Winslade graduated with a Master's Degree in Sport Psychology from JFKU in 2016. He has an undergraduate degree in Sport and Leisure Studies from the University of Waikato in New Zealand and a Graduate Diploma in Teaching from Victoria University of Wellington, New Zealand. Zane formerly played professional rugby in Romania, Portugal, and the national domestic competition in New Zealand. As part of his training at JFKU, he completed internships at a variety of different populations including high school, university, and semi-professional sporting environments. He currently works as a rugby coach and as a mental skills consultant with a variety of sports in Tauranga, New Zealand. He can be reached at zwinslade@ email.jfku.edu.

Think about this question: "What do *all* athletes, as a group, have in common?"

Surely you were able to name some traits or behaviors that might be *common* among athletes. Maybe you named things like dedication, mental toughness, speed, strength, or having *good* genetics. But now, think of an exception to your answer. You most likely can also think of an example of an athlete who doesn't have that trait. The same premise holds true for our clients. Instead of asking "how can I best work with a client of this group?", we need to ask "how can I best work with *this* client?" while accounting for any differences they may have, both from you and from any group to which they may belong (e.g. sport, culture, gender, socioeconomic, etc.). Therefore, this will not be a chapter outlining how to work with each specifically diverse group, but aims instead to help you examine yourself, and how you can best work with any client that differs from you.

Interpersonal functioning, defined as "developing self- and social-awareness in order to attain skills for relating effectively to others" (Silva, Metzler, & Lerner, 2007, p. 200), is a central component of professionalism in our field. Therefore, developing an appreciation of intercultural, socioeconomic, and gender/sexuality differences and enhancing knowledge on how they may affect a consultation is paramount to becoming a competent practitioner in sport psychology. Further, while AASP only recently (taking effect in 2018) started to require coursework in multicultural counseling for the Certified Consultant designation (AASP, 2017), it has required coursework in and knowledge of professional ethics and standards. For one to acquire the CC-AASP designation, she/he must be a member of AASP and membership requires adherence to the AASP Ethics Code (similar requirements exist for other sport psychology organizations, as well). The AASP Ethics Code states in Principle A: "Competence" and echoes in Principle D: "Respect for Human Rights and Dignity" that "AASP members are cognizant of the fact that the competencies required in serving, teaching, and/or studying groups of people vary with the distinctive characteristics of those groups" (AASP, 2011, paragraph 8) and:

> AASP members are aware of cultural, individual, and role differences, including those due to age, gender, race, ethnicity, national origin, religion, sexual orientation, disability, language, and socioeconomic status. AASP members try to eliminate the effect on their work of biases based on those factors, and they do not knowingly participate in or condone unfair discriminatory practices.
>
> (AASP, 2011, paragraph 11)

In addition, since applied sport psychology is also addressed by the APA in the U.S., it is important to be aware of that governing body's stance on addressing multicultural competence. The APA developed and adopted multicultural guidelines in 2002 that focused on three general areas: 1. multicultural awareness—understanding one's own cultural beliefs, attitudes, and values; 2. cultural knowledge—understanding other cultures' beliefs, attitudes, and values; and 3. cultural skills—the ability to navigate and integrate the two via communication and appropriate intervention (as summarized in Ryba, Stambulova, Si, & Schinke, 2013).[1]

Lastly, the ISSP has a position stand on culturally competent research and practice in sport psychology. This ISSP position stand outlined a plan to move toward creating culturally competent practitioners in sport psychology worldwide and calls for: (a) culturally competent sport psychology practitioners; (b) cultural awareness and reflexivity; (c) culturally competent communication; and (d) culturally competent interventions, defined as being free from client stereotypes based on group membership and treating clients in a manner consistent with social justice in sport psychology (Ryba et al., 2013).

In conclusion, in order to be an effective practitioner in the field of sport psychology and hold membership of many of the governing professional organizations in the discipline (i.e. be recognized by your field), you're *required* to refine your interpersonal functioning and be self-aware in this regard.

Exploring Self-Awareness

A good place to start assessing yourself is taking an inventory of your values and beliefs. Simply, our values are what we view as good and bad, what we prefer or don't prefer, and what is acceptable or unacceptable. Since humans are, by nature, social beings, we can't underestimate how much the society and culture that we were socialized into impacts the values that we hold as our own (Sage & Eitzen, 2016). In being culturally competent, it is important to acknowledge that our clients may have been socialized into other cultures and may not share all our values. Further, it is important to understand that the cultures and values of a society at large are a function of the cultural patterns of dominance (e.g. among race, gender, and socioeconomic status) in that society. Dominant groups are powerful in shaping cultural ideologies and values by the extent to which they can channel their resources into promoting their values to society. It is important to acknowledge your membership or non-membership in dominant or privileged groups in society and account for the impact that has had in shaping your values.

Samuels (2014) outlines the social identities that are generally privileged in Western culture. As you read these, keep a mental tally of how many of these groups you identify as a member of:

- Race: white
- Gender: male
- Class: middle-upper
- Sexual orientation: hetero
- Religion: Christian
- Physical ability: non-disabled/strong
- Mental ability: able/smart
- Age: 25–55
- Education: formally educated

According to prominent sociologists George Sage and D. Stanley Eitzen (2016), several pervasive values representing the dominant culture within the North American (or Westernized) value system include:

- Success: commonly measured by winning and economic achievements
- Competition: the valued means by which winning occurs
- Hard work: a valued and esteemed way to achieve success in North American society
- Materialism: the payoff from embracing the values listed above
  (This list is certainly not exhaustive and you're invited to reflect on the values you were brought up with in your own culture if you don't see them on this list.)

To see how our own values may influence our work with a client, sometimes without our awareness, let's imagine a consultation scenario: The client, a highly talented African-American senior college football player, has been referred to you by his coach for "being unmotivated." His coach, a white male, thinks the athlete could be a professional football player and wants you to help the athlete increase his motivation and output on the field during both practice and competition. He is also concerned that the athlete declined to attend his college's pro day (i.e. an on campus showcase for professional scouts) and has no plans to attend the upcoming NFL combine (i.e. an event organized by the NFL for select draft eligible players) after the season is over, despite being invited. He wants you to help the athlete "get his priorities right." While meeting with the client, the consultant begins with getting a general history of the client and his athletic career, and it is clear that the athlete had a relatively normal progression through the ranks of his sport. Upon probing further, the consultant asks the athlete about his motivation for playing football. It becomes clear to the consultant that the athlete is questioning whether or not to continue to play football. He says:

> I just love playing football. I have since I was a little kid. The feeling of running up the field with the ball in my hands, weaving in and out, with no one able to catch me—it can't be beat. I love my team too, they're like brothers to me and I'd do anything for them. They're some of the best guys I know. But after playing for four years here, the stuff I love about football just seems to be so little of what I'm actually doing: weights, study hall, team meetings, grueling two-a-days where we don't even touch the ball for days on end. I'm just over it all. It's like a job to me and it's just not enjoyable when it feels like that way. If I could just play football without any of that I'd do it for free for as long as I'm physically able.

The processing questions below will help guide your exploration of how your values may have impacted your consultation if you were working with the client in the above scenario.

Processing questions:

1. By the coach saying the athlete's priorities are not "right," he is comparing them to his standard of "right." What value do you think the coach is placing highest in this situation?
2. What value do you think the athlete is placing highest in this situation?
3. Assume that the consultant in this situation has been raised in the United States and would consider their values to be in line with general Americanized values, namely valuing winning, success, and materialism (for more information on the "universal" American values see Chapter 3 of Sage & Eitzen, 2016). How could the consultant's values affect their ability to help to the client make an unbiased decision?
4. If you were the consultant in the situation, what would you do with the client?

Think again about your answer to question 4 above. Likely, your values played some role in how you answered that question. If you were thinking along the line of trying to help the athlete increase his motivation for staying in football at his current level (or moving higher), you may have been reflecting on the value of maximizing success and not wasting potential if great success is possible. Or perhaps you were thinking of all the money that the athlete would make if he were to continue on the path of playing professional football, reflecting on a value of materialism. Or even greater, perhaps you once had strong aspirations of being a professional athlete and cannot imagine turning down such a precious (from your perspective) opportunity. If your answer was different than these, reflect on how your personal values and group membership may have impacted your decision on what to do with this client.

The intention of that scenario was to illustrate how our values can influence our consultations, sometimes without our realization. It's okay if you have any of these thoughts, or others not addressed in the scenario. What is most critical, however, is that you don't let your personal values interfere with helping the client determine *his* desired path forward. Before embarking on your consultations, it is important that you take an assessment of your values (both sport-related and not). Some general questions to assess your values include:

Social Issues:

- Do you support marriage for same gender couples?
- Do you think you can learn a lot about someone by how they are dressed?
- Do you believe that one should tell the truth at all times?
- Should athletes on the same team be permitted to date one another?

    o   Does your answer change for co-ed teams?

- Should conflict be avoided?
- Should children be disciplined by spanking?

Spiritual Issues:

- Do you identify with a particular religion?
- Do you believe that there is only one supreme being?

    o   If yes, how do you perceive another person believing in a different supreme being than yours?

- Do you believe in life after death?

Political Issues:

- Do you support the death penalty?
- Do you believe in a woman's right to choose to have an abortion?
- Should performance enhancement drugs be legalized?
- Should athletes who use performance-enhancing drugs be banned from sport?

Now, taking your answers to these questions into account, imagine a consultation where your client has a different answer to one of the questions than yours, and that is a primary component of their presenting concern. Would it impact your consultation? These types of questions should be explored before embarking on a consultation so you can be aware of any areas where you may have beliefs or values that would impair your ability to work with a client without bias (i.e. practice competently) and, if so, refer accordingly (see Chapter 11 of this book for information on how to handle referrals).

In addition to exploring one's values, it is also important to become aware of how you think about race, gender, sexuality, and socioeconomic status in society. Butryn (2002) explored the difference between *race thinking* and *racist thinking*. *Race thinking* involves the process of acknowledging race and its influence and presence in society (versus color-blindness, not acknowledging race, which is discouraged if trying to become more self-aware), while *racist thinking* involves dividing and ranking based on perceived (stereotypical) desirable qualities (or lack thereof), linked to phenotypical group membership. We will extrapolate that into considering issues of gender, sexuality, and socioeconomic status (SES) in society, as well. Thinking through these issues requires several components:

- Reflecting upon race, gender, sexuality, and SES differences and the impact of these on your life and on society in general (a sociology course or text is good place to start);
- Realizing that, while group membership is powerful in shaping experiences, every individual is just that—an individual, and should be treated as such;
- Acknowledging that, wherever you go, you bring yourself with you—we are inescapably linked to our experiences to some extent.

We have discussed exploring values and group differences as a very conscious process that we are aware of and can rationally think about. However, there are also subconscious forces at play that we are not aware of that can influence our consultations. These *automatic* associations are our unconscious biases that influence how we interact with others. Biases are largely based on *lazy thinking*, which is also the foundation of stereotypes and prejudices. But just because they are largely automatic and outside of your awareness does not mean that they cannot be controlled. In fact, simply being internally motivated to become aware of your biases and be free of them (versus just hiding them) is an effective way to reduce them (van Nunspeet, Ellemers, & Derks, 2015; Plant & Devine, 2009).

A highly recommended way to examine your biases is readily available to anyone with internet access. The Implicit Association Test (IAT) (Social Attitudes version) measures attitudes and beliefs that you may be unaware that you possess and is available free of charge online at https://implicit.harvard.edu/implicit/selectatest.html. The example given by the providers of the assessment states: "You may believe that women and men should be equally associated with science, but your automatic associations could show that you (like many others) associate men with science more than you associate women with science." The website provides options to assess your possible biases on several factors including race, sexuality, religion, gender, and age.

More specifically related to a mental skills consulting environment, it is recommended by Parham (2005) and by Silva et al. (2007) that a trainee/consultant ask themselves the following questions before a consultation:

1. Do I possess the skills, knowledge, experiences, awareness, etc. necessary to help this client effectively?
2. To what degree will my own values, ethnicity, gender, sexual orientation, etc. influence my ability to respond to my client? (If you have completed versions of the IAT you may be better able to answer this question.)
3. What do I objectively know about this client (not surmising or assuming)?
4. To what degree will my client's values, ethnicity, gender, sexual orientation, etc. influence this consultation?

After the session, the trainee/consultant is encouraged to reflect on these questions again. To further foster self-awareness of biases, the trainee/consultant should also consider the following questions (Parham, 2005): What have I learned about myself during this consultation? And what have I learned about my client during this consultation?

Increasing Self-Awareness of Cognitive Biases

Thus far, this chapter has explored how our biases can come from our value/belief system and the social environment in which we were raised. However, biases can also come from our own errors in cognition. If you have taken any cognitive psychology courses, you should be somewhat familiar with cognitive biases and heuristics (i.e. thinking shortcuts).

This is based on the career-long work of Kahneman and Tversky, where they were repeatedly able to demonstrate ways in which human judgment and decision-making strays from what is rational. One bias that practitioners may commonly find as a pitfall in a sport psychology consulting environment is the confirmation bias. The confirmation bias is a tendency to search for, or only regard, information that already supports your preconceived notion. Any information subsequently received to the contrary is, often erroneously, disregarded. Another bias related to the confirmation bias in a consultation is the anchoring bias. This bias occurs when people are over-reliant on the first bit of information that they hear. In conjunction with the confirmation bias, that first bit of information may be inaccurate, yet the consultant spends the whole session gathering information related to that first bit of information, without exploring other possibilities. It is crucial to your unbiased practice that you're aware of how these *thinking traps* may affect your consultation. For a more comprehensive review of cognitive biases and how they can affect your consultations, see the book *Thinking, Fast and Slow* by Nobel Prize Winner Daniel Kahneman (2011).

While undertaking my own training as a mental skills practitioner, I (Zane) completed an internship working with athletes who played rugby, the same sport I had played myself and had finished playing three years earlier. This situation can be difficult in that the consultant can be heavily biased by their own experiences of situations in which the clients may find themselves. In this example, a client had experienced trouble with recovering from mistakes made during a game; often one error would lead to another and the client attributed this to his own lack of ability to deal with failure. Through self-reflection of my own biases, guided by my supervisors, we found that I had made several assumptions about the thought process of the client, influenced by my experience in a similar scenario. While reflecting on the session with the client, I had found I had skipped questions that would have been crucial in helping to understand the client's thought process, and thus had assumed to understand what he was experiencing. This meant that I *jumped the gun* in my desire to intervene and help the client without actually understanding the issue. The process of reflection helped to identify the bias that existed, and enabled me to make changes in the way I approached clients in the future.

Reflecting on the example above, of interest to the trainee are the varieties of confirmation bias that can occur in initial consultations with individuals. When an athlete shows up for a sport psychology consultation, the practitioner may automatically make assumptions about that individual. As evident in the famous Rosenhan (1973) study, psychologists were influenced by their bias defined by their role when required to diagnose an abnormality. When the job was to find an abnormality, it was hard for them not to see abnormality wherever they looked. If your role is to find something abnormal, then you may be more likely to find behaviors to support that. As well as biases related to race, gender, and socioeconomic status, confirmation bias in sport psychology can be prevalent for trainees who have learned about new techniques in performance enhancement and are keen to make use of their newfound knowledge. Trainees may then only find opportunities to educate a client about a particular technique. The old saying "if the only tool you have is a hammer, then all you'll see is a nail" may have some relevance to the new practitioner. When the beginner practitioner is given a variety of new *tools*, they need to be careful not to be biased by these and look for specific problems that fit with the newly acquired tool. Open questioning and a client-led assessment process helps minimize the effect of this bias, as well as being self-reflective (see Chapter 5) and having adequate supervision/peer consultation (see Chapters 6 and 17). As a simple example, if a trainee in an internship had a client who happened to mention they experienced self-doubts before they performed, the trainee would have to be careful not to fast forward to an intervention such as thought stopping or another self-talk strategy before truly understanding the relationship that client has with these self-doubts. Newly developed knowledge can bias the practitioner to seek what they believe to exist. Confirmation and anchoring bias can influence what the trainee sees and how they act with a client, so the reflective process alongside strong counseling and reflective-practice skills are critical in minimizing the potential for bias to have a negative effect on the client-practitioner relationship.

As recommended earlier in this chapter, the process of self-reflection and evaluating one's own bias surrounding gender, race, sexual orientation, or social status is vitally important. In addition, a consultant must not let existing knowledge and beliefs about their new role influence how they interpret and consult within a session. Our own background and beliefs affect how we see the world, so understanding oneself and one's biases will help accelerate the openness with which one learns and develops as a sport psychology professional.

During the process of self-reflection, supervision, and in peer consultation, the trainee must be asked, or ask him- or herself, important questions that help to uncover personal bias. Of particular relevance to confirmation bias, the trainee must learn to ask themselves: Why have I favored this path of intervention? How has my own knowledge influenced my decisions with this client? And in what instances has my own bias prevented me from learning more about my client? This reflection should continue when you're a professional in the field.

Conclusion

This chapter has identified that uncovering biases requires more depth than one might imagine. To build a greater understanding of ourselves, and to apply that understanding to our own consulting, we must ask ourselves the important questions that this chapter has posed. We should ask ourselves about privilege and how that has affected us. We should ask ourselves about what we value and how we can work with a client whose values differ from ours. We should always be aware and ask ourselves how we may be influenced by our cognitive bias, so that an enthusiastic consultant does not just see things that they want or are prepared to see. Using the questions in this chapter as a guide, a trainee can learn to work more effectively with athletes from a variety of backgrounds and they will likely become a more competent and adaptable practitioner along the way.

A Trainee's Perspective on Acknowledging Biases

Philip Schmitz, M.A., student at JFKU 2013–2015

Currently, Phil lives in the San Francisco Bay Area and is the Athletic Director for two area middle school athletic programs. He continues to develop programs to allow for an enriching social, emotional, and physical experience for youth athletes while implementing basic mental training concepts in trainings with coaches and other professionals. He ultimately hopes to continue working within public recreation or in a higher level athletic department to continue to spread and enhance the positive impact of athletics to a greater, more diverse population. He also plans on working with area private coaches to complement physical training with his expertise in mental training techniques as it pertains to the middle school and high school populations. Email pschmitz@email. jfku.edu.

The first day of your internship is approaching. You try to mentally prepare for every aspect of the experience and preview the interactions you have. What does that involve? Most likely you'll imagine your interactions with your clients, coaches, and others. These imagined interactions will undoubtedly be formed from past experiences, assumptions, and even stereotypes you may not even be aware you possess. Understanding and examining all of these judgments and stereotypes you have experience with can help you better work with the client in front of you.

My second internship was with a private high school soccer team where students pay $30,000 in tuition. Honestly, I arrived thinking I was going to be dealing with spoiled kids with petty problems (harsh, I know). Part of my process in preparing for the internship was to dive into what I thought I was going to experience—I wanted to try to understand as much as I could before I met with anyone. After I started working with the team and my internship supervisor, I began to evaluate how my expectations compared with what I had experienced. Some preconceived notions were confirmed, yet many were quickly rejected. It was a constant fight with myself to encourage and seek out the client to tell his whole story, rather than assume that I already knew his story. Even when I did gather a significant number of the relevant details, judgments and stereotypes crept in. The work with my supervisor and my own personal reflections helped me continue to improve in my work with clients, particularly when it came to stereotypes and biases.

My next internship was with a women's NCAA tennis team comprised of ten international students, and I had several goals that I established with my supervisor. Among these goals were to ask more open-ended questions, listen more, assume less, and talk less. This process, particularly in the opening sessions, allowed me to get a clearer picture of the client without interjecting with too many of my assumptions, judgments, and stereotypes. It gave me the time to take notes, listen, and reflect later instead of having an instant reaction, which is usually laced with assumptions and judgments. This awareness doesn't mean that I simply forgot about or lost all of these stereotypes and judgments, but simply that I was more cognizant of how to work with them and evaluate afterwards. Though I definitely improved throughout this internship, I still wasn't where I wanted to be.

My final internship took place in a juvenile detention center. I chose this site as I knew it would be a challenge. I had very limited experience with the group so when I started all I possessed were stereotypes, biases, and judgments. I researched the demographics and understood the common crimes and living scenarios to educate myself. In this internship, I made the personal goal of working three sessions with each client before beginning any mental skills training. I found that, although sometimes difficult, particularly with quiet clients, this allowed for full stories, perspectives, and experiences to unfold from the client. I didn't have to guess to fill in the blanks, but would redirect the client to elaborate on any pieces of the experiences that were unclear to me. This—combined with my work with my fieldwork supervisor, group supervision, and personal reflection—allowed the optimal training experience for me in the program. Looking back over these experiences, it is clear to me now that I grew considerably. This is not to say that I enter every situation void of stereotypes and biases; rather, when I begin working with a new client, I understand that I need to let her or him tell their own story. Prematurely filling in the details based on my prior assumptions prevents me from really knowing my clients, which can prevent us from having a productive relationship.

Reflective Questions and Activities for You to Consider Before You Proceed

- What does a self-aware trainee look like?
- How do *you* compare with your picture of a self-aware trainee?
- Keep a journal; great journal entries will use theory and terminology appropriate for your educational level, be insightful about self/other/theory and recognize context of situations, illustrate that you're practicing divergent thinking and present multiple viewpoints, and describe events in a non-judgmental manner.
- Complete as many versions of the Implicit Association Test (IAT)—Social Attitudes as you can!

Note

1 For additional information on the APA Guidelines on Multicultural Education, Training, Research, Practice, and Organizational Change for Psychologists see www.apa.org/pi/oema/resources/policy/multicultural-guidelines.aspx.

References

AASP. (2011). *Ethics Code: AASP ethical principles and standards*. Retrieved from www.appliedsportpsych.org/about/ethics/ethics-code/

AASP. (2017). *Certification program updates*. Retrieved from www.appliedsportpsych.org/certified-consultants/certification-program-updates/

Butryn, T. M. (2002). Critically examining white racial identity and privilege in sport psychology consulting. *The Sport Psychologist, 16,* 316–336.

Kahneman, D. (2011). *Thinking, fast and slow.* New York, NY: Farrar, Straus, & Giroux.

Parham, W. D. (2005). Raising the bar: Developing an understanding of athletes from racially, culturally, and ethnically diverse backgrounds. In M. B. Anderson (Ed.), *Sport psychology in practice* (pp. 201–215). Champaign, IL: Human Kinetics.

Plant, E. A., & Devine, P. G. (2009). The active control of prejudice: Unpacking the intentions guiding control efforts. *Journal of Personality and Social Psychology, 96,* 640–652.

Project Implicit Overview. (2011). Retrieved from https://implicit.harvard.edu/implicit/education.html

Rosenhan, D. (1973). On being sane in insane places. *Science, 179*(4070), 250–258.

Ryba, T. V., Stambulova, N. B., Si, G., & Schinke, R. J. (2013). ISSP position stand: Culturally competent research and practice in sport and exercise psychology. *International Journal of Sport and Exercise Psychology, 11*(2), 123–142.

Sage, G. H., & Eitzen, D. S. (2016). *Sociology of North American sport* (10th ed.). New York, NY: Oxford University Press.

Samuels, D. (2014). *The culturally inclusive educator: Preparing for a multicultural world.* New York, NY: Teacher College Press.

Silva, J. M., Metzler, J. N., & Lerner, B. (2007). *Training professionals in the practice of sport psychology.* Morgantown, WV: Fitness Information Technology.

van Nunspeet, F., Ellemers, N., & Derks, B. (2015). Reducing implicit bias: How moral motivation helps people refrain from making "automatic" prejudiced associations. *Translational Issues in Psychological Science, 1*(4), 382–391.

5 Developing Self-Awareness

Have You Ever Looked in the Mirror?

Meg Kimball-Hodges and Perri Ford

Prior to beginning to work in applied settings, it is important to learn how to deliberately assess one's use of theory, knowledge, and skills in order to learn from experience. Reflective practice is an experiential approach adapted to help develop self-awareness and enhance effectiveness of professional services in applied performance settings. Through self-examination one can identify and overcome blind spots, social or cultural biases, assumptions, ideologies, and concerns within the work setting. By consciously creating a narrative of an event, the trainee (who will hopefully become a professional practitioner) recreates and clarifies meaning within experience and generates new perspectives of events. We learn much more quickly through reflection of trial and error experiences. The sole purpose of engaging in reflective narrative practice is to improve future actions by attending to and analyzing past behaviors, habits and patterns, interests, prejudices, and emotional reactions, and to create a new framework for understanding and action. This chapter will provide a definition of narrative reflection, guide readers through deliberate reflection, explore different venues for implementing reflection, and provide examples of reflection in action.

Background Information on the Authors

Meg Kimball-Hodges has a Bachelor's Degree in Psychology and Sociology from Bellarmine University in Kentucky, a Master's Degree in Community Counseling from Saint Mary's University in Texas, and a Master's Degree in Sport Psychology and a Doctorate in Clinical Psychology from JFKU. Meg is a veteran of the United States Air Force, a collegiate and world-class athlete in soccer, and an avid runner. She is currently in private practice in Colorado with a specialty in neuropsychology, sport psychology, and neurofeedback. She is also an adjunct faculty member with JFKU, where she teaches neuropsychology, assessment, cultural competency, and psychopathology courses while also supervising a few students each year during their internship experience where reflective practice is a key component of the work. Meg can be reached at mhodges@jfku.edu.

Perri Ford recently received a Master's Degree in Sport Psychology from JFKU. She also has a Bachelor's Degree in Exercise Science from the University of Texas at Arlington where she competed in track and field. Perri, who grew up in Calgary, Alberta, is currently an applied consultant with Bell Lap Mental Performance Coaching in Canada and works as a health coach designing and delivering corporate health programs to employees in unique workplaces. She credits much of her success and enjoyment during her time at JFKU to positive and impactful student-supervisor relationships. Learning about the process and experience of reflective practice has helped her to grow personally and professionally. Perri can be contacted at pford@email.jfku.edu. To learn more about Bell Lap Mental Performance Coaching, go to www.belllapmpc.com.

Why Practice Reflection?

Humans are creatures of habit. How many times have you witnessed a friend go through a breakup to only find that he/she chooses a similar mate once again? Or how about the person who goes on a diet every January yet falls off the wagon one month later, if they make it that long? In order to create change or walk a new path, you need to embrace awareness, discipline, and persistence. Critical reflection is the stopgap from reinventing the proverbial wheel; it's a process in which you question underlying assumptions, values, and beliefs, and consider alternate perspectives in order to open the gateway to new experience.

Recall Socrates, who expressed that an unexamined life is not worth living, emphasizing the role of self-examination as a foundation of mental clarity and happiness (see Navia, 2007). In many aspects, Socrates gave voice to the power of stepping back and objectively exploring what is going on in one's world as a way of increasing depth and purpose within one's life. Meaning and the development of identity is a byproduct of making sense out of our experiences within our community (Mehl-Madrona, 2010). Our beliefs about ourselves and what is considered appropriate behavior tend to start within our home. We learn at a very young age how to think, feel, and behave based on what we experience and the feedback we receive from parents, siblings, teachers, and other community members regarding how we act. These lessons then serve as a framework for assessing others around us, sometimes without even recognizing we're doing so. This ability to run on autopilot is actually a highly adaptive mechanism that frees up our brain's energy in order to focus on more complex, demanding tasks. As explained by French neuroscientist Dr. Dehaene (2014), non-conscious and pre-conscious processing is essential for processing language, vision, hearing, action, and of course, breathing. This automatic processing is necessary and useful for basic survival and when needing to respond quickly and reflexively.

There are some circumstances, however, in which autopilot can be counterproductive. What worked when we were kids may not be entirely adaptive as adults. Furthermore, what works in one environment can backfire in another entirely separate circumstance. As trainees and consultants, it's our job to attend to our client's way of life and adapt our skills to fit their needs. However, this doesn't naturally occur without bias. We make inferences of what we see, hear, and experience based on our own story. This is where reflection comes in; bringing to awareness that which has been stored at unconscious and pre-conscious levels (Dehaene, 2014). Through increased awareness of our responses to events, we can better tease out what is ours to own, what is interfering with client performance, and how to approach client change that best resonates with that person. Critical reflection is what we believe separates the mediocre from great consultants.

A key component of reflection is an understanding of how power comes into play within consultation. As the consultant who listens to another's person's story, including their trials and tribulations, you inherently hold power. Many times with power comes privilege—privilege of being the expert, of feeling less vulnerable, and sharing your own beliefs sometimes without having a clear understanding of where your client is coming from. Through reflection, you develop better control of your actions; you learn to pause and consciously consider your influence on the athlete before responding. Basically, you're practicing non-maleficence and beneficence, two of the tenets for ethical decision-making.

Reflective Practice in Sport Psychology Training

Like other mental skills such as imagery, mindfulness, and arousal control, it takes time to master reflective practice. However, the work is worth its weight in gold. The overarching goal is to increase our learning through experience in order to be stellar consultants. Enhanced learning occurs by giving attention to the nuances that come into play within consultation. For instance, you may unconsciously identify with your client or have strong feelings and beliefs that conflict with your client's beliefs or practices. At a surface level you can overlook these phenomena, yet with skillful reflection you are able to witness your own experience while also considering another's perspective, therefore bridging a gap in understanding.

Early on in the internship process, I (Perri) found myself identifying strongly with one of my first clients. I was working with Calvin, an athlete who played a team sport and who grew up in the same area as I did. Calvin was dealing with issues that I initially perceived to be similar to those that I had come across in my athletic career. While this felt like an advantage for our consulting relationship initially, I quickly learned that I was making assumptions about him rather than using our similarities to increase my ability to simply practice empathy.

These, as well as other forms of unconscious theme interference (Caplan & Caplan, 2001), frequently occur. Unconscious theme interference refers to the consultant unknowingly projecting themes from his or her own life onto the work or client. Themes can be thoughts or emotions triggered by an evocative cue in the characteristics of the client or in a feature of the client's case. Perception is subjective and the more attached you are to your perception the more likely it will interfere with consultation. When you hold onto judgments or have certainty around human behavior, you're holding onto preconceptions. Rather than focusing on solutions or ideas that tend to reside within your values and beliefs, you want to open yourself up to other perspectives, question your certainty, and create a space for you to grow. Critical reflection includes a level of vulnerability that can be uncomfortable. However, as you master the skill, your growth will far outweigh that initial discomfort.

Increased self-awareness of your thoughts, actions, and others' responses to your actions is integral to professional growth and development. Despite research that links effective delivery to reflective practice (Cropley, Miles, Hanton, & Niven, 2007; Cropley, Hanton, Miles, & Niven, 2010a), it has yet to be adopted as an official requirement for certification by organizations such as AASP. There are, however, professional bodies in and outside of sport that incorporate reflective practice, such as BASES (Rhodius & Huntley, 2014). Given that academic training programs, such as that in JFKU's Sport Psychology Department, have embraced reflective practice, and that it has been found beneficial for expediting growth, it is important to understand exactly what it is, how to do it, and the benefits of using it.

What Is Reflective Practice?

Reflection is something we naturally perform in our daily lives. We contemplate a response from a spouse or teacher, our performance on the sport field, and even our choice of food and clothing. The way that reflective practice differs from most everyday reflection is that it involves purposeful contemplation that leads to change in perception and action. Dewey (1933), who introduced reflection to psychology and pedagogy in the mid-nineteenth century, identified reflective practice as an active and deliberate cognitive process of milling over a subject to give it serious thought (Cropley et al., 2007). Rather than being a self-centered or narcissist approach, reflective practice engages our relationship with others—that which occurs between one's inner self and culture—allowing you to learn new ways of interacting and relating to others and the environment. The key ingredient in reflective practice is acting on changed perspectives grounded in stronger moral and professional judgment. As Bolton (2014) indicated, a critical reflective practitioner attempts to understand the heart of their work that can't be fully defined through evidence-based practice. This is what makes applied sport psychology an art of combining one's personality, interpersonal skills, and evidence-based practice into a sound working model. Reflective practice is a tool for integrating theory, performance-enhancement skills, counseling skills, multicultural competence, and one's own life experiences and personality for continued improvement.

Let's take a moment to revisit Calvin, the client to whom I (Perri) found myself relating during our consulting sessions. In our first few sessions I noticed that I would include my assumptions as a part of the learning process. I would ask a question leading with a sentence like "Wow, you must have been frustrated when . . .", and Calvin would nod in agreement without elaborating on the emotion. In my counseling skills classes, we had been working on active listening and I felt like I was doing a good job of using restatement as a way of encouraging conversation. Unfortunately, as I listened back to our audio tapes and discussed them with my supervisor, I realized that I wasn't restating Calvin's emotions, I was letting my assumptions interfere with his space to share. I consider my desire to build strong connections with people a personal strength; however, I quickly realized that there was a level of self-awareness missing as I tried to tie counseling skills into my own practice of mental skills consultation. If it were not for structured reflective practice, I may have never discovered the errors I was making in my work with Calvin.

As a mental skills consultant (MSC) in training, you need to not only develop sound knowledge and theory behind optimal performance, but you also need to practice the very skills you plan to teach others while gaining experience of *being* a consultant. Reflection is a means of integrating education, training, and experience in order to progress at a faster rate and with more efficacy. I (Meg) like to think of reflection as a form of mindfulness in which one creates a pause between experience and further action in order to assess what happened from a non-judgmental space and uncover hidden gems through self-inquiry. Through reflection, you explore areas you didn't realize you knew, had forgotten about, never set time aside to explore, or hadn't even considered in the past (Bolton, 2014). It's a method to reveal one's self with greater depth, including the reasons behind actions, inconsistencies in values and actions, and possible changes in action that resonate with one's authentic and empathic self. Reflective practice is a proactive approach toward discovery of self, one's work, and the world by facing one's fears, frustrations, struggles, and successes in a non-judgmental manner.

What does it mean to be non-judgmental or detached? With self-reflection, the aim is to increase your ability to observe and ask questions even while in the midst of a strong reaction. Certain powerful responses to an experience have the capacity to take command; we become reactive. Reacting restricts our worldview by limiting what we can see; it limits our perspective. By self-reflecting in the present tense and in the first person, we help remove the rigidity of our perception and quiet the reactive response without distancing ourselves from the experience. Self-reflection is an exercise in expanding our awareness and building up our capacity to be mindful in the moment.

Reflection is a powerful tool, but can be much more beneficial when practiced in a manner consistent with how the brain most efficiently learns. For humans, storytelling is a way of making sense of our world and connecting with others. As Benedict Carey (2015) described in "How We Learn," episodic or autobiographical memory has some of the same sensual and narrative structure as the original experience. Humans store episodes of experience in memory and share experience through storytelling. Similar to imagery, which involves creating a sequence of events using vivid sensory motor experiences, reflecting in narrative format is a recreation of an experience by putting sensory motor experiences into words. Narrative reflection brings the mental skills trainee closer to one's work by constructing and reconstructing changes in one's stories as new experiences arise (Browning, Brooks, & White, 2005; White, 2011). This is what, in neuroscience, is referred to as neural plasticity (Costandi, 2016; Doidge, 2016)—the ability of the brain to adapt and change in increased complexity as new events arise. These neural networks for memory of experiences are ever changing and the introduction of new memories alters the understanding of experience (Foer, 2012). That's what I (Meg) believe you're doing with narrative reflection, re-experiencing the event in a more detached sense in order to study it further. Doing this creates the space to alter your understanding of that experience as well as lay down new pathways to enhance your ability to respond more effectively in future related experiences.

Narrative storytelling is a natural phenomenon used by various cultures over many generations. Our brains are wired to tell and listen to stories and narrative communication helps us make sense of our experiences and give them meaning (Stelter, 2010). The field of narrative therapy takes advantage of the power of story for therapeutic change (Mehl-Madrona, 2010; White, 2007). Through the exploration of experience, the person progressively distances him- or herself from the known and familiar toward what might be possible to perceive, know and act—a form of roadmap for moving into the future (White, 2011). As social beings that relate through story, narrative reflection fits nicely into our biology. Furthermore, storytelling helps shed light on the themes, the power relations, and the strong emotions related to experience. By milling over (through reflection) what occurred in our own mind's eye, we can identify the meaning in the experience and learn perspective or alternate ways of acting. According to norm theory (Kahneman & Miller, 1986), humans derive a series of templates from experiences that are then used to compare imagined alternative realities. Basically, there's a template for the way people imagine scenarios. We modify our memories with new experiences, and by re-imagining past scenarios we can come to grips with the past.

Returning to the sessions with Calvin, narrative storytelling played a large role in understanding how to become a better consultant, and it was done in a number of ways. First, during my (Perri) one-on-one supervision I would give an account of the week's events and highlight areas that I felt needed to be discussed. It was through the retelling of the sessions' events that I came to realize that I needed to be sure I was taking myself out of the equation when I was working with Calvin. It became a running theme that I would feel distant or detached from Calvin on days that I was assuming his experience was the same as mine.

Because of the realization that I was sabotaging our work together (with well-intentioned efforts), I was able to change my preparation for our sessions by repeating the phrase "clean slate" to myself right before our meeting times. This is something I have continued doing with all of my clients to this day. I also found it helpful to write down the events as if I were telling the story in a journal format. In supervision, this usually came in the form of writing an email to my supervisor, or asking a classmate in group supervision about what they would do in my shoes. Now as a consultant, I continue to do this for myself as a part of the note-taking process. After each session I will reflect and write myself a brief note about how it went and look for areas that I may have missed in the moment.

What Are the Different Types of Reflection in Sport Psychology?

Donald Schön (1983), a trained philosopher, has provided remarkable insight into practitioner ability to quickly adapt to changes within environments. He emphasizes the need to enter the trenches, or "swampy lowlands" (p. 43), of the profession, learn from mistakes, and live with the consequences. In order to improve effectiveness, not only does one need to understand how to apply theory to on-the-job decision-making, but also how to embrace uncertainty. This ability to embrace uncertainty creates space for openness and flexibility, the ability to adapt to change, and lifelong growth through seeking knowledge rather than being all-knowing.

Schön (1983) described two specific forms of reflection: reflection-in-action and reflection-on-action. The former is a way to assess values, knowledge, theory, and skill

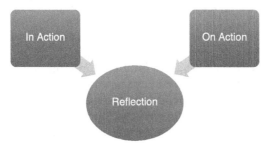

Figure 5.1 A model of Schön's (1983) Theory of Reflection

during work and make adjustments on the fly; this involves linking what we say we do (research-based knowledge) to what actually happens (hands-on knowledge). The latter, reflection-on-action, occurs after the event and when one is able to contemplate the situation in more depth and without urgency. It is a much more deliberate activity specifically designed to improve future performance (Cropley et al., 2010a). Both methods are important, with reflection-on-action increasing the effectiveness of reflection-in-action (Bolton, 2014). As you become more versed in reflection on your experience, you'll develop greater ability to use reflection on the fly during experience.

There are three formal situations during training in which to practice self-reflection. First is a guided reflection during individual supervision, in which you explore your experience with your assigned supervisor. This includes looking for themes and biases within your work as well as ways in which you decided to act based on knowledge and theory (i.e. decision-making). In this situation, the supervisor supports the supervisee in becoming more aware of thoughts, feelings, and behaviors that may not be apparent to the supervisee. This might include habits, conforming to norms, negative attitude, prejudice and racism, fears, expectations from others, over-identification with athlete, need for appreciation, and loyalty to staff versus athlete, to name a few. This type of reflection relies on trust in the supervisor and willingness to be vulnerable, which sets the stage for improved self-awareness and adaptability.

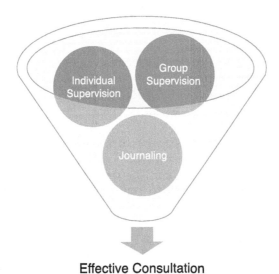

Figure 5.2 Diagram of the components of effective consultation

The second opportunity to practice reflection during training is in group supervision (or as we now call it at JFKU, "Group Soup"). During this forum, you can share your experience with peers by exploring the factors that contribute to your perception and adapting your perception based on responses from your peers. The vital component of group supervision is the ability of the group to refrain from input until the person sharing has had sufficient time to articulate his or her experience. Much of the time is spent asking questions that help uncover the story from the teller's perspective. Reflection is a process of exploring a person's experience with curiosity. It requires good listening skills and open-minded inquiry by the group to assist another's unfolding of their experience. Once the group has critically explored the event, members share their observations, recognized themes and inconsistencies, and their own experience of the event being shared. In doing so, everyone in the group learns from that experience. Cropley, Hanton, Miles, and Niven (2010b) emphasize the value of shared reflections, such as individual and group supervision, for promoting greater understanding of experience and the modeling of reflective process; however, this does not negate the third opportunity for formal reflection within the training environment.

The third venue for reflection is through individual narrative writing or journaling. This is a much more personal and multidimensional format toward growth that creates a space to reflect while writing. Through writing, more attention is given to the series of events, the players in the event, emotions felt and expressed, how one's own history influenced action, the consequences of actions, and how one might change future interactions based on this past experience. Writing is a great means of expressing yourself, your thoughts, ideas, and experiences in order to deepen your own understanding. While inscribing your narrative in ink, you work with the story rather than about the story (Knowles, Gilbourne, Tomlinson, & Anderson, 2007), reliving the experience and reformulating an understanding of what took place from your own perspective. You choose the questions to ask yourself and explore what you find important. Sharing writings with your supervisor enhances reflective writing even further. For some people, although it still creates feelings of vulnerability, this format feels safer than sharing with an entire group of peers. Topics or experiences that feel more threatening can be saved for this smaller and more intimate atmosphere. By sharing with the supervisor, the trainee has an opportunity to learn at a deeper level from an outsider with experience. In addition to the self-reflection methods mentioned above, Knowles, Gilbourne, Cropley, and Dugdill (2014) outlined a number of approaches to reflection that may be considered. These include:

- Mind mapping: a visual approach to understanding the relationship between different influences on a specific situation.
- Recorded narrative: a method of reflection that can be used to record thoughts and feelings immediately following a session or event.

During my time as an intern at JFKU, I (Perri) participated in group reflections, one-on-one supervision, and personal reflection through journaling. A particular situation with another athlete I worked with in my time as a trainee stands out as an example of how beneficial the three aforementioned styles of reflective practice were in helping me grow as a professional.

I was just beginning my work with a group of high performance youth athletes, most of whom were from very affluent backgrounds. During an initial session with an athlete on the team, I noticed that I perceived him to be stand-offish, and felt as though I was being talked down to by him. Every time I asked a question, he responded in a way that I believed was condescending and even sarcastic at times. Although I was able to maintain the flow of conversation with a good selection of meaningful assessment questions, I felt a shift in my demeanor with the athlete and was unhappy with myself for it. Throughout the session, I was struggling to label what I was feeling and had a lot of guilt for putting my own feelings above listening to the athlete. As a result, I left the session feeling as though I could have done better and hoping he didn't notice my change in attitude or my internal reaction to his answers.

The reflective process began by listening back to my audio file of the session and journaling feelings that came up for me or areas I noticed I could have improved on. Next, I met with my supervisor, who encouraged me to dig deeper into the reasons behind my reactions to the situation. During this exploration together we found that, during my upbringing in a middle-class home, I had developed a bias about socioeconomic status. Bringing awareness to the bias allowed me to confront the assumptions I had made about the client, and to revisit my analysis of the situation. Once I listened to the audio file again I realized that what I was hearing as arrogance could have in fact been nervousness. Next, I discussed the event with my peer group and was able to hear opinions from classmates who had been in similar positions. They offered suggestions about what they had done in the past, as well as different viewpoints to evaluate the athlete's behavior. When I returned to meet with the athlete again, I was able to approach the session with empathy and a heightened positive regard for the athlete. This new awareness of my own bias also positively impacted sessions with clients moving forward.

The reflective practice methods discussed here are all important for enhanced learning; this includes increased understanding in how to be aware, what to be aware of, why one needs to be aware, and what to do with this awareness. Now we'll transition to the meat of this chapter: how to go about narrative reflection.

How to Practice Narrative Reflection

Reflection is a personal process, one in which you explore questions appropriate for the situation with the sole purpose of personal growth. By sitting down and thinking through an event, you bring increased consciousness to your experience. For the supervisor reviewing the reflections, these audios and writings provide an inside look at what might be going on internally for the trainee. They provide insight regarding the depth in which the trainee approaches consultation as well as a venue for tracking trainee progress. The exploration of experience in narrative form brings in a stream of consciousness or succession of experiences to the reflective process, a term coined by William James in 1890 (see James, 1950). This delivery of consciousness to the forefront is a deliberate process that includes both the reflection of the event that unfolded and the internal process of experiencing the event in the first person.

Reflection on an event includes the sharing of what happened, thoughts and emotions around the event or series of events, the people involved, timing and location of the event, and what others may have experienced and felt about it. Exploration of one's own attitudes, theories-in-use, beliefs and values, assumptions, prejudices and habits, and what Bolton terms reflexivity (2014) emphasizes inter-relational dynamics. Being reflexive refers to an openness to explore the limits of your knowledge, incongruences in moral beliefs and action, and how your actions may marginalize or exclude others (Bolton, 2014). These components together provide an inclusive means to assess performance from an applied perspective, one that considers the trainee and future practitioner as a whole person rather than an object performing an act.

Like most learning experiences, developing skill in narrative reflective practice is something that happens with practice over time. However, it becomes easier and more

Table 5.1 Examples of Reflection vs. Reflexivity as expressed by Bolton (2014)

REFLECTION	REFLEXIVITY
Recalling sequence of events	Critically assessing one's attitude
Thoughts regarding event	Theories-in-use (ways of being/acting based on knowledge and experience)
Emotions related to event	Assess values, beliefs, and prejudices
Individuals involved	Assumptions
When it took place	Prejudices
Where it took place	Habits
Others' experience of event (perceived by trainee)	Roles in relation to others
Why sequence of events occurred (emphasis on relationships within event)	Influence of one's own culture and power/privilege on professional work

in-depth with experience. There is some debate regarding how structured the process should be (Anderson, Knowles, & Gilbourne, 2004; Gibbs, 1988; Kolb, 1984). Kolb (1984) developed a fairly structured format that can be helpful for the neophyte practitioner. It is referred to as the experiential learning cycle and includes four sequential stages: 1. having a concrete experience, 2. reflecting on the experience, 3. abstractly conceptualizing to build knowledge, and 4. planning for the next experience incorporating new ideas.

Anderson et al. (2004) suggest the use of Gibbs' (1988) model of reflection as an example of a simple structure for reflection. This includes a description of the event, thoughts and feelings about it, an evaluation, an analysis, a conclusion, and an action plan moving forward.

As you can see, using a model like this would allow you to explore the event and your reactions to it, as well as develop a plan for similar events in the future. This formal approach to reflective practice has been described by Cropley et al. (2010b) as important for developing good habits for a student and neophyte in the sport psychology field. However, such approaches can be limiting with their simplified and narrow vision of reflective practice. Since reflective practice is a multidimensional experiential process, I (Meg) recommend some leeway in what approach the trainee implements while keeping in mind models established by others in the field. Instead of focusing on stages of learning alone, I recommend placing emphasis on ways of engaging in the activity that allow for re-experiencing and exploring one's understanding of perception and action with more depth. Some simple guidelines when starting out include:

- Write in the first-person perspective.
- Engage yourself in the present tense.
- Include all the senses, re-imagining the experience.
- Form a learner perspective with a focus on digging deeper into experience.
- Look for themes and build on these themes through narrative reflection.
- Switch between experience and knowledge regarding the context (theory, prior experience, studies, stories from others, etc.) to transform tentative insights into a much wider understanding.
- Maintain an open mind, detached from your values and beliefs.

The active process of self-reflection allows for a consolidation of experience, planning, and organizing without ruminating over the passive judgment-based evaluation of all of the *shoulda, coulda, wouldas* of performance. Experience is not orderly with clear-cut beginnings and endings and smooth logical processes (Johns, 2010). Rather, experience is contextual, reflexive, and complex, and narrative reflection is an active, engaging process that allows an experience to evolve and connections between experiences to be realized. It is what Johns (2010) describes as resonant with chaos theory (Banks, Dragon, & Jones, 2003), as within the chaos of narrative there is order or pattern recognition that sheds light on the significance and meaning in action. What is extremely valuable about narrative reflection is the re-experiencing of tensions, similar to what I (Perri) described above when listening to my recorded consulting sessions. This re-experiencing sets the stage for self-realization and generation of new insights.

What to Reflect Upon

Getting started in narrative reflection can be the most difficult step. Some people find it helpful to spontaneously write for about 15 to 20 minutes without putting too much thought into the process. After completing the exercise, you can look back over the process—basically reflecting on reflecting to see what themes arise. Here is a list of questions adapted from Johns' (2010) text that provides possible areas of reflection to explore within an experience:

1. What issue(s) demand attention?
2. What feelings or behaviors did others express and what triggered it?
3. What were my emotional response and thoughts associated with those expressions?
4. What connections can I make to this response?
5. What was I trying to achieve with my response?
6. Did it have the desired effect?
7. What were the consequences of my response?
8. What physiological responses come up as I currently reflect?
9. What knowledge influenced this event?
10. Was my response congruent with my morals and values?
11. How might the event compare to similar experiences in my past?
12. How might I approach this experience differently?
13. What may be the costs and benefits of this new approach?
14. What constraints might hinder taking this new approach?
15. How do I feel now regarding this new approach?
16. Am I better able to support myself and others because of this reflection (reflecting on reflection)?
17. Have I developed new insights from reflecting on the experience?

This list is not exhaustive, but should provide a structured guideline for contemplating themes. By practicing switching between your personal experience and the experience of others, you'll improve your ability to do so more quickly during future work. This process also helps you develop empathy and connection with others by stepping outside your own perception of the world and learning to resonate with others' experiences. Lastly, by actively attending to the way you feel, you become more aware of the ways your own responses influence the efficacy of your work.

Audio Reflection vs. Written Reflection

Mental skills trainees at JFKU are given a choice of completing reflections in written or audio recording format. Instead of sticking with one format, I (Meg) recommend you experiment with both. I personally prefer completing written reflections as well as receiving the written format from students, the main reason being the focused attention needed for writing. I'll review here the benefits and challenges of both formats.

I recall feeling pressed for time during my graduate training. A wonderful benefit of audio reflection is that is requires less time and can be completed while performing less demanding tasks. You can audio-record reflections right after meeting with the client as an extension of the recorded session, while sitting outside, while doing dishes, etc. Multi-tasking has become increasingly popular with people, allowing the feeling they are able to accomplish more in a day than ever before. However, research has shown multi-tasking not only reduces our performance at tasks, but also results in decreased efficiency (Gorlick, 2009). Furthermore, those individuals who most believe they are stellar multi-taskers actually performed most poorly on multi-tasking during research studies (Gupta, 2016). When it comes to reflection, in order to reap the benefits you need to engage in focused attention. For me, this is much more likely when I have to contemplate details, write, and review what I have written.

Audio reflections can be completed during focused attention and should be considered as a viable option toward professional growth. However, it takes the mastering of guided reflection in order to know what to reflect upon. When reviewing sessions, you should look for themes, assess dynamics that play out in the relationship, analyze the interventions chosen, review the theory behind case conceptualization and intervention, and consider the outcomes of the interventions (Sperry & Carlson, 2014). Actually, as the consultant, you have a greater effect on your client than the method and techniques you choose to implement (Baldwin & Imel, 2013). As the client-consultant relationship accounts for the majority of service outcome, time should be allotted to reflect on this relationship (Duncan, 2014). For the trainee or neophyte consultant, audio sessions tend to be based more on free association than on guided reflection. Although this process is beneficial, the benefits have been lessened.

There are some instances in which audio recordings may be the preferred method. For instance, those who have dyslexia may find audio recording much more rewarding and beneficial than engaging in reading and writing activities that require increased mental energy and resources that take away from the reflective process. Additionally, the reflective process is much more beneficial when completed soon after the event. Memories of experiences change with time and one of the major memory-change agents is sleep. The brain processes and integrates what is learned during the day during sleep (Buzsaki, 2006). Audio-recorded reflections may be more beneficial on those days when time is limited and sitting down to review session details is unlikely to occur. Basically, audio reflection on the day of the event can be more authentic than completing a written reflection a day or two later.

The trainee can especially benefit from transcribing recorded audios and analyzing sessions from transcribed data (Newell & Burnard, 2011). Transcription is a time-consuming activity, yet provides a venue for teasing out the details and critically assessing nuances. Through transcription, the trainee can notice aspects of interaction otherwise easily overlooked. For instance, the rhythm of conversation, silences, interviewing technique, tones of voice, and transitions can be brought to light (Newell & Burnard, 2011). Reflection and analysis occur after transcription. Once these overlooked areas are identified, they can be noted and possibly addressed during future sessions. Some practitioners prefer writing reflections in the right margin of the transcript while others choose to do so on a separate sheet of paper. What matters most is the process rather than the location.

Transcriptions can be valuable within individual and group supervision. In collaborative settings such as these, there's an opportunity to focus on and work through one's thoughts, feelings, and decision-making process. By sharing with others, the MSC helps clarify, re-interpret, and reformulate his or her own reflection (Sperry & Carlson, 2014). Although this format can feel vulnerable for the trainee, the goal is growth, not judgment. When completed within a group setting, the MSC has an opportunity to hear others' responses to the events and learn from different perspectives.

In summary, reflection is a deliberate process of analyzing themes and meaning behind themes. It allows the consultant to identify key statements and phrases that reflect meaning, consider what evidence supports conceptualization and implementation of tools and techniques, review the outcome of interaction and interventions used, contemplate one's own values and biases that come into play, and determine the best course of action moving forward. Written reflection provides a richer venue for deliberate practice (Bassot, 2016); however, audio reflection should be considered, especially in times when thorough written reflection doesn't fit into the trainee's or professional's schedule. Sharing reflections with one's supervisor and peer group enhances learning even more by providing the opportunity to gain insight into different perceptions of the experience. This becomes a win-win situation in which the identified trainee and his or her peer group learn through experience.

Obstacles to Effective Narrative Practice

One of the main challenges in reflection is the awkwardness of chatting with one's self about one's self. The idea is to see yourself within a relationship. There's some vulnerability in engaging in this type of dialogue. It can stir up anxieties, doubts, and fears. Reflexive questioning can feel risky, especially when you plan to share your reflection with a supervisor or peers. Subjecting one's self to this task takes some humility, yet those willing to take the risk gain the most—greater emotional strength, agency, and transformative learning (Bennett-Levy & Lee, 2014; Bolton, 2014). To do it service, one needs to practice honesty and perseverance which can shake up a rigid identity with certain beliefs or worldviews. It may also force you to question your morality. In narrative reflection, you're tapping into a deeper understanding that changes your sense of self.

Another challenge with self-reflection is the ability for the practitioner to actually be aware of his or her biases, which will be discussed in more detail in the next chapter. For someone to look in the mirror and truly understand him or herself, one has to be sure the mirror itself is not distorted. As Watson, Lubker, and Van Raalte (2011) identify, a narcissistic practitioner would likely see her practice as unquestionably good and this belief may pervade throughout the self-reflective process. This further necessitates the need for consultants to not only just *look into the mirror* and reflect, but to step back and look upon the detail of the reflections and what self-serving beliefs might be distorting the narrative.

The expression of feelings through narrative reflection can be cathartic. However, there are times that it can have the opposite effect. Similar to using imagery within sport, when you imagine experience during reflective practice you want to harness feelings toward positive action. Mentally rehearsing can be debilitating when it involves rehearing a negative aspect over and over. It's important to modify the context of the specific emotion in order to empower the person rather than trigger stronger connections for a disabling event. Should you find yourself stuck, it is recommended you seek consultation through your supervisor, group supervision, or both. These venues provide rich learning experiences for all involved.

Benefits of Narrative Reflective Practice

One of the great benefits of self-reflection is increased practitioner awareness of professional progress, which inherently increases one's faith in the reflective process itself. This increased awareness of growth as a consultant furthermore encourages greater intrinsic motivation, providing a win-win situation as a professional (Anderson et al., 2004). The reflective process results in self-knowledge that can be classified as either technical, practical, or critical (Anderson et al., 2004; James & Clarke, 1996). A *technical* perspective might involve a practitioner using the reflective process to assess their own technical delivery of a particular psychological skills training program. An honest self-reflection on how the program was delivered as per the guidelines provided by empirical evidence and sport psychology theory would enable the practitioner to adequately identify areas for improvement. A *practical* perspective would involve more exploration of personal meaning, acknowledging and identifying biases and understanding the context through which they see certain information. A practitioner might explore the motives behind why they acted in a certain way or why a certain situation invoked a particular cognitive or emotional response. A *critical* perspective might involve the professional going through the process of questioning the traditional approaches to sport psychology as guided by organizational bodies to which the practitioners may belong (Anderson et al., 2004). This could include identifying the dominance of white privilege or inherent racial or gender biases. This form of reflective practice is often the most overlooked and is probably an aspect which will develop as the practitioner improves his or her reflective skills.

Conclusion

In summary, reflection is a powerful tool to improve depth and speed of learning. Similar to other mental skills techniques you teach athletes to use, practice improves your ability to reap the benefits. It takes some time and energy to develop the skill in the beginning, but with practice it becomes automatic and can be harnessed on the fly. Keep in mind that reflection can be a collaborative approach, and continue to reach out to classmates, colleagues, and supervisors to help you engage in the process. We are ever-changing with continued experience; even though our focus is on athlete or client change, we change in and among the relationships we experience. The chance of learning dramatically increases when we reflect on our experiences. Furthermore, we can assess growth through reviewing and reflecting on past reflections, or what I (Meg) term meta-reflection. Lastly, by becoming masters in self-reflection, we can better teach the skill to our clients so they can reap similar benefits.

A Trainee's Perspective on Self-Awareness and Reflective Practice

Richard Iacino, M.A., student at JFKU 2013–2015

Richard's goal is to work in Major League Baseball as a Mental Conditioning Coach. His career pursuits include gaining experience at the professional level, establishing a private consulting practice, and ultimately opening his own youth baseball academy with emphasis on the mental game. He would also like to be a part-time, adjunct university instructor. He can be reached at riacino@email.jfku.edu.

I have been working with clients for a little over two years now, including one year as a trainee, and must admit that one of the most important aspects of my applied work is the consistent use of reflection. The reality is that there will always be sessions that go well and those that do not go so well. By using reflection, I have been able to learn and grow regardless of the outcome. One of the key aspects of my reflection is the attitude I go into it with. When I first started out, there were times I was so critical of myself that I would find fault in nearly everything I did, and other times I felt so good after a session that I did not even bother reflecting. I learned that, when it comes to reflection, I needed to adopt a growth mindset (Dweck, 2006) so that I could begin to view every reflection as an opportunity to learn and grow, regardless of how the session went. There are many different reflection styles and models you can use, but the best lesson I learned is that the model you use is not nearly as important as the attitude you approach it with.

Once I learned how to view myself critically and constructively, I needed to find a model that fit my style. Structured reflection has worked best for me because it takes some of the emotion out of the reflection, and allows me to reflect in an organized manner. Personally, I gravitated toward Gibbs' Reflective Cycle (Gibbs, 1988) and still use an iteration of it today. My favorite part about this model is that it starts by simply looking at the facts; I can ask myself questions such as "Did I teach the lesson I had planned?", "Did the client walk away with something?", and "Did I stay within my time parameters?" These simple questions often help me realize that a session may have gone better than I originally thought, or possibly humble me. The key here is that it can ultimately help me build self-awareness around my applied work, and that awareness can help me focus on what I need to work on moving forward.

During my experience as a JFKU intern, I learned to use reflection to set goals for my applied work. After each session, individual or group, I would carve out 15–30 minutes to reflect on what went well, and what I could work on moving forward. These would ultimately become my goals of each day at internship (e.g. "Avoid double questions", "Sit with the silence", etc.). I would write the goals on a notecard and bring them with me to internship the following day. This would not only give me something to focus on throughout my day, but would also give me tangible results in my growth as a consultant. I was able to go back to my notecard after each day and evaluate my performance. This is a technique that worked wonders for me throughout each of my internships. It is important to get started as soon as possible because growth as a consultant will never stop as long as you do not allow it to.

Reflective Questions and Activities for You to Consider Before You Proceed

- Try out narrative storytelling for yourself! Choose an emotion-laden experience from your past that seems like a valuable time to reflect on and write about it using the guidelines mentioned above.

    o   What happened during the experience from beginning to end?
    o   How did you react and what did others do who were involved?
    o   What was most striking about the experience?
    o   What was your response and how was that response received?
    o   If you could approach it differently now, what might you ask or do?
    o   What did you learn from the exercise?

- Choose a recorded individual session with an athlete of your choice and transcribe that session. Once complete, go back through the transcript and annotate your thoughts, feelings, and observations in the margin of the transcript. Take into consideration the questions listed above.

- Think about the ethical considerations you will need to keep in mind during your own personal practice of self-reflection.

  o   What are the limits to confidentiality?

  o   How can you protect the privacy of your client?

  o   Was client safety a concern?

  o   What cultural components may influence client performance and the consulting relationship?

  o   Are any concerns of multiple relations present (seeing two athletes who are dating, competing against each other, or from the same family)?

  o   Are the athlete's beliefs or values in conflict with your own? If so, how might you broach this conflict?

  o   How might you handle being sexually attracted to the athlete? How about your response to an athlete being attracted to you?

References

Anderson, A. G., Knowles, Z., & Gilbourne, D. (2004). Reflective practice for sport psychologists: Concepts, models, practical implications, and thoughts on dissemination. *The Sport Psychologist*, *18*, 188–203.

Baldwin, S. A., & Imel, Z. E. (2013). Therapist effects: Findings and methods. In M. J. Lambert, (Ed.), *Bergin and Garfield's handbook of psychotherapy and behavior change* (6th ed.) (pp. 258–297). New York, NY: Wiley.

Banks, J., Dragon, V., & Jones, A. (2003). *Chaos: A mathematical introduction*. Cambridge, UK: Cambridge University Press.

Bassot, B. (2016). *The reflective practice guide: An interdisciplinary approach to critical reflection*. New York, NY: Routledge.

Bennett-Levy, J., & Lee, N. K. (2014). Practice and self-reflection in cognitive behavior therapy training: What factors influence trainees' engagement and experience of benefit? *Behavioral and Cognitive Psychotherapy*, *42*, 48–64.

Bolton, G. (2014). *Reflective practice: Writing and professional development*. Los Angeles, CA: SAGE Publications Ltd.

Browning, J., Brooks, B., & White, M. (ABC Radio National). (2005, October 1). Writing on the Mind, the power of story telling [Radio series episode]. *All in the Mind*. Retrieved from http://mpegmedia.abc.net.au/rn/podcast/2005/10/aim_20051001.mp3

Buzsaki, G. (2006). *Rhythms of the brain*. Oxford, UK: Oxford University Press.

Caplan, R. B., & Caplan, G. (2001) *Helping the helpers not to harm: Iatrogenic damage and community mental health*. New York, NY: Brunner Routledge.

Carey, B. (2015). *How we learn: The surprising truth about when, where, and why it happens*. New York, NY: Penguin Random House.

Costandi, M. (2016). *Neuroplasticity*. Cambridge, MA: MIT Press.

Cropley, B., Hanton, S., Miles, A., & Niven, A. (2010a). Exploring the relationship between effective and reflective practice in applied sport psychology. *The Sport Psychologist*, *24*(4), 521–541.

Cropley, B., Hanton, S., Miles, A., & Niven, A. (2010b). The value of reflective practice in professional development: An applied sport psychology review. *Sport Science Review*, *19*(3–4), 179–208.

Cropley, B., Miles, A., Hanton, S., & Niven, A. (2007). Improving the delivery of applied sport psychology support through reflective practice. *The Sport Psychologist*, *21*, 475–494.

Dehaene, S. (2014) *Consciousness and the brain: Deciphering how the brain codes our thoughts*. New York, NY: Penguin Random Books.

Dewey, J. (1933). *How we think: A restatement of the relation of reflective thinking to the educative process*. Boston, MA: D.C. Heath.

Doidge, N. (2016). *The brain's way of healing: Remarkable discoveries and recoveries from the frontiers of neuroplasticity*. New York, NY: Penguin Random Books.

Duncan, B. L. (2014). *On becoming a better therapist: Evidence-based practice one client at a time* (2nd ed.). Washington, DC: American Psychological Association.

Dweck, C. (2006). *Mindset: The new psychology of success*. New York, NY: Random House.

Foer, J. (2012). *Moonwalking with Einstein: The art and science of remembering everything*. New York, NY: Penguin Books.

Gibbs, G. (1988). *Learning by doing: A guide to teaching and learning methods*. Oxford Brookes, UK: Further Education Unit, Oxford Polytechnic.

Gorlick, A. (2009, August 24). Media multitaskers pay a mental price, Stanford study shows. *Stanford News*. Retrieved from http://news.stanford.edu/2009/08/24/multitask-research-study-082409/

Gupta, S. (2016, August 1). Your brain on multitasking. *CNN Health*. Retrieved from www.cnn.com/2015/04/09/health/your-brain-multitasking/

James, C. R., & Clarke, B. (1996). Reflective practice in nursing: Issues and implications for nurse education. In T. Ghaye (Ed.), *Reflection and action for health care professionals* (pp. 35–48). Newcastle Upon Tyne, UK: Pentaxion Ltd.

James, W. (1950). *The principles of psychology, Vol 1*. New York, NY: Dover Publishing (Original work published 1890).

Johns, C. (2010). *Guided reflection: A narrative approach to advancing professional practice* (2nd ed.). West Sussex, UK: Wiley-Blackwell.

Kahneman, D., & Miller, D. T. (1986). Norm theory: Comparing reality to its alternatives. *Psychological Review, 93*(2), 136–153.

Knowles, Z., Gilbourne, D., Cropley, B., & Dugdill, L. (2014). Reflecting on reflection and journeys. In Z. Knowles, D. Gilbourne, B. Cropley, & L. Dugdill (Eds.), *Reflective practice in the sport and exercise sciences* (pp. 3–15). New York, NY: Routledge.

Knowles, Z., Gilbourne, D., Tomlinson, V., & Anderson, A. G. (2007). Reflections on the application of the reflective practice in applied sport psychology. *The Sport Psychologist, 21*, 109–122.

Kolb, D. A. (1984). *Experiential learning: Experience as a source of learning and development*. Upper Saddle River, NJ: Prentice Hall.

Mehl-Madrona, L. (2010) *Healing the mind through the power of story: The promise of narrative psychiatry*. Rochester, VT: Bear & Company.

Navia, L. E. (2007). *Socrates: A life examined*. Amherst, NY: Prometheus Books.

Newell, R., & Burnard, P. (2011). *Research for evidence-based practice in healthcare* (2nd ed.). Iowa: Wiley-Blackwell.

Rhodius, A., & Huntley, E. (2014). Facilitating reflective practice in graduate trainees and early career practitioners. In Z. Knowles, D. Gilbourne, B. Cropley, & L. Dugdill (Eds.), *Reflective practice in the sport and exercise sciences: Contemporary issues* (pp. 91–100). New York, NY: Routledge.

Schön, D. A. (1983). *The reflective practitioner: How professionals think in action*. New York, NY: Basic Books.

Sperry, L., & Carlson, J. (2014). *How master therapists work: Effecting change from the first through last session and beyond*. New York, NY: Routledge.

Stelter, R. (2010). Narrative coaching: A community psychological perspective. In T. V. Ryba, R. J. Schinke, & G. Tenenbaum (Eds.), *The cultural turn in sport psychology* (pp. 335–361). Morgantown, WV: Fitness Information Technology.

Watson, J. C., Lubker, J. R., & Van Raalte, J. (2011). Problems in reflective self-practice: Self-bootstrapping versus therapeutic supervision. In D. Gilbourne & M. B. Anderson (Eds.), *Critical essays in applied sport psychology* (pp. 157–172). Champaign, IL: Human Kinetics.

White, M. (2007). *Maps of narrative practice*. New York, NY: W.W. Norton & Company.

White, M. (2011). *Narrative practice: Continuing the conversations*. New York, NY: W.W. Norton & Company.

6   Working with Your Supervisor

What, You Have Another Relationship to Think About?

Alison Pope-Rhodius and Michael Howard

Once the supervisor has been found or assigned, there are many aspects that go into making this a successful relationship. This chapter will address considerations specific to the supervisory process, such as learning about important aspects in this professional relationship, being clear on ground rules, responsibilities, and applicable deadlines, acknowledging one's own strengths and challenges, being open to feedback, and how to make the most of supervision time. Being a trainee can be a daunting task, especially at first, and a good supervisor will help guide the logistical elements involved. Additionally, supervisors assist with the intellectual and emotional journey that training in applied sport psychology can involve, thus making a strong supervisory relationship important. The supervision model at JFKU includes individual and group supervision modalities to support the students' growth, and the benefits of each will be highlighted. As reflective practice is an excellent tool for trainees, ways to use it for supervision will be addressed in this chapter.

Background Information on the Authors

Alison Pope-Rhodius is the Chair of the Sport Psychology Department at JFKU (see Chapter 1 for more bio information) and has been supervising trainees for close to 20 years. She has written about supervision and presented on this topic internationally, and feels strongly about the importance of supervision and training for supervisors and meta-supervisors. Her co-author for this chapter used to be one of her interns a wee while ago, so she has a lot to say on this topic! She can be contacted at arhodius@jfku.edu.

Michael (Mike) Howard is a native Oregonian who currently lives in the Flint Hills of Kansas while working as a performance and resilience enhancement specialist with the United States Army. He has a Master's Degree in Sport Psychology from JFKU and a background in utilizing sport and performance psychology to benefit under-served youth in various urban and rural communities. In this role, he helps to train community organizations on how to implement enhanced recreational programming for their clientele. Mike is also a CC-AASP. Mike loves to supervise sport and performance trainees and help them to maximize their potential. Much of his personal philosophy on sport psychology practice and life is to build confidence through reflective self-awareness and to cultivate a strong sense of optimism through gratitude and deliberate future-mindedness. He can be contacted at mhoward@jfku.edu.

We're assuming if you have reached this chapter then you're about to start (or are planning to start) your supervised applied work. You are now embarking on the beginning of an important relationship: that between you and your supervisor(s). There are some situations in which you might find yourself being assigned a supervisor (e.g. when you're in an academic internship experience) and there are other times when you need to find your own supervisor. Chapter 3 of this book covers finding your supervisor, so if you still need to find a supervisor, make sure you read that chapter first as we will now discuss the ins and outs of supervision.

In recent years, there has been some debate about the terms *supervisor* and *mentor* in our field (see, for example, Castillo (2014) for more information on the different definitions and their use in our field). For the purposes of this book, and congruent with the terms used by the Sport Psychology Department at JFKU, we will be using the terms *supervisor* and *supervision*.

"Supervision occurs when established practitioners guide others in their development to become effective consultants" (Rhodius & Sugarman, 2014, p. 331). Mentoring, by contrast, "can be formal or informal; faculty to student; student to student; and experienced professional to student/less experienced professional" (Rhodius & Sugarman, 2014, p. 331). Supervision can include elements of mentoring, but it also connotes a level of ethical and legal responsibility for the trainee typically under the auspices of an academic program and/or supervisor. Due to the nature of internships and the responsibility that trainees have to work professionally and ethically with their athletes, we therefore provide supervisors and supervision at JFKU.

Despite the lack of formal training for supervisors in our field (Rhodius & Park, 2016), there have been a few articles addressing this topic over the past two decades (e.g. Barney, Andersen, & Riggs, 1996; Van Raalte & Andersen, 2000; and Watson, Lubker, & Van Raalte, 2011) that aim to provide more understanding of this process. Notably, Mark Andersen's edited book *Doing Sport Psychology* (2000) has four chapters on the topic of supervision and, more recently, Cremades and Tashman (2014) edited a global practices book with 17 chapters solely devoted to this critical topic, from being a neophyte supervisor (Cropley & Neil, 2014), to ethical issues in training supervisors (Castillo, 2014), and peer mentoring and peer supervision (Titkov, Bednáriková, & Mortensen, 2014). In their follow-up 2016 global case study approach text, Cremades and Tashman (2016) have 16 chapters covering case studies in supervision, which include incorporating technology in supervision (Tashman & Cremades, 2016), illustrating various practices around the world (e.g. Fogaça & Lee, 2016; Stambulova, Johnson, & Linnér, 2016), supervising the millennial (Vana Hutter & de Bruin, 2016), and more. These texts offer a great variety of advice and in-depth illustrations about supervision and are well worth a look if you're about to start supervising or wish for more professional development related to supervision.

At JFKU, we have close to three decades' worth of cumulative years of supervising interns in the department and several thousand joint hours of supervision experience from our 40+ supervisors. From these experiences, this chapter is a practical guide for helping you understand how to get the most from your supervisory relationship and how to avoid various pitfalls that can happen in the supervisory process. There are elements throughout this chapter that offer ideas for *both* trainees and supervisors.

What Happens During Supervision?

During individual supervision, there are a whole host of events and discussions that occur including (but not limited to):

- Initial supervisory help with some logistics in the internship
- Providing advice about ethical issues
- Developing professional relationships with each other (supervisor/supervisee)

- Conversations about referrals
- Guidance on sport-specific mental training exercises
- Delineating appropriate assessments
- Reviewing case notes
- Listening to audio, watching video, and in-person observation of the intern's work
- Reading reflective journals
- Advising on closure meetings

At JFKU, we also require our interns to attend group supervision (nicknamed "Group Soup") every week that they are in one of their four internships. During Group Soup, we first check in about urgent matters; we either use a color coding system, where red is the most urgent, or we use numbers and a five-alarm is the most urgent to address as soon as Group Soup begins. Group Soup enables interns to share and discuss internship-related issues that have arisen during the week, or that they wish to plan for and preview. The interns get to share ideas, brainstorm new ways of teaching/assessing/facilitating, test out strategies, voice concerns about their internship, share ethical dilemmas, feel supported by their peers, and consider the impact of theory and research on their work. This work usually takes place under an AASP-certified group supervisor who offers guidance and facilitates the discussions.

Being a supervisor can be incredibly rewarding, but it can often be tricky to balance the roles of supervisor and mentor whilst also being an evaluator of the interns' work. On one hand our job is to help problem-solve, be empathetic when challenges arise, and act as a guide through the journey of applied work. However, it is also a great responsibility to the field of sport psychology to adequately monitor the quality of work and assess whether the intern is ready to move onto another internship experience, eventually graduate, and practice in the field. At JFKU, all active supervisors meet quarterly to discuss our interns' progress, complete professional development on new ideas, and support each other toward offering the best supervisory support we can.

Philosophy of Practice

Before the first meeting between a trainee and their new supervisor, the supervisee should already have some applied sport psychology knowledge (history, theory, and research of the field and related topics) and some training in the skills and overall concepts. Some of the initial work between the supervisor and supervisee will incorporate the inception of what the trainee's early philosophy of practice will entail. At JFKU, students develop their philosophy of practice in terms of describing their main theoretical foundation, other key theories and/or research that is important to them and resonates with their style, and how it all fits together to form a marketable package once they graduate. Likewise, an effective supervisor also has a philosophy of practice for the way that they supervise. It is therefore useful to know what your supervisor's philosophy is in terms of the way that they consult and the way they supervise; this can help better understand the work being executed and foster a successful working supervisory relationship from early on.

The benefit to having a clear philosophy of practice is that there are many facets to how a sport psychology professional approaches work with clients. Eventually, the philosophy of practice may also include how you like to approach building rapport within individual and team sessions with your clients, what you hope to establish as a set agenda in the working time you're given, and what are some of the outcomes you hope clients take away from your time together. Starting out, we don't expect a trainee to have a comprehensive philosophy of practice, but rather begin to understand that eventually one will be a necessity and what that entails. A philosophy of practice exercise is certainly something to address before finishing with supervisory experiences and graduating from our program.

Top Tips for Engaging in a Successful Supervisor–Supervisee Relationship

As with any relationship, there are various ups and downs in terms of how much enjoyment (and productivity) you may get out of working together. This is because you cannot control how the other person thinks, feels, or behaves, nor should you try to! Even though you are only one half of this relationship, there are a number of top tips that we want to share that may help you get the most out of this important connection. We will break down information in the next sections to specifically address trainees and supervisors, but we encourage you to read all of it regardless of which side of the relationship you are on.

Build Rapport in Supervision, Like You Would with a Client

For Trainees

Remember that your supervisor is a person too and is trying to balance the two key aspects of being both supportive and evaluative. Your supervisor will appreciate the effort you make to be friendly, courteous, and personable. This will also benefit you for those moments when you might not agree with their feedback on an approach to the work, or the direction you've taken with a client. It's easier to debate something when you have built a rapport and know the other person a little better than someone you may have put on a pedestal.

Trainees often feel the imbalance of power given the evaluative nature of this relationship. However, interns must be self-aware and reflective in order to have an open dialogue and discourse within supervision about the details of the interactions and the work that occurs between them and their clients. When a balance is struck, the relationship between the supervisor/supervisee will feel as though it progresses naturally between thoughts and topics alike. Supervisees will be confident and comfortable authentically expressing their thoughts and actions without fear of judgment. This is the stage where interns get to discuss freely what they attempted to achieve with their clients and what worked or didn't, all while being open to creative suggestions about how to advance with their work in the future. This balance and comfort can take time to develop, but try to remain open to building a positive relationship with your supervisor even if you experience initial discomfort in the process of supervision.

For Supervisors

Supervisors can also make a point to work on building rapport, taking into account that trainees often feel nervous about what is to come. You can allay their concerns and even add in anecdotal stories that help illustrate what going through the process was like for you or other trainees you have worked with. You may also wish to address concerns around how they will be assessed, as the worry of evaluation can be a roadblock to building rapport. At JFKU we have a comprehensive set of rubrics for each program learning outcome (PLO, included in Chapter 1 of this book) that the interns are assessed on. These are given ahead of time (in their orientation to the fieldwork experience) and are reinforced throughout their supervised training.

Despite the obvious power differential, it should be understood that creating a balance between the supervisor and supervisee forms a healthy, psychologically safe relationship. Supervisors don't have all the answers and even if you did, it's probably not the greatest help to give them all to the supervisee. Thinking of the multitude of experiences that a well-trained supervisor holds could feel overwhelming if imparted all at once to a trainee.

Be Clear on the Rules of Engagement

For Trainees

As each supervisor comes from a different perspective, she/he may not have been trained at the institution where you are learning and will see the world through different lenses from you and any other supervisors (as they should). Each supervisor will have slightly different expectations about what they want to see and hear, which is great for a diverse training experience. However, this can sometimes be anxiety-provoking if you're not sure what they want from you as a trainee. So, it's important to be clear on what their expectations of you are. If your supervisor doesn't start their first meeting with their own ground rules (in addition to any set by an academic training program), then ask them "What do you expect from me each week in terms of XYZ?" This will show them you are professional, prepared, and ready for action.

For Supervisors

Supervisors will help the working relationship by having clear ground rules about what you expect from the supervisee as a person (around professional issues such as attire and punctuality), and as a trainee (in terms of knowledge and skills). Make sure you clearly delineate how they can be successful in your eyes. This should not only help ease their concerns somewhat, but also help them set clear attainable goals that you can facilitate and support.

Time Commitments and the Importance of Being on Time

For Both Trainees and Supervisors

These suggestions apply to supervisors and supervisees and, when both parties adhere to them, this will help to keep the relationship strong with a healthy mutual respect. Time is one of those valuable resources which nobody seems to have enough of. When it comes to making the most out of your supervisory experience, time management and scheduling tools become a must. This not only ensures the successful navigation and completion of all your weekly supervision sessions, but all your other responsibilities as well. Frequently you will have to travel between responsibilities of your life that may be a great distance from each other, e.g. your internship, a paying job, and school. These may or may not be close to where you live, thus presenting challenges for time management.

Arriving late (even if you call to notify someone of your tardiness) to even one planned session may reflect poorly on the trainee or the supervisor as an individual and as a professional. Additionally, ongoing tardiness gets in the way of optimal learning opportunities in supervision. Recurring tardiness may be due to the buildup of inevitable everyday tasks that are certain to occur with a busy schedule, but may also reflect poor balance or time-management skills. Of course, everyone will be late from time to time if they're fully maximizing their scheduled commitments, and unforeseen events happen. Examples may be that a client will arrive late, a class will go long, traffic will be at a stand-still, etc. However, the key is to control and influence your schedule as much as possible so that these situations are minimized and don't hinder you from securing and maximizing weekly supervision sessions. If a *worst case scenario* happens, make a phone call or send a text message (not whilst driving!) to let the other person in on what's happening. It's on both parties to make the most out of the time you can secure. Additionally, it's important not to make a habit of canceling meetings, or having slow responses to setting up meeting times for supervision. Both of these actions can convey disrespect and poor time management. It is often a good idea to set a regular day and time for your meetings, and then you will both be able to get into a rhythm about supervision.

Receiving Feedback and Guidance

For Both Trainees and Supervisors

Everybody likes to receive feedback in a different way and we all have habits regarding how we deliver feedback to others. Related to hearing feedback, some people are the "Give it to me straight, Doc!" type, and others would prefer to primarily hear about all the amazing things that they do, especially at first. It is important for trainees to know how they like to receive feedback, so as a trainee be prepared to communicate this preference to your supervisor, and to be aware that the supervisor's style may be different from what you prefer. Supervisors should be able to communicate about their process for giving feedback and be open to adjusting this process and style for the student. Hopefully with this foresight in mind though, supervisors and supervisees can strive to find a balance of feedback delivery through good communication that fosters a strong relationship and productive growth for both parties at all times.

One time I (Alison) listened to an intern's work via audio recording and she kept saying "OK" many times as a verbal validator/reinforcer for the client. However, she said it so often that I wanted to shout "stop it" at the machine several times! In our next supervision meeting, I gave her a challenge: for every time (over a max of five times) I heard her (in her audio recordings) say "OK", she had to give me $5. She accepted the challenge and the next time we met, she had her "OKs" down to zero! If I hadn't spent the time listening to her work and giving her feedback, she might still be saying "OK" to this day. The creativity and the humor in the situation enabled us both to laugh about it for many years after (she even tells this story to her own supervisees now). For a different supervisee, this may not have worked well, but from what I knew about this intern, I decided this was an approach worth trying.

Being Prepared for Supervision

For Trainees

It is of paramount importance that you come prepared to discuss and reflect upon your past and future efforts in your internship to maximize the growth opportunity you have with your supervisor. For example, come prepared with specific questions for your supervisor, bring handouts for your supervisor to review, or come with questions about a particular theory relevant to a case. If your supervisor asks you to submit items such as audio recordings by a certain day or time, be sure to plan for this in your schedule as well.

For Supervisors

Supervisors can also be prepared for the sessions by following some kind of broad structure that helps create familiarity for the trainee and helps them reflect on their progress. Perhaps set time aside to talk about the takeaways from the previous supervision session, or talk about their audio/video work that you have reviewed. Remember to role model the professional attitude and behaviors you want to see in your trainees.

Assess Your Current Strengths and Weaknesses

For Both Trainees and Supervisors

We all have strengths and challenges in our applied work, so addressing them in supervision is beneficial. Nobody likes to enter into a supervisory relationship with someone who thinks that they know it all and have nothing left to learn; this applies to both the supervisor and supervisee. In his book "Give and Take", Adam Grant (2013) discusses the idea that being able to establish competence while also displaying vulnerability with our shortcomings allows us to build greater rapport throughout the relationship by maximizing both individuals' strengths and setting goals to target potential weaknesses. Showing a little humility or vulnerability might make us more endearing and likeable to those who tend to have their guard up during initial interactions. This may also enable your supervisor to warm up to you (the supervisee) and enable trusting rapport to grow.

To have the most successful working relationship possible, ensure that both the supervisor and supervisee have discussed the areas that they do well in their respective role and the elements that may not be as much of a strong suit. These could be factors such as how well a supervisee may build rapport with a client or difficulties with following a line of questioning. Maybe supervisors understand that their strengths come from postulating different intervention strategies to supervisees or that they need to supervise in a less assertive nature during supervision. By allowing both parties to pre-emptively plan, both individuals can navigate some of the nuanced facets of their work together a little more easily. Sometimes this might not be possible at the beginning (especially if the trainee is new to this work); however, engaging in honest and frank discussions about roles and styles (on both sides) throughout the process will be helpful. This is not the time or place for anyone to be on a pedestal.

Specifically for supervisors, empower open and honest communication about all situations that a trainee encounters, especially about areas where improvement is needed. Validation is a key component to maintaining a positive relationship while giving feedback to a trainee about their work. Remember that new learners will make some mistakes (as do we all), so look at the effort the trainee is putting in and search for the teachable moments. When we can empower interns through an empathetic approach by assertively discussing and vulnerably hearing out constructive criticism regarding their trials and tribulations, we can help to motivate interns throughout the supervisory process. As Carol Dweck (2006) discusses in her book "Mindset", and as laid out in Goal Perspective Theory (Nicholls, 1984), heightened awareness to continually seeing effort as the key to mastering new skills will help individuals reach higher levels of personal success.

Training Goals

For Both Trainees and Supervisors

Goals need to be established from the first contact between the supervisor/supervisee; supervisees should enter the working relationship with their own goals in mind, but the process of setting or refining those goals can be facilitated by a good supervisor (as happens in mental skills consulting). These goals should be based on past work as well as a general direction in which they are looking to further their knowledge, skills, or experience. If the student has had prior supervision, it would be helpful to come to the current supervisory relationship with information about the supervisee's previous training experiences, past goals, and progress with those goals. In academic programs, it is advised that the program provide current supervisors with evaluations from previous supervisors. In doing so, supervisors can help craft goals based upon where they believe the intern should be regarding skill level, learning outcomes (in academia), or criteria for certification/ accreditation. It should also be noted, though, that it is in the best interest of the relationship if the supervisor anticipates coming into their role and meeting their intern where they reside in terms of development.

By making goals a priority in the supervisory setting, the relationship and focus of work will be kept strong in deliberate and measurable ways from day one. Though sometimes it may seem like a supervisee might be capable of accomplishing more or less than anticipated over the duration of an internship, by consistently reflecting back on what work has been accomplished and is left to be achieved, a solid balance will prevail throughout the supervisory relationship.

Maximizing Meetings with Creativity by Using "Sweet Spots" of Time

For Both Trainees and Supervisors

For interns who have a difficult time adhering to the structure laid out by the supervisor, such as recording work with clients, reflecting on sessions, analyzing past challenges, previewing future work, etc., the relationship will not be as fruitful as it possibly could be. It will feel much more like a new driver trying to learn a manual transmission as opposed to a seasoned driver who knows how to shift smoothly and adjust appropriately when the inevitable challenges present themselves during the internship. Supervisors and supervisees who are able to solidly construct the foundations and structures of the internship, and allow for flexibility and creativity, help to create a stable and efficient relationship from the beginning.

To continue this path of maximizing the supervisor/supervisee relationship and the time structured for the supervisory sessions, perhaps there is a *sweet spot* we should aim for that follows an inverted U-shaped curve. At one end would be supervisees who complete their supervisory preparations too soon; they may lack the openness to be as fully creative with their responses as those who prepare and prime themselves for the upcoming work to be accomplished. To the other extreme (and the other end of the inverted U-shape), however, individuals who wait too long to address a task may also do so to the detriment of the work they're trying to complete. The sweet spot lies in the middle somewhere and involves preparing yourself for the work and priming what you need to think about accomplishing over the coming supervisory sessions without last minute scrambling. With that in mind, talk to your supervisor/supervisee and discuss how to both find *your* sweet spots in the timeframe you have.

Be Honest in Your Reflections

For Trainees

You can waste a lot of time in supervision simply going through the motions to get credit, rack up the hours, and pass, but a good supervisor will also push you to reflect deeply, helping you set goals that push you and allow for growth. It's quite important, therefore, to be honest with your supervisor(s), be willing to be vulnerable in front of them, and to try to tap into your emotions as you reflect on your work. Reflective practice is a great way to enhance learning during supervision (and beyond). If you haven't read up on and/ or been trained in using reflective practice (RP), then you need to do so (Chapter 5 of this text also covers how to utilize RP during your internship experience). It can be defined as "an intentional process that enhances self-awareness and understanding through thinking about applicable 'events'" (Rhodius & Huntley, 2014, p. 91). There are helpful texts available to further your understanding and use of RP, such as Knowles, Gilbourne, Cropley and Dugdill (2014). I (Alison) also wrote a chapter about using RP for supervision (see Rhodius & Huntley, 2014).

For Supervisors

Practical ways that we incorporate RP in supervision at JFKU are by using audio reflections. This is where the trainee records a brief reflective audio piece (often no more than 10 minutes) after working with a client. The focus is on the experience of the intern and not on the client per se. The reflection can take place immediately after the applied work, or it can be several hours later. An insightful exercise is to try both time strategies and see how the reflections change over time about the same event. Once the RP has been completed, the supervisor can then listen to this audio prior to the next supervision meeting and it can help facilitate the discussion; the process can also be very helpful for the trainee. Elements to discuss based on RP and the session itself might be areas of agreement or disagreement between the trainee's and supervisor's perceptions of the direction of the work or the quality of the work done.

I (Alison) have found listening to audio reflections incredibly valuable in supervision because not only does it give the trainee an opportunity to reflect on their thoughts and feelings about their work and learn from it, it also gives the supervisor clear insight on *what* the trainee is thinking and feeling about it. At JFKU, we use written, audio, or video reflections as a key piece to allow the interns to learn more about themselves.

Illness and Family Affairs

For Trainees

Trainees get sick, which is especially true if you are burning the candle at both ends, like many trainees frequently are. Ideally you can take care of yourself to help ensure healthiness, but sometimes illness cannot be avoided. When you are sick, often the best course of action for all involved is to get some rest. Your clients don't want to get ill and neither do your classmates, friends, family, or supervisor. If you can't attend something due to illness, be sure to respectfully contact and inform those that have expectations of, and rely on, you. It doesn't require much in terms of honesty and effort to keep a relationship strong and healthy. Even in those times when you are feeling somewhere between "Today's not my day" and "I think I've got the plague," communicating such in an appropriate manner will go a long way to maintaining strong and healthy relationships.

For Supervisors

The hiccups in relationships (trainees with supervisors, and also clients, instructors, and even peers) can start to occur when a lack of respect is perceived due to poor communication; it's important to role model such communication with your supervisees. Good supervisors should also abide by such rules when they're ill or have pressing family matters to attend to. Sometimes we find events and emergencies that are outside of our control, yet still require our utmost attention. A good balance in any relationship means that there's an understanding of when priorities in life shift. Practice what you preach in terms of timely communication about changes in schedule and try to only reschedule supervision if emergencies arise.

Midpoint of the Internship and Much Work Is Still to Come

For Both Trainees and Supervisors

When a supervisee has a designated sports team they are working with, there's usually a midpoint of their time together. This provides the opportunity for a *half-time* evaluation where the supervisor and supervisee can reflect on goals, including what has been accomplished and where the work might be coming up short. During these half-time check-ins, certain topics of consideration might arise such as: "Have I been meeting the needs of my clients adequately?", "Has my supervisor been helping me to meet the goals that we laid out at the beginning of our work together?", and "What would I most like to help my clients accomplish with the remainder of our time together?" This is also a good time to check in to make sure that the trainee is on track to meet the requirements for total hours so that, if they are not, this can hopefully be rectified before the end of the applied experience.

This opportunity to have a half-time regrouping between the supervisor and supervisee can be immensely productive to ensure that the relationship remains strong between the two individuals and that the intern is maximizing their efforts with their clients. We have it as a standard recommendation in our supervision process at JFKU. Quite frequently, if this half-time check is bypassed or neglected, the conclusion of an internship can approach abruptly and leave the relationship between the supervisor and supervisee feeling as though less was achieved than either had hoped. Additionally, if an intern is running the risk of not passing their internship for some reason, the midway check-in is a good time to determine if changes can be made. It can be unfair to a trainee to wait until the end to confirm that their efforts will not lead to credit for the internship experience.

Potential Hurdles the Trainee May Experience and Ways to Handle Them

Two potential hurdles commonly experienced by trainees in supervision are around conflict with your supervisor and feeling micro-managed.

Conflict with Your Supervisor

If you have followed some of the guiding principles above, then hopefully you are in a good space with your supervisor; however, conflicts can occur from time to time. Keep in mind though that, even with conflict, a healthy working relationship can still be fostered between the two of you. In order to resolve the issues and improve on the relationship, it's helpful to reflect on whether this is a conflict that stems from a specific issue or instance, or if it is due to a number of issues that have built up over time. The distinction is an important one because it will help inform how you may want to proceed, though by preparing yourself in advance through these chapters the likelihood of issues diminishes substantially.

If you hit a roadblock with your supervisor due to a single issue, then we encourage you to address it sooner rather than later. Ensure that before undertaking this process you are clear in the message you're attempting to communicate, and that you are controlled in the manner in which you approach the conversation. This will ensure the best chance of being heard in the conversation without the other party becoming defensive or attacking.

In communicating with your supervisor about an issue between you both, it is helpful to follow a few guidelines: 1) State as clearly and simply as you can the challenge you experienced, 2) say why it was challenging for you, 3) explain how you felt about it, 4) discuss what you had hoped to gain originally, and finally 5) share what do you hope to accomplish moving forward that will best suit the needs of everyone involved. Yes, it can be awkward, but this is an opportunity to learn more about having mature conversations about issues you find challenging. A good supervisor will recognize that it may be hard for you, will rise to the challenge to support you, and will role model dealing with confrontations, even if they disagree with you. It's a great teachable moment.

This approach to discussing the specific issue that arose and created conflict in the first place should help to air grievances, while setting the relationship between the supervisor and intern back on track. Of course it should be anticipated that this will be a two-way conversation where both parties have the opportunity to be heard and the ability to agree upon reasonable and appropriate steps to proactively move forward, all in a respectful manner.

If the conflict has evolved over time and is still there, the supervisory relationship has declined over time, or either of the individuals no longer feels like they have resolved the issues on their own, then it may require third-party mediation (often a meta-supervisor, which at JFKU is one of our Fieldwork Directors) to see if things can be put back into healthy, functional working order. Situations that may lead to this degree of conflict could be when a trainee feels distrust with the supervisor's oversight of their work, or when the core beliefs about the supervisory process do not align (e.g. one person believes trial and error is key to learning and the other has the belief that strict guidance and support are the best ways to enhance personal progress).

If you can discuss conflict and disagreement even in these deeper circumstances, then that is great and we hope that your supervisor has the skills to be able to resolve these kinds of issues. If you need additional assistance, this third-party mediation would ideally be someone in a position of power over both individuals (or a trusted, mutual peer). If you're unable to completely resolve the issue with or without outside intervention, or you cannot meet with a third-party quickly, it may be helpful to focus not on what happened to disrupt the relationship but focus more on pro-active goals that will be used to measure the work of the supervisor/supervisee moving forward. This structure can often lead to a narrowing of focus for both parties to the most pertinent supervision needs and a better grasp of the knowledge being imparted/received from the individuals in the relationship in question.

When I (Mike) was going through my graduate studies, I experienced an instance when my supervisor and I didn't quite see eye to eye on the way I was going about doing my work. A portion of this could be attributed to our mode of communication on a regular basis (emails, text messages, etc.) getting lost in translation, but most of it had to do with different beliefs about what made a practitioner of applied mental skills services most effective. Tough fight to have, right? This conflict eventually reached a tipping point where we decided to meet with a third party who oversaw us both (the meta-supervisor) to help get our work together back on track. One of the greatest benefits to this approach was that it really allowed for me as the supervisee and my supervisor to recognize that both of us had the best intentions at heart for the clients and work being accomplished. Once we were able to start focusing on our similarities and agree upon a solid foundation from which we could base our work going forward, I think that my supervisor and I accomplished even more than we might have without proper intervention!

Again, much of this came down to the willingness to be vulnerable about my needs as a supervisee/intern and also the ability to ask for help when things weren't going quite right. Though I was capable and willing to discuss our differences in beliefs, this did not mean that I would get everything I had wanted in terms of the resolution. To the contrary, I got *more* than I wanted in the long run because I was able to better meet the expectations of my supervisor, my program, and my personal long-term expectations because I had realigned what was important to me as a learner and practitioner. That experience in turn proved to be a solidifying moment in which today I can say that my supervisor helped me grow more than I may have anticipated I could.

When I (Alison) have come across these instances, I find it helpful to recognize what is happening and gently confront the intern about the dynamics. It may be that they're pulling a face when you make suggestions, they may be vocally disagreeing with any recommendations you make, or they may be purposefully not doing any homework you assign them in an effort to derail the relationship to deflect their own perceived challenges. Addressing these issues in a gentle, yet firm, manner can let them know that they are in a supportive environment, but they also need to be honest about their feelings, even when it is awkward. Help them understand that this can be a teachable moment around being comfortable when feeling uncomfortable—something we aim to instill in our performing clients.

"My Supervisor Is Micro-Managing Everything I Do"

Some supervisors want to be very aware of the work that you are doing and your plans for doing it so they can help you, or some may wish to control your work a little more than they should. Regardless of the intent of the supervisor, for some trainees, this can feel like micro-managing. If you are starting to find yourself at odds with your supervisor's style because they request to see all of the items related to your work every week (for example, all case notes, all reflections, appointment book, etc.), you may need to have a direct conversation about it. While keeping in mind that your supervisor's role includes being aware of your work and helping you execute your work well, ideally there can be more of a balance that works for both of you. If you are feeling that there may be too much involvement from the supervisor, we would encourage you to bring this up in a supervision meeting to try and establish a structure that will work best for both parties involved.

Many times, supervisors have your best intentions in mind and may not realize that they are asking too much of you (especially if this is one of your later internships/applied experiences), or you may not realize the method to their seeming madness. A good supervisor is probably trying to help create a strong foundation for, and execution of, your work. If you can discuss the structure that you're aiming for with your clients and work, then you'll likely be able to negotiate more slack from your supervisor and perhaps not feel so micro-managed. You may still need to submit plenty of audio/video/reflection sessions to have reviewed, as well as upload any documentation handouts and worksheets you utilize, but in discussing your approach to working with clients and then demonstrating a healthy awareness and willingness to reflect accordingly on the work you've accomplished, many micro-managing conflicts can be subdued before they get out of hand.

Conclusion

In this chapter, we have tried to highlight various ways to be a *good* intern and supervisor, how to develop a strong working relationship, and gave some examples of less productive ways of thinking and behaving. Done well, a supervisory relationship can blossom into one that lasts many years, where levels of trust deepen and may even evolve into peer-to-peer support and friendship. We hope that you are able to follow some of the guiding principles in this chapter and focus on ego-less interactions on both sides that allow for growth and learning.

A Trainee's Perspective on Working with Your Supervisor

Joy Marquez, M.A./Psy.D. student at JFKU 2013–2018

As a military veteran, Joy's professional interests include clinical work with veterans, integrated behavioral healthcare, and exercise as complementary therapy. Joy's goal is to work as an integrated behavioral health psychologist in a medical setting, and build a private sport psychology practice. Joy can be contacted at jmarquez@email.jfku.edu.

Supervision has played a prominent role in my professional development outside of school, and through my internship experience I developed a deeper understanding of myself beyond academic or applied work alone. Because of this, my sport psychology supervision experience exceeded my highest expectations. At first, I felt nervous to be paired with the JFKU Sport Psychology Department Chair because of her depth of expertise. Being completely inexperienced by comparison, I wondered what she might expect in terms of my abilities to perform in the role as an emerging mental skills consultant. My nerves quickly dissolved at our first meeting when she established rapport by clarifying our roles and reminding me of the developmental stage of the work I was about to begin. In doing so, she set the foundation for an amazing working relationship.

Developing clear goals with action steps at the outset helped me focus my effort and energy toward what I thought was important for this internship and allowed my supervisor to understand my priorities. More specifically, I identified my internship goals to be: 1) gaining proficiency of performance enhancement skills, 2) learning about and applying walk and talk sessions, 3) creating my physical workspace, and 4) prioritizing weekly self-care. During supervision, I reflected on my level of accomplishment for each goal, monthly and at the end of the internship, allowing me to realize that, overall, I made significant progress toward these goals.

Throughout my internship, my supervisor validated my efforts and offered recommendations for improvement, which had an almost immediate effect on my work with clients week after week. I could go into supervision frustrated or dejected, and come out refreshed and ready to work again because of the insights I gained. My supervisor was consistently thoughtful and kind in providing her feedback, and I eventually developed confidence from being treated as a colleague-in-training. In many ways, my supervision experience paralleled my internship: we applied the work I wanted to do with my clients in our supervision sessions, such as walk and talk meetings and making theoretical terminology more relatable to athletes.

The highlight of supervision was working together with my supervisor to develop a workshop for an annual tennis clinic and tournament that she supports. I had the opportunity to observe my supervisor presenting this workshop and interacting with clients, while I simultaneously worked with her in small group breakout sessions. After this vicarious experience, I approached my internship clients with increased confidence. I would highly recommend that interns experience work alongside their supervisors in a real-world setting with clients to create additional learning experiences and deepen the intern's understanding of applied work.

This internship provided an opportunity to experience what consulting could be like when I earned my M.A. With guidance from my supervisor, I learned how to manage my time, communicate with clients, and apply theory to session content. I also developed an understanding about how my consulting business could operate. The classroom came to life for me through my applied work during internship with the ongoing support and encouragement of my supervisor.

Reflective Questions and Activities for You to Consider Before You Proceed

- What strengths do you bring to the supervisor–Supervisee relationship?
- How can you communicate these to your supervisor/supervisee?
- What challenges might you face with a new supervisor/supervisee?
- What can you do to help the relationship be smooth, professional, effective, and efficient, i.e. how can you take responsibility for these elements?

References

Andersen, M. B. (Ed.). (2000). *Doing Sport Psychology*. Champaign, IL: Human Kinetics.

Barney, S. T., Andersen, M. B., & Riggs, C. A. (1996). Supervision in sport psychology: Some recommendations for practicum training. *Journal of Applied Sport Psychology*, 8(2), 200–217.

Castillo, S. (2014). Ethical issues in training future practitioners. In L. Tashman & G. Cremades (Eds.), *Becoming a Performance Psychologist: International Perspectives on Service Delivery and Supervision* (pp. 252–259). New York, NY: Routledge.

Cremades, G., & Tashman, L. (Eds.) (2014). *Becoming a Performance Psychologist: International Perspectives on Service Delivery and Supervision*. New York, NY: Routledge.

Cremades, G., & Tashman, L. (Eds.) (2016). *Global Practices and Training in Applied Sport, Exercise and Performance Psychology: A Case Study Approach*. New York: NY: Routledge.

Cropley, B., & Neil, R. (2014). The neophyte supervisor: What did I get myself into? In G. Cremades & L. Tashman (Eds.), *Becoming a Performance Psychologist: International Perspectives on Service Delivery and Supervision* (pp. 219–227). New York, NY: Routledge.

Dweck, C. (2006). *Mindset: The New Psychology of Success*. New York, NY: Random House.

Fogaça, J., & Lee, S. M. (2016). Multicultural supervision: Experiences in an international Master's program. In G. Cremades & L. Tashman (Eds.), *Global Practices and Training in Applied Sport, Exercise and Performance Psychology: A Case Study Approach* (pp. 307–314). New York: NY: Routledge.

Grant, A. (2013). *Give and Take: A Revolutionary Approach to Success*. New York, NY: Viking.

Knowles, Z., Gilbourne, D., Cropley, B., & Dugdill, L. (Eds.). (2014). *Reflective Practice in the Sport and Exercise Sciences: Contemporary Issues*. New York, NY: Routledge.

Nicholls, J. (1984). Achievement motivation: Conceptions of ability, subjective experience, task choice and performance. *Psychological Review*, 91(3), 328–346.

Rhodius, A., & Huntley, E. (2014). Facilitating reflective practice in graduate trainees and early career practitioners. In Z. Knowles, D. Gilbourne, B. Cropley, & L. Dugdill (Eds.), *Reflective Practice in the Sport and Exercise Sciences: Contemporary Issues* (pp. 91–100). New York, NY: Routledge.

Rhodius, A., & Park, M. (2016). Who's supervising the supervisor? A case study of meta-supervision. In G. Cremades & L. Tashman (Eds.), *Global Practices and Training in Applied Sport, Exercise and Performance Psychology: A Case Study Approach* (pp. 322–329). New York: NY: Routledge.

Rhodius, A., & Sugarman, K. (2014). Peer consultations with colleagues: The significance of gaining support and avoiding the 'Lone Ranger trap'. In G. Cremades & L. Tashman (Eds.), *Becoming a Performance Psychologist: International Perspectives on Service Delivery and Supervision* (pp. 331–338). New York, NY: Routledge.

Stambulova, N., Johnson, U., & Linnér, L. (2016). Student's supervised practice on helping an elite Swedish golfer: Application of the Halmstad applied sport psychology supervision model. In G. Cremades & L. Tashman (Eds.), *Global Practices and Training in Applied Sport, Exercise and Performance Psychology: A Case Study Approach* (pp. 280–289). New York: NY: Routledge.

Tashman, L., & Cremades, G. (2016). Incorporating technology in supervision: Using interpersonal process recall to enhance reflective practice. In G. Cremades & L. Tashman (Eds.), *Global Practices and Training in Applied Sport, Exercise and Performance Psychology: A Case Study Approach* (pp. 343–351). New York: NY: Routledge.

Titkov, A., Bednáriková, M., & Mortensen, J. R. (2014). Peer mentoring and peer supervision: Nordic experiences. In G. Cremades & L. Tashman (Eds.), *Becoming a Performance Psychologist: International Perspectives on Service Delivery and Supervision* (pp. 293–299). New York, NY: Routledge.

Vana Hutter, R. I., & de Bruin, A. P. (2016). Supervising the millennial. In G. Cremades & L. Tashman (Eds.), *Global Practices and Training in Applied Sport, Exercise and Performance Psychology: A Case Study Approach* (pp. 262–270). New York: NY: Routledge.

Van Raalte, J. L., & Andersen, M. B. (2000). Supervision I: From models to doing. In M. B. Andersen (Ed.), *Doing Sport Psychology* (pp. 153–165). Champaign, IL: Human Kinetics.

Watson II, J., Lubker, J., & Van Raalte, J. (2011). Problems in reflective practice: Self-bootstrapping versus therapeutic supervision. In M. Andersen & D. Gilbourne (Eds.), *Critical Essays in Applied Sport Psychology* (pp. 157–172). Champaign, IL: Human Kinetics.

7 Doing the Work

Can You Go from the Classroom to the Field?

Megan Byrd and Noelle Menendez

Working with performing clients is the reason why many individuals choose to study applied sport psychology. While applied work is often enjoyable and rewarding, for individuals starting out it's common to feel uncertain and uncomfortable. For a first-time trainee, it may seem unclear what one actually does when working with the clients, and they may be less-than-confident in doing so. The classroom and the field are vastly different arenas, and this chapter discusses how trainees can apply what they have studied to actual applied work with clients. When a team or site has been secured, the trainee may feel as if there is a solid client base, and that their schedule will be full, but this may not automatically be true. Trainees must understand how to market their services to the clients at the site while making the work and themselves appealing. To hit the ground running, trainees need to have plans for how to create a busy schedule and then understand what to do with the clients when working with them; this chapter will give guidance on both. Through this chapter, trainees will be encouraged to preview potential situations and ways to handle these topics, with guidance given for how to come to appropriate decisions within the setting.

Background Information on the Authors

Megan Byrd is the Research Director and an Assistant Professor at JFKU. Megan earned a Ph.D. in Sport and Exercise Psychology from West Virginia University (WVU). Additionally, Megan has a Master's Degree in Community Counseling from WVU, a Master's Degree in Sport Behavior and Performance from Miami University, and a Bachelor's Begree in Psychology from Eastern Kentucky University. Megan has eight years' experience as a sport psychology practitioner and has worked with clients ranging from youth sport to professional athletes, although her work has predominantly been with elite collegiate athletes. Megan's main area of research is emotional impacts of sport concussion, for which she was awarded a research grant from the National Collegiate Athletic Association (NCAA). Other research interests lie in perfectionism, anger, aggression, and professional ethics. Megan can be contacted at mbyrd1@jfku.edu.

   Noelle Menendez earned her Master's Degree in Sport Psychology from JFKU and her Bachelor's Degree in Psychology from Florida State University. She was highly active within the program at JFKU as the Sport Psychology Student Association President. Noelle pursued the research track with a thesis on female sport psychology professionals in collegiate athletics. She is now a contractor for the United States Army and National Guard as a Master Resilience Trainer and Performance Expert.

Noelle provides performance, resiliency, team building, and academic training to soldiers and the Department of Army Civilians. The training she delivers for the military aims to increase mental strength and readiness for both soldiers and their families. She is passionate about her work and the opportunities to travel across the U.S. providing these services. Noelle can be contacted at nmenendez@email.jfku.edu.

Securing the first internship site is exciting, yet it comes with a new set of roles and responsibilities. You are now moving from student to teacher, and may be experiencing feelings related to performance that are similar to the feelings of the athletes and clients you will be working with. Just as you would prepare an athlete for competition, you want to prepare yourself prior to embarking on this new journey.

As Chapter 2 highlighted, internships require much of your time when you are there with your clients. You also want to make sure you have adequate time set aside for planning the various sessions you will conduct. Planning and research hours are imperative to your success, so you will want to keep that in mind as you create your schedule. This is true in the time leading up to when you begin, as well as on a daily or weekly basis for the duration of your internship. Some of your planning will involve others, such as your supervisor, the coach, or peers, and other planning and preparation will be done on your own.

In this chapter, we share a timeline for preparation and how to best transition from being in the classroom to working in an applied setting. Your timeline may vary, but we want to help you understand the points to consider and steps to take that will allow you transition effectively from classroom to field.

Two to Four Weeks (or More) Before You Begin

Planning Travel to, and Access at, Your Site

Before your first day in your first internship, you will want to work out logistics related to your internship site. Take into consideration the location of your internship and if you will be traveling during peak traffic times or not. It may seem obvious, but if this is your first time visiting the site, or you have only been once, you may be unaware of construction or travel patterns. Consider various routes for driving, and research public transportation if that's part of your plan.

You might want to ask if you need a parking pass for the location, especially if you will be at a college or somewhere in a city with limited access. Leaving your site to a towed car or parking ticket would not make for a good day! Also consider identification or access cards to get into facilities. For example, my (Megan's) first day at a new internship site did not go as planned, as I was unable to get into the building where the team was practicing. I only had the contact information of one coach. I knocked for about 30 minutes until finally an athlete left the building and let me in. Luckily for me the athlete had to leave practice early, or I would have been even later than I was. The coach was understanding and even apologized for not thinking of access, but it was hard to overcome that first impression of being late on day one. Coaches juggle many balls at once, so something like a parking pass or ID card are likely not on his or her radar. It's better to ask than to be stuck outside! Your peer group and other student-interns may also have advice or experiences you can learn from and apply to your work, especially if they have been at the site before you.

Meeting Locations

When planning your sessions, you will also need to know where you will be able to have your meetings. Will your sessions be indoors or outdoors? Will there be a place to use electronic media or sound if you want to show a video? Is there a whiteboard or blackboard? The amount of space may also dictate the kind of group activities that you can do with the team. You also want to know what kind of space you will have for individual sessions so you can take confidentiality and privacy into consideration; if a private space is not available, what alternative locations might you use?

Attire

What will you wear on your first day and throughout the internship? This is a logistical concern you shouldn't overlook. Your program or school may have attire guidelines, but also check with your site. In your conversations related to confirmation of the internship and getting approval from the site (as outlined in Chapter 2), you might consider asking what the coach/administrator prefers for you to wear to sessions and observations. Do not ask for gear! This is a mistake that interns and first-time consultants often make when working with a team. If a team or site wants you to have gear, they will provide it to you. If the coach does not specify what they want you to wear, a polo from your school with khakis or business casual pants will suffice. You can, of course, dress in a way that is true to you and your style but you need to be professional and appropriate in your choices. Remember that you may be on a field, mats, or in a gymnasium, so plan your clothing and shoes appropriately. Another aspect to keep in mind is to refrain from wearing the logos or gear from other teams you have worked with, or a team you support as a fan. You want to look professional and make your current team feel as if they are your only focus.

If you're working at a college, another consideration is licensed gear. I (Megan) interned with a university who, unbeknownst to me, had shifted their sponsorship from Under Armour to Nike. I showed up one day wearing a school polo with an Under Armour logo, and the coach told me I could not wear it around the facilities or when working with the athletes. In hindsight, the blunder wasn't that big of an issue, but at the time I felt embarrassed. Feeling embarrassed coupled with the nerves of a new internship is not a winning combination. I was relieved that it did not occur at a competition, as I didn't bring another shirt to change into and I likely wouldn't have been able to stand on the sidelines. The more questions you ask about clothing, the better prepared you will be. The more comfortable you are in the new situation, the more comfortable the athletes and coaches are likely to feel. If you are not given information on attire, an alternative plan is to mirror the coaches and other staff. Research shows that athletes perceive sport psychology professionals who wear athletic attire more positively and with higher perceived effectiveness than those who wear more formal attire (Lovell, Parker, Brady, Cotterill, & Howatson, 2011; Lubker, Watson, Visek, & Geer, 2005). However, if the coaches are wearing business casual on the sidelines, especially at games, you should follow their lead.

Marketing

Marketing for your internship is essentially self-promotion, and is necessary. Even though you have secured your site, you will still need to market yourself and the services that you offer. Think of marketing as your billboard to gain client interest. You may be working with teams who are not familiar with what sport psychology can offer, so you may need to include some education with your marketing. If you are not in a team setting, but a location such as a tennis club or gym, you will need to market yourself to get clients. Ask the location if you can put up flyers detailing your services ahead of your start date. The flyers should follow the 7 Cs of communication: clear, concise, concrete, coherent, complete, correct, and courteous (Cutlip & Center, 1952). Use simple language, with brief, direct points. The flyer should explicitly say who you are, what you can offer, and how people can reach you. Think of the flyer as the front door of your consulting: what should potential clients leave with (information) and how do you want them to feel (like you have something they want)? In addition to flyers, bring business cards to leave out at the front desk (if one exists) or provide to coaches ahead of time. Your cards should be clean (not overly designed or hard to read), and include your contact information (phone number, email) and title (i.e. mental skills intern, performance coach).

Your Elevator Pitch

If you are in a team setting, the athletes will need to buy into what you are selling if they are going to want to work with you in individual sessions. This is where your *elevator pitch* and first impressions are going to be crucial. Consider arranging your speech with the following structure: an introduction, establishment of proof and support, and a conclusion. The introduction is used to state the situation in which the services would be needed, and that those services provide opportunities, address the problem, or are the solution. Establishing proof and support is where you provide your expertise in the matter and can share supporting ideas of what you present. In your conclusion, you are selling to the listener by getting them agree to your suggested next steps such as a future meeting or phone call (Simpson, 2016).

Another trick for an effective introduction involves using your hand as a guide for delivering the five elements of an elevator speech (Finta, 2016). Your thumb is the introduction, the attention grabber. Here is where you want to share why someone would want to listen to you and what your services provide. Your index finger is point number one: what makes you unique? Point number two will be represented by your middle finger. People are moved by fear or desire, so explain how your training will make the potential client better. Your ring finger solidifies the need for your service now by offering proof or an example case study. That is point number three. Lastly, with your pinky finger you will move the listener to action, and conclude your elevator pitch. The goal is to leave the potential client wanting more from what you have already shared. You have introduced your service with your thumb, provided three impactful take-away points with your three middle fingers, and concluded your pitch with your little finger. Once you have practiced your hand-guided elevator pitch you can tailor it based on the situation (clientele, environment, etc.).

Paperwork

In addition to marketing yourself, you should ensure you have all the necessary paperwork completed for you to do your job. It is best practice to send consent forms prior to the first day if you will be working with minors as parents/guardians will need to give consent before the youths can give assent (agree). We recommend asking the coach if there is a parent or pre-season meeting you can attend where you can properly introduce yourself and have athletes and/or parents sign the consent form while you are present in case they might have any follow-up questions or concerns.

One to Two Weeks Before You Begin

As you get closer to the start of your internship, and the logistics have been addressed, now is the time to prepare for the actual work you will do. There are several points to consider when meeting the team or individual clients for the first time. First impressions are crucial; you want to start off on the right foot. Introduce yourself including your educational background, your philosophy of practice, what you offer the athletes, what is expected of them, and create buy-in. These are essential objectives to address in the first meeting and will be discussed in more detail below. The introduction to the team or individuals initiates the season-long relationship you with have with one another; use the following information to help you plan and execute your work.

How You Will Introduce Yourself

The title you give yourself is important as it helps clients understand what it is you do and how they may address you. It's important to be confident and comfortable with your title. "Mental Skills Intern," for an example, may be used to stress that mental skills is at the core of your work and to diminish any "laying-on-a-couch" assumptions. The intern portion of the title is to emphasize that you are a student or trainee, are learning, and that you are required to get a certain number of contact hours. It is important to be upfront and clear about your title and role. You can use your educational program, state, or country's guidelines to help you determine an appropriate title. Additionally, educating clients and staff about the required qualifications for being a psychologist or sport psychologist helps to clear any preconceived ideas of what your role includes.

An example of how you can teach coaches and athletes what to call you is by emphasizing your additive role to the team as a coach. You can reiterate that your scope of practice focuses on the role the mind has on performance. This is important for legal reasons, and for remaining an ethical member of the applied sport psychology field. Your title and role are areas you will have to repeatedly address, as athletes and coaches are likely unfamiliar with our work. You may be referred to as the "sport psychologist" regardless of your title and how you have explained it. Be aware that you will be labeled with the incorrect title, and preview when and how you re-educate and reinform what your title is and why.

Describing Your Philosophy of Practice

A philosophy of practice is a framework of interventions and theoretical models that you use to support your work. Your framework can be developed from personal values and beliefs, but is supported by scientific models of behavioral change. Describing your philosophy and how you will approach your work provides comfort for your clients and a foundation for you as a practitioner. "Professional philosophy significantly shapes the consultant's approach to the essential elements of the consulting process [and it] can serve to provide direction when confronted with the unique situations where there is not an established textbook solution," (Poczwardowski, Sherman, & Ravizza, 2004, p. 446). When sharing this information with the team, for example, you might describe your philosophy as a collaborative effort, meeting the client where they are currently situated, and emphasizing that you are not here to fix them because something is wrong with them. You are there to help them as athletes to develop skills they can use during athletic performances and in life, to be their best selves. You will all have different approaches, but your philosophy must remain true to who you are as a trainee and ultimately as a professional.

What the Athletes Can Expect from You and the Work

Athletes may question if there is something wrong with them due to having a sport psychology trainee on board for the season. To help avoid this incorrect assumption, explain what you can offer in your role, and how clients can view working with you in a positive light. It is crucial to educate performers and athletes about what sport psychology is all about and how it is applied. Within your role, you offer a set of tools that athletes can deliberately practice to enhance their performance. What concepts do these tools address? You can provide techniques to build confidence, manage energy, control attention, efficiently set goals, teach imagery skills, and more. An additional perspective to present to your clients is that you offer a fresh set of eyes and ears, you have no control over playing time, and you solely work on the skills that can help enhance their performance.

We recommend you help the clients understand *how* the work is done. The mental skills training that you offer is mainly done in three ways: team or group sessions, one-on-one sessions, or on-the-spot consulting. Consider letting the athletes know how team sessions will be set up so that they understand what to expect. Trainees may lead meetings that are more lecture-based, some are more activity-based with debriefs to aid in learning, and other trainees like to have a mixture of both. Internships are a great opportunity to find your style and how you prefer to facilitate sessions. It's encouraged that during your first meeting you facilitate an activity to give the athletes an example of what you mean by interaction and engagement via team sessions.

What You Expect of the Athletes

It is crucial to set clear expectations for the team so that everyone is on the same page and so that your service delivery is set up to benefit all those involved. Be clear to the athletes that you are a facilitator of these skills and, while the skills can help, they are not an instant fix. Just as sport skill development requires physical repetitions, the mind needs its mental repetitions too. Help them understand that you will teach skills and present ideas, but it will be up to them to utilize these skills (with your support) if they want to see change.

Ideally you will meet regularly for individual meetings with many of the team members. It is helpful to request that each athlete meet with you at least once. Keep in mind you personally cannot mandate this so a proactive conversation beforehand with the coach is helpful. Can you come up with an agreement to have the coach require athletes meet with you at least once? Consider a proposal where those who are completely against individual sessions can approach you or the coach privately to agree upon an alternate plan.

Doing Your Research

When presenting yourself and the mental skills the athletes will develop with you, be sure to offer examples of how this applies specifically to their sport. Here is where your preparatory work and research is imperative, especially if you have not worked with that sport before. When working with a softball team, I (Noelle) was sure to present various scenarios and aspects of softball where mental skills apply—in the outfield maintaining focus even if you are not involved in the play, or as a pitcher remaining confident with a high ball count or having walked the opponent at bat. These examples will help to create athlete buy-in and give specifics as to how mental skills can be utilized within their performance.

In addition to prep work and research on your own, you may also want to have conversations with the coaches about the sport and their athletes. How might they describe the team dynamic? Is it a new team starting from scratch, or is there history and tradition built into the culture? What are the goals the coach has for his or her athletes this season and what are some challenges? Additionally, you may want to have done research on the rules of the sport, and learn information relevant to your athletes' performance. My (Noelle) first internship was with a lacrosse team, a sport I knew very little about. Prior to beginning I looked up the general rules of the game, learned about positions and equipment, and watched highlight videos. I also utilized a classmate who played lacrosse competitively to gain insight into the culture of the sport. I learned the lingo and that lacrosse tends to be a tight-knit community where everyone knows everyone who plays. This information helped me feel prepared and allowed me to connect with my clients because I had some initial understanding of their sport.

Planning for the First Meetings

It is best practice, especially for your first internship as a trainee, to prepare a content outline for your first team meeting with supporting handouts or activities. Planning this outline or template of what you need to cover ahead of time can be a checklist to ensure you have touched on all critical matters and have the proper tools for execution (e.g. supplies for activities, collection of consent forms, business cards, etc.). Once you know your internship site, assessment tools can be modified to best fit the sport you will be working with, and you can research the sport if you are unfamiliar with it, using videos, books, or reaching out to any known athletes in that sport.

Logistics of Group Work

The logistics of team sessions are a little more complicated than working with an individual, simply because you have more people to coordinate. Team or group sessions will most likely need to be arranged with the coaches and scheduled around training and competition. If possible, involve captains or seniors in the organization of team meetings as this often helps to enhance team buy-in. Try to set up a routine where once a week, or once every other week, you conduct a team session. If the mental training becomes part of the routine just like their physical practice, this will reinforce the skills you are teaching to athletes and normalize the sessions you do. This regularity also works best to ensure you get the team contact hours you need and so that the athletes know what to expect. If team sessions are scheduled last minute or inconsistently, it will be difficult to guarantee turnout and will likely impact the effectiveness of the mental training. One suggestion is to be creative and implement something like *Mental Mondays* to better integrate your work within the team's culture and schedule.

You will also need to consider where the sessions will take place, and hopefully you planned for this ahead of time. It is best practice to avoid places that have a lot of foot traffic so you are not combating external distractions. Locker rooms sometimes make for good meeting space, depending on size of the room and team, and who else is in there at the time of your meeting. If you are at a college/university or school, consider using a classroom or other athletic department room for your session. This will give you more space and likely access to a whiteboard, chalkboard, or media equipment. If you can, hold sessions either before or after practice; the athletes are already on-site and this timing reinforces the idea that mental skill development is part of their training, not a separate entity. The disadvantage to holding sessions after practice is that athletes will likely be tired, or are focusing on what they have to do after practice (e.g. eat, homework, etc.). Though they will not be able to immediately implement the skills you discuss, the athletes can relate what they experienced in practice to the day's topic. If your session is before practice, then you can talk directly about how to implement ideas from the meeting into practice. Once you know when the sessions will take place, use these pros to your advantage and then work out how to combat the cons.

The First Week or Two of the Internship

Holding the First Team Meeting

Now is the time that all the planning is put into action, and you get to hold your first meeting. Once you have introduced yourself, your scope of practice, and addressed some of the logistical aspects of your role and time with the team, you can move into doing *the work*. How do you start? An icebreaker is an interactive, generally brief, activity used to engage participants. An icebreaker interaction is an excellent way to introduce to your clients the type of engagement you'll expect of them during team/group sessions. "Using icebreakers brings humor . . . establishes rapport, fosters a safe learning environment, and overall assists with content learning" (Chlup & Collins, 2010, p. 34). Valuable resources for icebreakers include *104 Activities That Build* by Alanna Jones (1998), *101 Teambuilding Activities* by Dr. Greg Dale and Scott Conant (2004), and online sources such as www.icebreakers.ws. Consider participating in the icebreaker during the first meeting so that the athletes can get to know you a little better, but be aware of your comfort level in participating, and the information you disclose. To gauge whether self-disclosure is appropriate before sharing, ask yourself if the personal information about you will benefit your clients.

Typically, icebreakers do not have an in-depth debrief, but to properly wrap it all up as a facilitator you can summarize the activity with questions pertaining to any take-away points. After an ice breaker, if you choose to use one, you will likely want to assess the team so that you can learn more about their strengths, areas to work on, begin to understand their dynamics, and then use this information to prepare for upcoming sessions. I (Noelle) always recommend that interns bring a handout to the first day with their contact information and a brief description of the work they will be doing. I also suggest using diagrams and models over text, as visual representations are often easier to understand and digest. This will set the tone for your first meeting and give you a structure to follow on the off chance your nerves creep in and you need a little assistance from a handout.

At the first session, we encourage you to show enthusiasm as a facilitator, as you are getting to know your clients and you ideally want them to feel comfortable being themselves around you. If you bring energy to the activity, that energy will likely be mirrored. Observation and assessment start as soon as you walk on the field or into the room, so take notice of athlete interaction during the activity. You can point out any observations you had from the activity in the debrief. In terms of group management, be sure to explain all instructions clearly before beginning, and decide strategically when to distribute materials in order maintain the athletes' full attention. A successfully run first team or group activity can set the tone for the remainder of sessions throughout the season; you want to declare your role as an effective facilitator from the start. Showing your professionalism is recommended by having your equipment ready and easily accessible, including enough copies of handouts and pens or pencils for your clients to use. If you do not have consent forms back, the first team meeting is a good time to remind them to complete this (bring extra copies with you).

Once you have introduced yourself and have educated the group on mental skills training and how you will implement the work, you might want to conclude with a handout of some sort and an exchange of contact information. A handout is a great resource for the players and staff members to refer to regarding the specific mental skills or techniques you explained, structure of team or individual sessions, and might include information about you. Another trick to consider trying at your first meeting is to have everyone (if applicable to age group) take out their cell phones and enter your number into their contacts. This diminishes any excuses or errors for the players not being able to get ahold of you and, in return, have them text you their name so you too have access to them as well. If you are working with youth athletes, who need their parents to sign their consent forms (younger than 18 years of age), then it would be imperative to include on that form information specific to communication channels you will be utilizing during your work with minors. On the form, you would explicitly state the use of text messaging and phone calls to set up individual meeting times and locations and to send reminders and confirmations. You will want to clarify that there are parameters in effect for sending and receiving texts such as the time of day that texts can be sent (e.g. no texting during school hours or after 8pm); this way you are clarifying how and when you and their child will be in communication.

Introducing the Idea of Individual Sessions

Team meetings are a great time to introduce and have sign-ups for individual sessions. Be clear on your academic requirements for these meetings, but generally these are one-on-one, confidential, and are focused entirely on performance and the mental aspects you can assist with. Historically in psychology these sessions are 45–50 minutes long, but the duration of the meeting can vary. For example, on a golf course you might work with an athlete for longer than the traditional 50 minutes on the front nine of the course. Shorter meetings, such as 20 minutes, are sometimes enough and may be the time the athlete has in between school and the start of practice. The duration of your meetings with an individual athlete is dependent on what is most useful for them and fits within their schedule. It can be helpful to change it up, and be flexible. One-on-one meetings allow for specific, customized mental skills training for that individual and can be implemented for the entire length of the internship. More details of what to include in these sessions is coming up shortly. Audio or video recording all sessions is one tool the JFKU Sport Psychology Department uses as a teaching aid. The recordings are shared with the intern's supervisor for feedback, reflection, and learning purposes. Recording your sessions is advised regardless if it is required by your program; recordings help you review and learn, and may be required later by certifying bodies (e.g. AASP certification). It is useful to get comfortable with this as a trainee. One-on-one sessions will likely be a large part of how you get your contact hours. At times the tricky part of one-on-one sessions is getting clients to sign up.

Buy-In

It's suggested that you ensure and prioritize athlete buy-in during your first meeting. Many athletes, parents, and coaches may not yet understand how mental skills training can add value to performance. When you have an internship site, you cannot assume that, just because the coach wants you, the athletes will fully understand your work and its benefits. It takes more than being assigned to a team to have a full schedule with the players. You may need to be a salesperson for your discipline, in terms of what you have planned, and the eventual results your service can help provide. According to Heath & Heath (2008), there are six principles to include in your communication with potential clients about your services to make the message stick. When pitching your idea (mental skills training), it is stickiest (sticky, as in not forgotten about) when it is simple, unexpected, concrete, credible, emotional, and includes stories. These traits will more likely ensure your "sticky idea is understood, it's remembered, and it changes something" (Heath & Heath, 2008, para. 1). Once you have piqued their interest you are more likely to have athletes signing up to work with you one-on-one.

I (Noelle) learned to announce that my goal was to meet with every player at least once during the season at the first meeting with the team. This early expectation helped not only to reach but exceed the required number of individual contact hours, and provided ample practice assessing players in their first individual session. It also allowed me to have that private conservation with every player; often, once they met with me, they further understood what an individual session was, realized it was helpful, and signed up for more one-on-one work! Keep in mind that generally these sessions happen outside of practice time and hopefully you have already planned for this in your schedule.

Getting Clients to Sign Up for Meetings

Once you have the athletes interested in signing up for sessions, there needs to be a way that they sign up and that you organize your time for these meetings. Sign-ups can be done in several ways including a physical, paper sign-up sheet or with the support of technology. You need to consider the logistics for individual meetings: how they sign up, the times you are available, and a meeting place (which you have hopefully already addressed before the start of the internship). It's critical to make it as easy as possible for the athletes to sign up for your meetings, and to do it in a way that helps you stay organized.

Manual sign-ups can be done, allowing the players to physically sign up with you while you are at practice or meetings. If done in this fashion, privacy can become an issue. Other players see who signed up for a meeting, and when those sessions are by looking at the paper. In addition to privacy concerns, pen and paper sign-ups tend to be less efficient as opposed to online access.

Online sign-ups seem to be advantageous, especially for collegiate athletes, so consider if this is the right choice for your population. Using something like the online platform SignUpGenius.com allows you to post time slots you are available, before or after practice, for example. From there you can email blast the link for your entire month's availability. Once the athletes have access to the link, they can log in and sign up for a certain day and time. When using online tools, be aware of privacy concerns. Be sure that the schedule sign-ups are set to private so no one else can see who signed up, but only that a time slot is taken. We would also strongly suggest that you remind your athletes of their meetings at least 24 hours in advance, for example via text or email. With reminders, be sure to check what works best for your client and consider confirming with the parent as well if the client is a minor. Your confirmation serves as a reminder and allows for any changes to be made ahead of time to limit the chances of being stood up or waiting for a no-show.

Another factor to consider for individual sessions is location accessibility, especially if you are working with youth, particularly those who cannot drive themselves to meetings. Can they get a ride to or from a meeting with you if it is scheduled outside of practice times? Additionally, consider meeting space for minors: Is there adequate privacy in your meeting location if the parent or guardian must hang around for the session? A final point to keep in mind is related to those athletes who are injured. Injured players may still be present at practice and could benefit from mental skills training even if they are not physically able to participate in training. If approved by the coach, you could take time during practice to have a one-on-one with the injured athlete, to work on mental skills such as imagery for their rehabilitation or helping them build their confidence even while inactive.

What Happens in Sessions with Clients?

Individual Work

The logistics of one-on-one sessions have been covered in terms of typical session length, location, and tools for getting athletes to sign up. But what do you do in your meetings with clients? We present an example outline that you can follow within your one-on-one meetings with clients. Keep in mind that this outline can be revised to best fit the situation and each step is given an approximated amount of time. In this example, we use a more traditional 50-minute session, with each part examined in more detail below:

1. Introduction: Lay out what is planned so that the athlete knows what to expect for the next 50 minutes (adjust the time to meet your needs); confirm that the topic is still what they would like to focus on and that they are still available for that designated amount of time (3–5 minutes).
2. Review: Highlight the major themes from the previous session; for the first meeting this is where the assessment takes place (Review: 5–8 minutes, Assessment: 30 minutes).
3. Topic of the day (in the second meeting and beyond): Teach the mental skill(s) (30 minutes).
4. Preview: Pre-plan the when, where, and how of the skill or technique (10–20 minutes).
5. Wrap up: Summarize information and implementation of skill, ask for a take-away point from the athlete, and remind them about continued work before the next meeting (5 minutes).

Introduction Section of the Meeting

An example introduction that can take place during the first individual meeting is as follows:

> Hi [athlete's name], how are you? Thank you for meeting with me today. I want to first lay out for you what the next 50 minutes will look like before we get started. Are you still available for around 50 minutes? [Response from the athlete]. We are going to briefly go over the informed consent, including the purpose for the recording, and address any questions you may have. Then, afterwards we'd typically review what we talked about last time, but since this is our first meeting there's no recap needed. Third, we will get into the actual mental skill followed by its implementation. We'll preview the how and when part of the skill. For our first meeting today, I am going to spend time getting to know you as an athlete rather than teaching or working on mental skills. Together we'll discuss your strengths and areas of improvement. This process is known as assessment and allows us to properly identify what to work on. Lastly, we'll wrap it up with a summary and your personal take-away from our meeting. Any questions about the layout before we begin?

I (Noelle) personally like to use "we", especially during one-on-ones, to emphasize that mental skills training is a collaborative effort.

In subsequent sessions, your introduction would include the review portion following the meeting's introduction. The review allows the athlete to reflect upon what was discussed previously to make the connection of the skills' next steps. A review might sound like this:

> Let's recap where we left off last week. As your take-away, you shared how you found it helpful to brainstorm where and when you could use diaphragmatic breathing when

you're performing. We discussed the various benefits of this type of breathing and the effects it has on the body. Were you able to implement this skill in real time since we last met?

Review Section of the Meeting

The review portion of the individual work is as it sounds, reviewing the previous session and skill(s) taught, and is an ideal segue into the continual use of the skill. This section of the meeting can also provide you with insight as to what work was done by the athlete outside of the meeting. Did they use and execute the skill? What went well? What did not go so well? Taking the time to reiterate or review the athlete's understanding will only improve the chances of the skill's application.

If this is your first session, you will likely do an assessment—an evaluation of the athlete. This process allows you to collect information, make interpretations to gain understanding, and efficiently facilitate the intervention plan. As a trainee, you can utilize internships to practice administering different assessment tools such as the Performance Profile (Butler & Hardy, 1992), a SWOT analysis (Strengths, Weaknesses, Obstacles, and Threats; Chermack & Kasshanna, 2007), or a client intake form you have created. At JFKU, in addition to students learning about various assessment measures, styles, and strategies, we typically suggest that trainees have a guideline of questions they wish to ask their clients in the beginning such as:

- What mental skills training have you done prior to this if at all?
- How do you mentally prepare to compete, if at all?
- What are the specific demands of your sport and/or position?
- How might performing poorly make you feel?
- What did your best performance look and feel like?
- What is your sport history?

Topic of the Day Section of the Meeting

The beginning of mental skills training is generally done after you have completed a formal assessment. This is where you are teaching mental skills to clients, or refining their use of skills they already possess. There are nuances of how real consulting works when you go from the classroom to the field. This part of the one-on-one is where many trainees want to zoom through multiple mental skills that the athlete could use and/or they set out to teach one new skill per session. Rather than sharing everything quickly and in little detail, select one skill to focus on and work toward mastery; move on when the skill has been learned well and is utilized efficiently (see Chapter 12 for more detail on assessing how well your clients have learned and are utilizing their skills). Taking this approach throughout the season is most effective for the athlete. A tip I (Noelle) learned from a professional in the field is that, after assessment, present the athlete with three primary skills you think would most benefit them. You provide a briefing on each of the mental skills and explain why and how it can enhance their performance. From there, you allow the athlete to select which skill they want to develop first. You can then move on from there when ready. I have found this to be effective in that it often provides your client with increased motivation and autonomy (Ryan & Deci, 2000) and allows the client to contribute to the process. However, it is possible to meet with an athlete who knows exactly what they want to work on or they already have interest in a specific skill. Even in this case, take your time, teach the skill well, and make sure that the client's use of the skill is effective before moving on.

Preview Section of the Meeting

At this point during the individual work you have introduced to your client the layout of the session, recapped any pertinent prior information, and taught the mental skill itself. When getting into the preview part of the one-on-one, you are now facilitating the when and where of the skill. Specifically, when can this particular athlete use the skill in training and in their performance? How can he or she execute the skill? In this phase, you are pre-planning the action the athlete will have to take for them to reach complete or improved comprehension of the mental skill. The more specific scenarios you can discuss with client, the more it will allow them to follow through with integrating the skill into practice, performance, and other settings. You will not be there every time the athlete can utilize the skill so it is crucial to preview and set them up for success on their own. Remember that this may need to happen in more than one session before the client is ready to shift to another topic or technique, and that the skill or idea may not be fully covered until the third or fourth meeting.

Wrap-Up Section of the Meeting

At this point in the session you have spent quality time teaching the client a new skill or technique, which entails a lot of information. A summary of the key points of the lesson lets the athlete leave with those points prominently in their mind. Before ending the session, we suggest asking the athlete for at least one take-away from the meeting. Their take home point may be something new they learned or an application tip they plan on using. There is no right answer. As a sport psychology professional or trainee, this question shows what sticks out most in the mind of the athlete. This conclusive piece of information can then be recycled and used at the next meeting as part of the starting review.

Potential Challenges of Individual Work

What can you do if an athlete does not want to meet for individual work? This scenario is plausible and is something you should be prepared to handle. You cannot force an athlete or client to meet with you; the training will be ineffective if it is forced. It is important to keep the door open for possible work later in the season. I (Noelle) have found this approach helpful: *"I know you do not want to meet with me one-on-one which is not a problem. I wanted to be sure you know that I am here if you ever change your mind or have a question for me."* Depending on the timing and the rapport with that athlete, you might feel comfortable inquiring why they do not wish to do individual work. It is possible that they have worked with a mental skills coach before and had a bad experience or they feel they know enough already. Regardless, as a trainee or professional, respect their decision and maintain accessibility.

How do you approach an athlete about working together if this type of proactive communication is not an area of strength for you? Approaching people about work is a reality that you will face in this field and, if this is a personal weakness, it can be strengthened with practice. From my (Noelle's) experience as an intern, I learned quickly that the real growth comes from being uncomfortable. Your internships are a time to make mistakes and to experiment with and find your own style, while you have ample supervision. Get comfortable being uncomfortable and you will learn the most doing so.

Group and Team Sessions

In addition to individual work, you will hopefully be able to conduct team or group sessions related to mental skill building and development of team dynamics. Speaking in front of a group of athletes or participants may seem intimidating, but there are some basic skills that can help with group facilitation. I (Megan) always recommend to interns and those starting out in sport psychology to get as much practice as you can talking in front of groups. The best way to get comfortable in front of a group is to practice being in front of a group! Coaching youth sport teams, presentations at conferences, and public speaking classes are great ways to practice. The more you practice, the more comfortable you will be in these settings. If you are going to be working with teams, seek out classes in team dynamics and team building.

The more prepared you are, the smoother the group meeting will go. There is nothing is worse than getting in front of a group and forgetting what you wanted to talk about or not using the entire time allotted by the coach. If you're given 45 minutes, use all of it! Having a plan that is written out and that you have in front of you also seems to help with nerves. Even if you do not ever refer to your plan, knowing it's there just in case feels good. Remember that you can use time before you begin an internship to tentatively plan some of your meetings.

Structure of Group Meetings

Earlier we outlined how you will likely want to approach your first team meeting. From there, your team meetings will likely be focused on team dynamics and/or mental skills. Now let's talk about how you might want to structure and organize your team meetings after the first session. At JFKU, we often encourage trainees to aim for 45-minute to one-hour meetings on a weekly basis. You might have to be flexible based on training time and team availability, so consider how you might need to alter these ideas based on the amount of time you have. Below is a sample breakdown of a 45-minute group session on goal setting, which will then be covered in more detail. We also suggest that in this outline you include the materials needed for this session, to aid in preparing but also as a reminder for the future.

1. Introduction: Each athlete describes a current sport goal. Write each goal on the board (or have another athlete write) as they share. (5–8 minutes)
2. Content: Explain about types of goals (process, performance, outcome) and how they relate to each other. Use examples from athletes to explain points. Ask about team outcome and performance goals. (12 minutes)
3. Activity: Split athletes into groups to work on staircase worksheet to plan the process goals for their team performance and outcome goals. Have enough worksheets for each athlete to keep with information on goal-setting content. (5–10 minutes)
4. Debrief: Talk about what athletes wrote down, their own experience with goal setting, how they've used it before, and challenges with goal setting. Ask each what they can do in practice today (or tomorrow) to help the team process goals. (5–10 minutes)
5. Preview next session (topic, date/time); remind about individual meeting sign-ups. (2 minutes)

Items needed for session: white board, marker, worksheets, pens.

This type of plan/outline is something that we encourage you to create for each meeting; it allows you to stay on topic and ensure that you cover what you want in a short session. These notes are also great to keep so that you can refer to them later in the season to recall what you have covered and how to build on topics as you continue to work. Here is a bit more detail on each part of the meeting.

Introduction Stage of the Meeting

We encourage you to get the athletes invested from the beginning. Use a dynamic or multisensory approach from the start. Get the athletes talking and, when possible, moving! One of my (Megan) favorite ways to start a group session is to go around the room and have each athlete tell me something they did well in practice earlier that day or the previous day. It sets a tone that you will be focusing on their strengths and, if nothing else, each athlete's voice has been heard at least once. In early sessions, you may want to check in with clients, hear about how they have been since the previous meeting, and work on addressing their mental skills needs.

CONTENT: CHOOSING A TOPIC

When preparing for group work, you might want to have a concrete topic or point of focus for each session. To start your list of potential topics, begin with the coach. Prepare a list of general topics and then ask the coach which topics seem to fit the needs of their team. You can offer input based on your observations (if you had time to make any), but remember whose team it is. If the coach really wants you to do a session on goal setting, do a session on goal setting. Next, through assessment, learn about the needs of the team and ask the athletes what topics they think would be helpful. Maintain a balance between coach and athlete wants and needs while delivering your best work! Keep the goal of team sessions in mind when you prepare meetings and during delivery. Think about what you want the athletes to leave the group with and work backwards. If the purpose of the session is to set team goals, build activities and lessons around that.

Lastly, when choosing your topic remember that less is more. We do not have to teach everything we know about goal setting in one 30-minute session. Teach them goal setting in small chunks, much like you learned it in your classes. Think of your sessions as constantly building on each other. Plant a seed for an idea or skill in group session one and then come back to it later to continue teaching it. When we give athletes too much content in one session, we turn into lecturers instead of facilitators of a group. In addition, do not try to cover more than one area in one session. Connecting skills to practice and other skills is great (and encouraged) but, for example, do not teach them how to set goals and how to focus in the same session.

Activity Stage of the Meeting

When planning the group activity, try to use a multisensory approach that addresses different learning styles. Think back to your favorite classes in college. I (Megan) would imagine those were from professors who moved beyond a lecture format. Most likely you want the athletes to learn, but you do not want them to feel like they are in school. Some things to try are showing videos, breaking up the educational portion with activities, or breaking the group into smaller discussion pods. I (Megan) find that a lot of trainees are hesitant to try an activity in a team session, but will readily use it in an individual session. It does take some skill (and practice) to facilitate an activity in a group session, but it can be done!

During the activity, be sure that all athletes are getting involved. Typically, seniors and captains will readily be willing to respond to group prompts and questions. Try to get all members engaged so that your team session looks like a team meeting and not an individual session with others watching. Use techniques that cut off (nicely) and redirect the conversation, such as "I'd like to hear from a freshman on this question." or "Thanks [senior athlete], I'm curious if anyone else had another experience?"

Debrief Section of the Meeting

A common mistake I (Megan) see when supervising trainees (and one that I made a lot) is not leaving time in sessions for the athletes to process as a group. Group sessions need to maintain a balance of content (what are you teaching them) with time to debrief. You want to set up the group so you will have time to spend on processing what you've just explained or whatever activity you have used. This is where athletes really learn how to put mental skills into practice and into their sport.

During the group process or debrief, encourage all athletes to speak and pay attention to the athletes who have not spoken. This may provide insight as to who the group leaders are and the general makeup of the team. If you have an athlete who is generally outspoken but in a group session appears timid or reserved, this would be the time to check in with that athlete discreetly after the session. Any abnormality in behavior should be a mental note for you as the facilitator. There will also be times when the team needs to process an experience or event. Perhaps they're coming off a loss, or someone has left the team. You want to allow for these moments to be discussed and learned from; be willing to shift away from your plan to meet the group's needs and allow them to process their thoughts and feelings. We recommend creating an environment where athletes can learn from each other. Remember, some athletes may already be utilizing these skills; we are just there to help them get better, and giving time for debriefing and processing allows for improved learning.

Preview Section of the Meeting

End the session by previewing to athletes when you will see them next. This reminds athletes that mental training is part of their routine and helps to maintain a schedule. If you know the next topic, introduce it as well. This may spark some ideas the athletes have or plant a seed for them to think about. When you have just had a great team session, keep the momentum going and get them excited for the next mental skill you will teach them (or that you'll be helping them even more with the current topic)! I (Megan) also like to close sessions with each athlete sharing if time permits. This can be a summary of what they are taking away, what they liked best, what they are looking forward to in practice/ when they get home, etc. After your closing round, best practice would be to preview the next section for your athletes and remind them of when you will see them again.

Final Notes about Real-World Work as a Trainee

Case Notes and Client Files

Case notes are a way to keep track of and record pertinent information discussed during individual work. As a trainee, you might want to figure out what best serves you in terms of writing your case notes. Some find it most beneficial to jot down notes during the session while others designate 10–15 minutes after each session to write down the information needed into their case notes. It can be helpful to create a template to follow so that you have a systematic way of record keeping for each one-on-one. On your case note form you might consider including the client's initials (to protect confidentiality), date of session, current mood of the client, main topics discussed, plan of action, a section for notes on conversation, any assignments given, and next appointment date and time. A common note format in sport psychology is a SOAP note. SOAP stands for Subjective, Objective, Assessment, Plan (Cameron & Turtle-Song, 2002). The purpose of the note is to keep track of your client's progress as well as to provide documentation for the work you have completed with the athlete. Notes must be filed in a confidential place so that your client's identity is protected. Note-taking can seem rigorous and tedious, but is a necessary part of the job. One suggestion is to audio record case notes on your phone. Take 5–10 minutes to talk about what was discussed and replay that voice memo later when needed to complete written case notes. Regardless of how you take your notes, remember that these notes are an important part of being a professional in the field and help to serve your clients well.

Additionally, consider how you will keep each individual athlete's information organized. For example, will you file them away, have a designated folder for each, an accordion file, or something else? Ideally, you have given and received a completed and signed informed consent form before your first one-on-one meeting and/or team session. Treat a consent form for what it is, a confidential document and contract between you and your client, and you need to keep track of it in your client's file.

Conclusion

When thinking about your internship, it's important to keep your expectations aligned with reality. The reality is you will make mistakes and may feel anxious that you have to *do everything perfectly*. As one student-practitioner explained, she felt as if she was "thrown to the wolves" in her first internship; translating what you've learned in a classroom regarding theories and mental skills is often much more difficult than expected (Tonn & Harmison, 2004). Mistakes can lead to growth, as long as you maintain consistent supervision and are open to feedback. We encourage you to view making mistakes, and learning from them, as a crucial addition to your professional growth. In this chapter, we reviewed points to consider before starting your internship and tips for doing *the work*. The classroom serves as the foundation to teach you the material and concepts, and the field is where you learn to apply that information to athletes. You become the teacher and will soon learn that being a mental skills consultant is both art and skill.

A Trainee's Perspective on Transitioning from the Classroom to the Field

Ava Blennerhassett, M.A., student at JFKU 2014–2016

Ava is a Mental Performance Coach in her private practice, AMB Peak Performance. She enjoys working with individual athletes, teams, and coaches to achieve success in sport by improving their mental game. Ava works with collegiate and youth athletes and teams. She can be contacted at Ava@AMBPeakPerformance.com.

Going from the classroom into my first experience as a trainee I felt excited, nervous, motivated, and sometimes overwhelmed. After securing my first internship site I felt I was prepared and ready to start working with groups and individuals. Learning the skills and techniques in the classroom was critical for my work. However, being able to take what I learned into my internship and making it a creative, enjoyable experience for the individuals and teams was just as important. There were various moving parts constantly going at once, so staying organized, previewing each day, and being prepared was important.

I worked predominantly with youth athletes (under the age of 18), which involved getting buy-in (and consent) from the parents/guardians. Their receptiveness was as important as having buy-in from the athletes, coaches, and Athletic Directors. In my experience, attending a parent-athlete meeting at the beginning of the season worked well, especially when the coaches provided time for me to introduce myself. This way I could explain my role, the work I would be doing with the athletes, and go over the consent form with the parents without having them attend another meeting. Presenting at the initial meeting (typically pre-season) allowed the parents to get to know me and feel more comfortable about my work with their young athletes throughout the season.

As I began my work with clients, I quickly learned that being prepared and understanding how to best present the skills appropriately was crucial. For example, changing the terminology and my approach, which differed from my classroom knowledge, was needed. This way the athletes, coaches, and parents could comprehend and apply the mental skills I presented. I had to adjust my academic language to be client-friendly.

Other strategies that helped me transition from the classroom to the field included:

- Learning about the sport: what was involved with playing and competing. I found it helpful to go out on my own or with a friend and practice some of the technical skills used in the sport. This allowed me to grasp the terminology used and provided some insight into the physiological and psychological components of the sport.
- Having specific examples ready to use that the athletes could identify with and relate to. This not only helped to build rapport, but also to help them understand how they could apply the tools and techniques discussed.
- Knowing recognizable professional athletes or figures in the respective sport became a useful conversation starter, especially in the early stages.
- Using videos I had incorporated in class presentations into the internship. I showed athletes motivational videos and videos of elite or professional athletes speaking about their personal use of mental skills and how this impacts their performance. Videos and the inclusion of inspirational figures are excellent tools for engaging athletes on mental skills training.
- Previewing different situations that might arise within my internships allowed me to be as prepared as possible. Individual and group supervision, as well as peer support, helped with challenging moments.
- Accepting feedback and criticism helped me grow as a student-intern and in turn helped improve my work with the athletes.

At each internship site, I gained new tools and strategies for my service and built upon my previous experiences. I found myself being timid in the beginning, especially in my first internship. The exposure I received with each applied experience as a graduate student expanded my knowledge immensely. I was not always confident in myself, but having a supervisor and trusted peers assisted in my learning and transition from the classroom to the field.

Reflective Questions and Activities for You to Consider Before You Proceed

- What have you completed in your education that might need refining or reworking for you to be prepared for your internship?
- How comfortable are you in pursuing clients at your site to gain a full schedule? If you're not comfortable, how might you work on that?
- How will you market yourself?
- How are you going to create buy-in from your athletes?
- What are your one-on-one meetings and/or team sessions going to look like?
- What are you most nervous or anxious about when starting your internship? What are you most excited about?
- What supervisors, mentors, or peers are in your network that you can reach out to for guidance and support during this transition?

References

Butler, R. J., & Hardy, L. (1992). The performance profile: Theory and application. *The Sport Psychologist, 6*, 253–264.

Cameron, S., & Turtle-Song, I. (2002). Learning to write case notes using the SOAP format. *Journal of Counseling & Development, 80*, 286–292. doi:10.1002/j.1556-6678.2002.tb00193.x

Chermack, T. J., & Kasshanna, B. K. (2007). The use and misuse of SWOT analysis and implications for HRD professionals. *Human Resource Development International, 10*(4), 383–399. doi:10.1080/13678860701718760

Chlup, D. T., & Collins, T. E. (2010). Breaking the ice: Using icebreakers and re-energizers with adult learners. *Adult Learning, 21*(3), 34–39.

Cutlip, S. M., & Center, A. H. (1952). *Effective Public Relations: Pathways to Public Favor.* New York, NY: Prentice Hall Publishing.

Dale, G., & Conant, S. (2004). *101 Teambuilding Activities.* Durham, NC: Excellence in Performance.

Finta, D. (2016, November 22). Re: A perfect pitch: Giving an effective 30–60 second elevator pitch every time! [The Kennedy League]. Retrieved from http://blog.jfku.edu/a-perfect-pitch-giving-an-effective-30-60-second-elevator-pitch-every-time/

Heath, C., & Heath, D. (2008). Made to stick success model. Retrieved from http://heathbrothers.com/download/mts-made-to-stick-model.pdf

Jones, A. (1998). *104 Activities That Build.* Richland, WA: Rec Room Publishing, Inc.

Lovell, G. P., Parker, J. K., Brady, A., Cotterill, S. T., & Howatson, G. (2011). Looking the part: Female sport psychologists' body mass index and dress influences athletes' perceptions of their potential effectiveness. *The Sport Psychologist, 25*(1), 82–93.

Lubker, J. R., Watson, J. C., Visek, A. J., & Geer, J, R. (2005). Physical appearance and perceived effectiveness of performance enhancement consultants. *The Sport Psychologist, 19*, 446–458.

Poczwardowksi, A., Sherman, C. P., & Ravizza, K. (2004). Professional philosophy in the sport psychology service delivery: Building on theory and practice. *The Sport Psychologist, 18*, 445–463.

Ryan, R. M., & Deci, E. L. (2000). Self-determination theory and the facilitation of intrinsic motivation, social development, and well-being. *American Psychologist, 55*(1), 68–78. doi:10.1037/0003-066X.55.1.68

Simpson, D. (2016). "Going up?" A sport psychology consultant's guide to the elevator speech. *Journal of Sport Psychology in Action, 7*(2), 109–120.

Tonn, E., & Harmison, R. J. (2004). Thrown to the wolves: A student's account of her practicum experience. *The Sport Psychologist, 18*(3), 324–340.

8   Collaborating

Are You a Team Player?

Tyson Holt and Daniery Rosario

Within the modern competitive environment there are a number of stakeholders who work to support athletes/performers and positively influence performance. Many performers work with a number of different coaches including, but not limited to: their head coach, various assistant coaches, and strength and conditioning coaches. Dieticians, athletic trainers, and doctors may also have a regular presence within many performance environments. All of these individuals, including the trainee, have similar goals: to help the performer reach his or her potential. Navigating the structure of athletics and other performance domains can, at times, seem treacherous. This chapter will help the student learn how to leverage relationships with these various stakeholders while simultaneously keeping their clients' best interests as the chief concern.

Background Information on the Authors

Tyson Holt received his Master's Degree in Sport Psychology from JFKU in 2009. After graduating he worked as a Performance Enhancement Specialist for the U.S. Army, teaching mental skills to soldiers. For the past five years he has been employed by the Pittsburgh Pirates baseball team/organization as the Mental Conditioning Coordinator. It is his responsibility to oversee the mental skills development within the minor leagues as well as assist the organization in creating an overall culture of mental toughness. Tyson can be contacted at tholtmcc@gmail.com.

   Daniery Rosario graduated from JFKU with his Master's in Sport Psychology in 2011. While at JFKU, he interned with Stanford University's women's swim and crew team. His thesis, with the help of Drs. Alison Pope-Rhodius and John Kerr, "The Experience of Aggression among Mixed Martial Arts Athletes Interpreted Through Reversal Theory", was published in 2014 in the International Journal of Sport Psychology. Over the past five years, he has served as the Athletic Director at one of the country's top performing charter high schools in California, Leadership Public Schools Richmond (LPSR). Daniery can be contacted at daniery.rosario@gmail.com.

The Importance of Being a Team Player

In the work environment, everyone has a role and a job to fulfill. Being a team player means being committed to the overall mission of your organization or team and carrying out your responsibilities to the best of your ability while being able to support others in a time of need. It also means respecting everyone's role. This is important because a team's success is a result of everyone's collective effort. As an intern, you will receive support from a number of people who are committed to both your development and the team's success. It is in your best interest to balance the support you receive by contributing to the team's mission. When everyone can successfully collaborate together, so much more can be accomplished.

Knowing Your Setting

One of the first steps in preparing to work with athletes as a trainee (and eventually as a practitioner) is understanding the type of setting that you will be stepping into. In every setting, there will be many moving pieces. Some of these may directly impact your work, and others may not. Regardless, you should always be aware of what is shaping your environment in order to adapt and thrive.

Rules and Policies

In each setting there are rules and policies that will govern your work. For example, if you are stepping foot onto a high school campus you will want to know the school's policies regarding school hours and calendar events, visitors, fingerprinting/background checks, parent consent forms, etc. At Leadership Public Schools Richmond (LPSR), where I (Daniery) have served as the Athletic Director for the past five years, we (and JFKU) require all interns to complete a tuberculosis exam. We ask applicants to submit a Live Scan Request form, which is an inkless fingerprinting process that is sent to the California Department of Justice for review, along with completing a packet of volunteer forms that must be turned in to our home office at a separate location. Failure to do any of these things can result in delaying your start date, or even worse losing your internship. In addition to the paperwork, you will want to be aware of the all the legal issues around working with minors on school campuses, such as having sufficient insurance coverage and a valid driver's license on file with the school if transporting students. It is also recommended to obtain a signed consent form from a parent or guardian which allows you to provide sport psychology/mental skills services to minors. My strong suggestion would be to contact the school beforehand and get in touch with the Athletic Director. They can help you get all the information you need to ensure you are cleared for your first day.

If you are planning on working with collegiate athletes, as was my case when I (Daniery) interned at Stanford University, you will want to be familiar with the National Collegiate Athletic Association (NCAA). The NCAA is the governing body for collegiate sports in the U.S. The association lays out all the rules and policies for all universities, coaches, and athletes to follow. Any NCAA violation can result in the athletes losing their scholarships, universities being fined, and coaches being suspended or terminated, so it's important to understand those rules as well.

A typical collegiate athlete has a very busy schedule that can include team meetings, tutoring sessions, academic classes, strength conditioning, outside travel for competitions and more. The NCAA also has rules that dictate the maximum number of hours an athlete can spend at practices and when coaches and other personnel have direct contact with them. It's important to communicate with the coaching staff and players ahead of time when scheduling group and individual sessions as this may contravene one or more of these hour rules.

Top Tip: Adhere to all the policies that are in place in your internship setting, and if you don't know, ask. It's your responsibility.

Stakeholders

In order to be an effective team player when you're in an internship/applied experience, you will want to get to know your team. There are countless people that are involved in helping your athletes and teams to reach their goals, so identify the stakeholders. Depending on your setting, this may include parents, coaches, assistant trainers, directors, teachers, administrators, general managers, agents, and the list goes on. Stakeholders have the most influence over the athlete's performance, and they are the gatekeepers to a wealth of information that can be critical to your success.

What are the best ways to approach stakeholders?

- Find an opportunity to introduce yourself in person. Do not go for weeks on the job, or as a trainee, without having met the people who influence your work. They will likely be hard to find at times, but make the effort to meet them in person. This does not have to be an hour-long conversation, but a brief introduction can serve a purpose.
- Keep it positive. When meeting new people on the team, focus on the task at hand and stray away from any negatives. Some staff members will want to gossip, so be careful not to get caught up in it. You never know who is listening and how these interactions can come back to bite you. Be mindful of all your interactions to help keep things in perspective.
- Provide help when needed. This does not mean driving athletes to and from games (e.g. if you are in a high school setting), but if there is an opportunity to give a hand on a task, such as carrying something for the team, do it. Assuming your help will be brief and will not require you to go beyond your area of expertise, we see no harm. However, be sure to have your work covered before committing to anything.

Top Tip: It can be intimidating to meet new people and enter in a new environment that is already established, but don't let that stop you from making your presence known. Keep in mind that your role is important, they have often sought out your help (even as an intern), and you are providing a meaningful service.

Climate

The climate refers to the social-motivational constructs of your setting, a term coined by Ames (1992) in her research on achievement motivation. Most schools and organizations have a mission statement that you will easily find online. Reading and understanding their mission statement prior to your internship can help you gain a sense of what the overarching goal is at your site. Later on, as we will explain, it is important to have conversations with your boss, school dean, supervisor, or anyone else who is in charge; this will allow you to develop a deeper understanding of what the organization wants to achieve.

You will also want to become familiar with the level of professionalism at your site and how work-related issues are addressed. Take your attire as an example; some places may require you to follow a dress code or allow you to dress a certain way in order to set yourself apart. At JFKU, we were encouraged to wear something simple and professional, such as khaki pants and our program's affiliated polo shirts with the JFKU logo on. This allows people to easily identify you as an intern. Even the smallest decision, such as your clothing, can affect or add to the atmosphere you are hoping to create with your team.

Every place is different and each will have their own unique approach that goes beyond attire. Successful teams and organizations spend a considerable amount of time setting expectations and goals that dictate the mindset and work flow within their setting. At LPSR, we have what are considered high academic and behavioral expectations for schools in the "iron triangle" of Richmond, California. Therefore, it is important for sport psychology interns who join our teams to know that we are a college prep school and our students are consistently exposed to rigorous academic work. Knowing this information beforehand will help you understand the type of motivational climate your athletes are accustomed to and the level of difficulty at which you can teach them.

Top Tip: Assess the climate and use these experiences to determine your own comfort. Internships and early work are great opportunities to help you figure out which type of environment you prefer to work in.

Essentials for the Working Relationship

Ok, you have the lay of the land. You know who has a vested interest in the athletes' performance. You have done your homework and have a pretty good idea of what you are getting into as well as the rules and regulations that will impact your work. You know where you will spend your time and who you will spend your time with. The next question is *how* will you spend your time? There are some critical steps to take from the beginning to the end of your working relationship to ensure that both you and the people you are there to serve benefit from the relationship.

Preparation for the Job

As we reflect on our experiences in the field as interns, professionals, and supervisors, one point that seems obvious, but is often overlooked, is knowing who your boss is. When you are working in a team or organizational structure, your boss is the person that is bringing you in to do the work. It might be a coach, an Athletic Director, or in the case of professional baseball it is a farm director or general manager. In these settings, the boss is not the athlete. A common mistake is to be so excited to start working with the athletes that you set your goals and expectations around how you can best help them achieve performance excellence and then drive full steam ahead. The problem with this approach is that you are leaving a critical person out of the planning process: the person that brought you in to do the work in the first place. They brought you in for a specific reason; they have expectations for what it is that you will be doing, how you will be doing it, and what you will achieve in the process. If you want to have a successful experience on the job, the first thing you need to do is sit down face-to-face with the boss and collectively determine how you are going to work. This is especially critical in our field because of the wide spectrum of qualifications, competencies, and education levels that fall under the umbrella of "sport psychology professional" (or related terms). There are also a vast number of misunderstandings and misrepresentations of who we are and what we do. These meetings are critical as trainees and professionals. If you want to make a positive impact, work to clearly define your job description to include expectations, roles, and responsibilities.

An important aspect of this first meeting is defining expectations. Stated simply, you are collaborating to set your goals for your work. Besides thanking your employer for the opportunity to impact his or her athletes, the first thing you should work to uncover is why they brought you on board. There are two incredibly important parts of this task: 1. you are going to learn a lot about what services they think you offer to the clients, and 2. you are going to begin merging your goals for what you hope to accomplish with what they want you to accomplish. The ideal scenario is that there is a lot of overlap. They ask you to do a lot of things you were hoping to do and some things that are a little outside your comfort zone. At the same time, you reaffirm and expand their vision of your role. The end state of the ideal scenario is that everyone gets better. But as we all know, the ideal scenario is very rarely reality. Reality is that the boss may ask you to do some things you cannot do based on competency or even ethical concerns. In this case, you will have to educate your employer on what you can and cannot do. The worst-case scenario is that you walk away from this meeting and your collective goals seem at odds. If this is the case, you probably need to seek advice from your supervisor or mentor on how to proceed. However this conversation goes, it is an improvement over the alternative of assuming the team, school, or organization you work for has no expectations outside those of your own.

During this conversation, here are some example questions you may want to ask:

- What are your goals for me?
- How would you prioritize those goals?
- What do you think is the best way to achieve those goals?
- What obstacles do you think I may encounter?
- How will you determine (measure) my success?
- Would you like progress reports?
- Do you prefer email, phone, or face-to-face communication?
- How often would you like me to be here?
- Are there important dates or events I should know?
- What meetings or events should I be a part of? Can I be a part of? Can't I be a part of?
- How should I dress?

This is by no means an exhaustive list. However, you will have a good idea about how you are going to be evaluated. Because whether you establish these collective expectations or not, you and your work will be evaluated.

Top Tip: Assume nothing! Leave the first meeting with specific goals and specific actions based on specific conversations.

Communication with Your Team

Working as a full-time staff member in player development in baseball, my (Tyson) team includes front office staff, coordinators, managers, hitting and pitching coaches, strength and conditioning coaches, athletic trainers, and other support staff members. All of these stakeholders have one common goal, which is to provide the highest quality of support in their respective area of expertise. However, because it is a fast-paced, demanding environment, and time is limited, sometimes your goals can feel at odds. When this happens, it is usually because there has been a breakdown in communication. Therefore, there are some things you should keep in mind in order to be the best teammate you can be:

- Invest in the relationship. Find at least one thing you have in common with your teammates to start building bonds. The stronger the bond, the more durable the relationship will be when there is turbulence.
- Be a collaborator, not just a communicator. Communicators share their goals and know the goals of those around him. Collaborators work on their goals and the goals of those around them.
- Be empathetic. Know the challenges your teammates face in accomplishing their goals.
- Be flexible. Keep in mind that your number one priority may not always be the team's number one priority. Expect and welcome changes because they are going to happen. The United States Marine Corps has an unofficial mantra that is worth adopting: "Semper Gumby," or always be flexible.
- Communicate early and often. Relationships and the environment are both dynamic. Good starts do not guarantee good finishes. Establish relationships, standards, and expectations, and then continue to feed into them with your words and your work.

Top Tip: Make teamwork the priority. This is a big distinction from making teamwork a priority. When it is a *priority, other priorities can lead you away from making team-centered decisions. When you make it* the *priority, you will find that your goals and the goals of your teammates will benefit.*

Collaboration on Mental Skills Development

In the competitive setting, you have a team of trained professionals dedicated to helping the athletes improve. As the resident expert in mental skills training, you can leverage your relationships with your team. Collaboration on mental skills development can lead to a team culture dedicated to mental toughness, maximizing the mental game growth of the athletes.

Collaborating with the Team

As one stakeholder among many stakeholders in the competitive setting, collaborating on mental skills development has many advantages. By sharing the principles of mental skills such as confidence, composure, and concentration, you are helping the other stakeholders become better coaches. You are also increasing the chances that your messages to the athletes are being reinforced when you are not around. In most cases as a student and a professional in the field, the time you are absent will be far greater than the time you are present. Many, if not most, of your fellow stakeholders who interact frequently with individual athletes will recognize specific strengths and weaknesses across mental skills. The challenges that most coaches face are knowing how to proceed and what to do about it. This is where your training comes in. By training the other stakeholders on mental tools such as self-talk, goal setting, and visualization, they can go one step further than identifying barriers to the athletes' success. You can even share the work you are doing with individual athletes as long as you have the athletes' consent. This is another opportunity for you to collaborate with the other stakeholders to maximize your impact on mental skills development.

While many of the teams you work with may value the services you provide to the athletes, professionals in our field have a responsibility to empower the other stakeholders with the knowledge we possess. With every interaction, each stakeholder is coaching the mental game and they are either helping it or hurting it. With your expertise and your observations, you can ensure that they do much more helping than hurting. As a mental skills professional that is part of a team of stakeholders, you have an obligation to your team as well as the athletes to make sure each person sees you as a resource. By educating both your team and the athletes to the best of your ability, you can ensure that the mental training done in the environment you are working in is based on science and best practices.

Confidentiality

When collaboration is one of your main goals, the respect for confidentiality has to always be in the forefront of your mind. Based on AASP's Ethical Principles and Guidelines (2011), confidentiality should be used to respect your client's right of privacy and welfare. In doing so, you create an environment where your clients can feel safe being vulnerable, allowing you, the practitioner, to best assist the client in identifying the most beneficial path for growth. Setting up an expectation of confidentiality also assures your client that what is shared will not negatively impact him personally or within the team or organization. The key mantra with confidentiality is do no harm.

In a setting where you are collaborating with others, it will be important for you to always educate the athletes on how you operate within the team of stakeholders. One important aspect to share is that working on the mental game is necessary to be an elite performer. This is to ensure the athlete that, by working with you, he/she will not be negatively impacting his/her standing on the team. This is especially critical in sport settings where most of your work will be highly visible. It is also important to encourage the athletes to share what they are working on and inform them that you would also like to share what they are working on. It is essential to always ask if there is anything they are uncomfortable with you sharing with the other stakeholders. Even if you are in a climate that encourages mental skills training, you must respect the athletes' desire for privacy.

A Case Study of Collaboration

It is understandable to feel unprepared to collaborate as a team member in our field. There are not a lot of examples in the literature available yet. Because of that, I (Tyson) have provided an example of what collaborating as a sport psychology/mental skills professional might look like based on my own stumbles and lessons learned to complement the foundational information provided above. This is a case study about a fictional professional baseball player named Jeff. Though he and his story are fictional, each element is based on my real experiences and the Pirates' protocol for dealing with individual players.

Jeff is an infielder who has been struggling lately. He has not had a lot of good results in the past several games and he is allowing his emotions to get the best of him. This is something that has challenged Jeff throughout his short career. As the mental conditioning coordinator, my role in helping Jeff has to go beyond coaching Jeff. I also want to arm the coaches with the tools and information they need to help Jeff improve his mental game. When I collaborate with the coaches who will have daily interactions with the players, I can be sure that his approach to the mental game is being coached when I am not around.

This consistency in coaching Jeff's mental game will be the key to making significant strides forward.

Mental conditioning is a constant part of every player's development, not just when players struggle. Collaboration is essential to our process. For Jeff, our work began a couple of months after he was drafted. Our mental conditioning process starts with the Pirates Mental Game Profile, a self-assessment that has them evaluate their mental game based on the mental skills and mental tools we teach to improve performance. After scoring the assessment we compare those results to our observations and the observations of the coaches, and then players provide final thoughts or context on their scores. We then meet with the players individually. During these meetings we are going to try to identify some strengths in their mental game and one area they could set goals to improve. This helps the player and the coach for the upcoming season narrow their focus onto a specific mental skill. For Jeff, that skill happened to be composure. Once we determine a mental skill for development, such as composure, we collaborate with the player and coaches to make sure that a specific plan is in place for them to build the skill. A specific plan is put into place by the end of Spring Training.

During the season, a large part of my time is spent traveling between each of our minor league affiliates to spend four or five days with each team. I will see a team roughly every six weeks. On one particular trip, I arrived in Charleston, WV, where one of our minor league affiliates plays. My number one priority when I get there is to collaborate with the staff. My second priority is to follow up with the athletes. I check in with the staff to see how the players are doing and see how I can help. The hitting coach tells me that Jeff is more aware of the situations that challenge his composure, but he is still really struggling keeping his emotions in check. In this conversation with the coach, I have a couple of goals. The first is to help the coach help Jeff. In most cases this is a continuation of an ongoing conversation. The second is to broaden the coach's understanding of the mental side of the game. In this case, I work to improve the coach's understanding of composure—the science of how the brain and body work and the art of practical ways to talk about or improve it. For Jeff, we decide that something he would benefit from is a *reset* or some way to let the frustration of one pitch go so he can commit to the next one. The hitting coach is going to take some extra time with Jeff in the batting cages to talk through a specific routine of stepping out, taking a purposeful breath and getting back to his hitting approach.

Next I meet with Jeff and look for an opportunity to talk about his mental game, specifically his composure. Jeff happens to have a game where he is not in the lineup. When we are in the dugout watching the game, I rest up against the dugout rail beside him for a couple of innings, checking in on him. The conversation ranges from family to "frolf" (Frisbee golf). Ultimately I look for, or create, an opportunity to reinforce the coach's message and learn about the player. In this particular conversation with Jeff, he tells me that he understands the technique the coach shared but does not think it is impacting performance. I reiterate the importance of repetition and practice and tell him to keep after it. I also take the coach's advice one step further by giving him a deeper rationale of how a *reset* helps physically and mentally.

There are some important things I keep in mind when collaborating with my team on a player's mental game. First, I always communicate with the player about what I would like to share. As Jeff and I are wrapping up, I recap what we discussed and ask if it is okay if I share the highlights with the coach. Some players will want to keep some things between you and him and that is okay—not everything needs to be shared. Some players will come to you with personal issues. Our background of training using counseling skills tends to make us very effective listeners so we may have more conversations like this than most coaches. However, like any good coach, teacher, or friend, I am going to be there and listen to their personal struggles. If that is all they need, it stays between us. If they need professional counseling/therapy, I am going to find someone to help them. If it is a performance-related issue, I am going to encourage and remind them that their struggles are normal and that they should loop their coaches in to help because the goal is not normal, the goal is to be elite. For example, one reason that Jeff had been off his game is because he and his girlfriend were having a hard time with the distance and he had missed out on some sleep trying to smooth things over. He did not want me to share that with the coach, so I did not.

In summary, my team is the developmental staff and I respect the relationship between myself and the players. I communicate in ways that help Jeff get the most out of his physical and mental abilities. I also communicate in ways that are focused on what he *can* do and *is* doing rather what he lacks. This is especially critical in a high stress, high stakes environment where it is many people's job to evaluate what a player can and cannot do. I am in player development and I am very thankful I do not have to make those calls.

Conclusion

Working within a collaborative environment can be difficult. Each day a member of a team has to navigate different settings, situations, personalities, and decisions. However, as the saying goes, "nothing that is worthwhile ever comes easy." Working in a collaborative environment offers multiple opportunities to invest in the lives of others and enrich your own life through personal and professional development. Preparation in areas of an organization that range from the depth of policy to the nuance of culture can help you feel comfortable in various settings and situations. Considering the goals and perspectives of others can provide you with confidence that you are making the right choices. Buying into the standards of the organization you are serving, the field you are representing, and your own personal code of conduct can provide you with conviction in how you operate. Prioritizing collaboration as a means to maximize an athlete's development while always keeping the athlete's best interest at heart is a recipe for success for creating an organization dedicated to mental skills development. It is our hope that we have provided you with some guidance for how to achieve some comfort, confidence, and conviction as you navigate your current or future opportunities.

A Trainee's Perspective on Collaboration

Tommy Muir, M.A., student at JFKU 2014–2016

Tommy's passion is helping people to maximize their innate abilities, no matter their chosen endeavor. He resides in the Los Angeles area, where he actively works with individuals in sporting and non-sporting environments through his part-time consulting practice, Mindset Elevated, and his full-time work at a law firm. Having extensive experience leading teams comprised of up to 180 individuals, Tommy intimately understands the importance of cohesion and collaboration. While we possess the ability to accomplish whatever we set out to, Tommy believes working with others significantly increases the ease with which we arrive there. His other pursuits include triathlon, writing, and continued education, and someday he would like to be a part-time, adjunct instructor at a junior college or university. He can be contacted at tmuir@email.jfku.edu, and his website is www.mindsetelevated.com.

The whole will always be greater than the sum of its parts, no matter the situation or circumstances. Furthermore, it truly takes a village and behind each and every one of us lies a plethora of individuals who have contributed to the success we ultimately achieve. As a student-intern, understanding and genuinely believing we play a small yet consequential role with the athletes with whom we work is paramount. In varying degrees, we are a piece of the puzzle working toward the betterment of the athlete.

No two athletes are the same, just as no two athletic environments are the same. With this in mind, it is important for trainees to understand approaches will need to be varied, accommodations will need to be made, and fluidity is necessary. Ultimately, finding success while deeply immersed in a dynamic new site begins from the onset. Immediately developing an awareness of the situation, specifically focusing on the individual personalities of the athletes and the coaching staff, as well as understanding any and all formal policies or procedures which must be adhered to while on-site are integral. The firmer the understanding of the comprehensive situation on-site, the more thoroughly a trainee is able to develop their initial plan. In short, maximizing one's time on-site begins with gaining a firm, all-encompassing grasp from the beginning.

No matter how efficient we are at performing the work, we will only advance as far as we are enabled to go. Ultimately, there is someone who has chosen to bring us into the fold as the gatekeeper (e.g. coach, Athletic Director, parent, athlete, etc.) and we are on-site at their behest. The work we do with athletes is best served through developing a relationship with these stakeholders, built upon a solid foundation steeped in open and honest communication. For me, having a face-to-face liaison with the stakeholder prior to commencing the internship was preferred but it may not always be possible. In these instances, a phone call may be needed. In either regard, this meeting needs to be a top priority.

A successful approach to this meeting begins with the utmost professionalism and a clear understanding that this is the first impression which you are making with someone who holds the keys to the proverbial kingdom. I found it best to do some research on the primary stakeholder prior to the meeting so I could gain a better understanding of what drives them in the position they are filling. If they are a coach at an academic institution or a club, chances are they have a biography on the associated website. Additionally, any supplemental information, excluding anything confidential in nature, which may be gleaned from previous interns who worked at the site will prove beneficial. This may disclose areas where friction occurred or where a different approach may have worked better.

As interns going into a new internship armed with a more thorough understanding of the environment and associated personalities, we are better prepared to develop our questions which enable us to better formulate our initial plan. Having a list of questions or concerns outlined prior to the meeting is essential. It not only prevents an important question from being overlooked, but it also distinguishes us in the eyes of the stakeholder as being prepared. Additionally, inquiring about the stakeholder's expectations of us as well as their vision of how we will be employed leads to a more thorough understanding. Finally, and most importantly, I found it essential to openly state my expectations. Ultimately, we are our own advocate and openly disclosing our needs from the beginning better enables the stakeholder to create an environment ripe for our success.

As the work moves forward, building and maintaining relationships with all parties is a continuing process. In doing this, it is essential as budding practitioners that we remain cognizant to the needs, desires, plans, and styles of all those associated. In the end, we are but one cog in the process. However, the end product would be dramatically altered if our contribution was removed, just as it would were anyone's contribution removed.

Reflective Questions and Activities for You to Consider Before You Proceed

- What types of challenges have you faced when stepping into a new job? How did this help or prevent you from doing your work?
- Are you able to connect with the organization's mission statement?
- What role do you play in collaborating and how will you communicate this to the team?
- How do you plan on addressing confidentiality with your boss and colleagues?

References

AASP. (2011). *Ethics code: AASP ethical principles and standards.* Retrieved from www.appliedsportpsych.org/about/ethics/ethics-code

Ames, C. (1992). Achievement goals, motivational climate, and motivational processes. In G. C. Roberts (Ed), *Motivation in sports and exercise* (pp. 161–176). Champaign, IL: Human Kinetics.

9 Being Your Best

Are You Looking After Yourself?

Sara Robinson and Alexsandra Walton

Being at one's best over a stretch of several weeks, even months, is a challenge. By looking after and taking care of oneself, the people around the trainee, including clients, teams, coaches, supervisor, friends, and family, will also benefit. A trainee who is practicing strong self-care tends to have healthier, more productive, and more efficient interactions with whom he or she works. Being at your best during training and beyond includes utilizing the mental training skills one teaches to others for self-benefit, maintaining a work-school-personal balance, having peer consultations for extra support, participating in one's own psychotherapy as needed, and recognizing the signs of burnout and what to do about it if it arises. This chapter will highlight the potential short-term and long-term pitfalls of not using some of these strategies and outline ways to incorporate them into applied work.

Background Information on the Authors

Sara Robinson received her M.A. in Sport Psychology from JFKU in 2006. She began working as a supervisor there in 2008. In the next year, in addition to her own consulting business, she added teaching, online course development, and coordinator of the Sport Psychology Department's non-profit program to her duties. Self-care became a critical part of managing it all. When she became a mom in 2012, she began to shift more focus to her mental skills consulting work and in 2016 she launched *Get Mom Balanced*, a website that aims to support moms in using mental skills in their own lives to help create balance and find new avenues for self-care. As a parent, wife, and professional, she is keenly aware of the importance of taking care of yourself in order to be able to do your best work in all aspects of life. Sara can be contacted at srobinson@jfku.edu.

Alexsandra (Alex) Walton, received her M.A. in Sport Psychology from JFKU in 2015. The program not only provided her with the education to work as a mental skills professional, but also allowed her to acquire well over 400 hours as a sport psychology intern in settings ranging from youth camps, to elite high school athletic programs, to collegiate basketball. It was during her time as an intern that it became clear that she was lacking in self-care. With the support of her professors and class-mates, Alex was able to strike a balance between school, family, and self-care. Alex is the mother of three sons: twin teenagers and an eight-year-old. She has also been married to DeWayne Walton for 15 years. They met at UCLA, where she received her BA in History. Self-care is a topic that is tremendously important to Alex. As a professional, she continues to make self-care a priority. Whether it's a weekly workout or a date night with the hubby, it's always on the calendar! Alex can be reached at awalton.mentalskills@gmail.com.

The Need for Self-Care: A Personal Example from Alex

During each week of group supervision at JFKU, the professor would ask "What are you doing for yourself this week?" Every time I heard this question I would try to come up with something that sounded good. "Ummmm, I am going to go for a run and then go to a yoga class." My professor would nod with approval. On my drive home I knew that I would be doing no such thing. I was the mother of three sons, a wife, and a graduate student in my third internship. Oh, and did I mention I was working full time? There was no way I would get in any time for me. That just was not an option. However, I felt that if I said it out loud, I would make it happen. I wanted badly to make time for myself and I truly believed that, if I said it enough, I would do it. I knew that it was important, but it was the easiest thing for me to push to the side if I felt overwhelmed. I just could not figure out how to make taking care of myself a priority.

Each week I would continue in the same way, running from place to place, showing up to group supervision, and promising to take care of myself that week. Until one day, everything came together like a tornado and hit me. And it hit me hard. It was my turn to talk about my week with my team and I could barely speak. I was exhausted and completely overwhelmed; my professor could see it all over me. She kept me after class and I fell apart. I cried until I could not cry anymore. I felt like I was losing myself in all of this. She said "You haven't been taking care of yourself have you?" I couldn't even respond. She saw right through me.

The Reality of Internships

As you prepare to start work with your clients, it is important to have a strong understanding of the realities of being in an internship. If you don't, and if you're not prepared for the amount of time and work an internship requires, you may find yourself in a position similar to what Alex experienced.

Generally speaking, your internship(s) will take place over an extended period of time. At JFKU, students are required to work with their team from the start of their season to the end of it. With some teams this may be three months, for other teams this could be closer to a year. The requirement to be with a team from start to finish is beneficial for you and your clients; rapport can be well established, there is time for the clients to develop and utilize mental skills, and you are able to be consistent with clients through the closure of their competitive season (if there is one). As you probably know, our role is to help and support our clients. How might you feel as an athlete if your mental skills consultant left mid-way through the season? With this idea in mind, before agreeing to a site, be sure that you can commit to your team for their entire season. Preview what else will be happening during that timeframe; for instance, what will your course load(s) be like? What are your family and work obligations? If the team's length of season or schedule does not match up well with your availability, or you are not in the mental space to be completing an internship, then you may find that no amount of self-care helps you through the experience.

Having supervised numerous interns and worked in the field for a decade, I (Sara) have observed interns who have not taken self-care seriously in their own lives. In life we all benefit from ongoing self-care, but especially those of us who choose helping professions and work in mental health (Barnett, Baker, Elman, & Schoener, 2007). Baker (2003) puts it this way: "We need to replenish if we are to share with others" (p. 17) and we have a responsibility to remain aware of our own needs and tend to them. However, oftentimes the need for self-care becomes much stronger when we are over-tired and over-worked and, as Alex experienced, these are also the times where self-care feels the hardest. As has already been discussed in this book, there is much preparation that happens before you begin an internship (see Chapters 1 & 2). This chapter aims to help you understand not only the importance of self-care, but also prepare you with your own personalized self-care first-aid kit.

Self-Care

Before we go any further, let's define it. Self-care is a term thrown around quite a bit, both in academic literature and the popular media, but what does it really mean? At first glance, the term defines itself: self-care means to take care of oneself. However, it is more than that. It is being *intentional* about focusing on your needs: physical, emotional, or mental (Beauchamp & Childress, 2001). This chapter aims to bring clarity to what self-care is, along with providing ideas for how to fulfill your own needs.

The Importance of Self-Care

Self-care is not only important for your personal well-being, but professionally as well. The APA Ethics Code (2002) discusses the need for professionals to be aware of their own physical and mental health and the possible impact of it on their work. Without taking care of ourselves, we are not able to best serve the clients we work with. Those in helping professions are no different than other individuals; we have our own challenges and circumstances along with helping others with their own circumstances. Norcross and Barnett (2014) present the idea that self-care is an "ethical imperative" (p. 1) for those in mental health and counseling. While we may help others with their own self-care, Norcross and Barnett say that while "[lack of self-care] is so easy to see and diagnose it in other people; it is so hard to get off the treadmill ourselves" (p. 1). Self-care is included in this book to highlight its importance, clarify what self-care may mean for you, and give you practical ideas for engaging in self-care.

As a professional in the field, I (Sara) have truly become aware of the importance of self-care and discuss this with my students, supervisees, and clients. When you are not taking care of yourself, you cannot be your best or meet your potential within any of the roles you take on. In the field of applied sport psychology, we are working with others and we owe our clients the best version of ourselves, which can only happen when we take care of ourselves and have the self-awareness to realize that self-care is needed (Baker, 2003; Richards, Campenni, & Muse-Burke, 2010).

When you are aware of your own needs and you work to meet them as best as possible, you will likely find that you are more productive in and out of your internships. For example, if you get behind on sleep you will begin to feel sluggish, will be less able to maintain focus in your sessions, and probably will not be as productive with your time when planning and preparing for your work. All of this can lead to stress or anxiety which can affect your sleep. When you take care of yourself by getting the right amount of sleep, eating well, being physically active, taking time for activities you enjoy, etc., you are in the mental and physical space to be more effective in the work you do. If we are not paying attention to our own needs and actively taking care of ourselves, it can be a challenge to put any of our issues aside when we step into our sessions.

What does it mean to actively take care of yourself? This means that you are thoughtfully, intentionally, and proactively taking steps to put yourself first and nurture your relationships with others. In addition to being a trainee, you may be a parent, significant other, caregiver, friend, or employee. When we are not at our best and are not taking care of ourselves, these relationships can suffer. It is difficult to show up and fully engage with others when we have not tended to our own needs. When I (Alex) was a graduate student and had not taken care of myself, I noticed that I felt even more overwhelmed when interacting with my kids. My patience was shorter and trying to tend to all of their needs was challenging. I would feel guilty and frustrated all in one. I also noticed that when I did not actively take care of myself stress worked its way into all areas of my life, especially with my husband. I found myself feeling like I was being neglectful and that was not my intention at all. I (Sara) agree with this and notice that my home life is negatively impacted when I am neglecting my self-care. Though I may be able to *hold it together* with my clients, the stress seeps out at home. It is not fair to my family.

Though we (the authors, and the broader "we" of professionals in the field) know that self-care is critical, it can be easy for practitioners to be less than perfect when it comes to self-care. We talk with our clients about the need for self-care, help identify what self-care may be for them, and remind them about the importance. And yet, we also struggle with making the time for self-care. I (Sara) regularly go through phases where self-care falls to the back-burner and I (Alex) distinctly remember an internship meeting with a high school hurdler where my own self-care came up. The athlete was stressed out about maintaining her grade point average, making it to the state championship meet, and pleasing her parents. When I asked what she did to take care of herself when she felt like this, she stared at me and said "Nothing. What do you do?"

Though clients may not always directly ask us about our own habits, and we likely want to limit self-disclosure, honesty went a long way in this situation. Instead of fibbing a little and responding "I do yoga, run, meditate . . ." I shared, "That is actually an area of growth in my life. I am working on finding ways to take care of myself as well." The athlete smiled and said "Thanks for that." This story is a great reminder that we need to practice what we preach to our clients. If, as a trainee or consultant, you are talking to your client about the importance of taking care of oneself and encouraging the athlete to practice self-care but you are not doing so, the athlete may be able to tell that you are not at your best. And if you are not at your best, how can you help your client to reach their own potential?

What Constitutes Self-Care?

Remember that many of the performance enhancement skills you are teaching your clients are life skills as well. And we do not just mean life skills for our clients, we mean life skills for ourselves. You may already be using many of these skills to help with your performance as a practitioner: calming down before presentations, using imagery to practice your work, or setting goals for yourself. However, in using these mental skills for yourself outside of your work, you may notice additional benefits. Ideally you will become a better teacher of these skills because of your own personal use, but these mental skills can also be an important part of your self-care.

A good way to think of self-care is that it is like a first-aid kit. If you are not familiar, a first-aid kit has a variety of supplies and equipment that help a person to deal with a wound or emergency situation. First-aid kits have an assortment of items in them allowing the user of the kit to deal with several issues or situations. For a first-aid kit to be utilized, it must be brought with you and available when the need arises. The box that holds the items in the kit is the foundation and structure; we want to present the idea of mindfulness as a foundation for self-care. Practicing mindfulness on an ongoing basis will allow you to notice thoughts without becoming attached to them. You may have experienced trying to manage your thoughts and find that this is a challenging task. When being mindful, you work to stay in the present, noticing your thoughts, feelings, and reactions, and you move on. When we fixate on thoughts, this can cause stress and anxiety. With regular use in all aspects of life, mindfulness can create the ability to respond more objectively to thoughts and situations rather than react emotionally. For additional information on mindfulness see *Mindfulness and Performance* (Baltzell, 2016).

With the foundation of mindfulness comes better awareness, and the ability to know when we might need to utilize the items that our first-aid kit holds. What follows is not an exhaustive list of mental skills, but is a starting point for you to begin to think of your own self-care first-aid kit and what yours may need to include.

- Breathing skills—*similar to the concept of a Band Aid (utilized easily and at any time)*
  Using diaphragmatic breathing will help to bring oxygen into your body, slow down your heart rate, and possibly quiet your mind. Utilize deep breathing at moments where you are experiencing stress, but also to begin any event from a calmer place.
- Thought management techniques—*could be considered similar to an Ice Pack (where you can get focused relief in a particular area)*
  It is normal to worry about and over-analyze situations, or to experience many competing thoughts when you have numerous responsibilities. Consider how you can cognitively manage those thoughts, such as using a thought-stopping cue and a replacement thought that is helpful and productive.
- Imagery—*like taking an Aspirin (it may take a little time to impact your system, but works well when it does)*
  While imagery can be used in many ways, consider creating a relaxing place that you can visit through vivid imagery that will help you to feel more calm and in control. Imagery can also be used to help you prepare for upcoming moments, allowing you to feel more confident and calm when you begin.

In addition to the skills listed above, there are other ways to practice self-care. Dr. Barbara Markway (2014) discusses the pathways to self-care and that any of these paths can help an individual better handle stress and be able to calm down.

These pathways include:

- Sensory: focusing on the sensations around you and includes activities such as listening to running water, staring at the sky, or listening to music.
- Pleasure: being involved in something that is enjoyable to you, such as walking your dog, journaling, or going for a jog.
- Mental/Mastery: taking on a task that engages your brain or allows you to tackle a task, such as doing a crossword puzzle, or organizing an area of your home.
- Spiritual: finding ways to connect with the more abstract, personal aspects of yourself (or something bigger), regardless of what spirituality means to you. For example, praying or connecting with nature.
- Emotional: acknowledging and dealing with your emotions. If you're stressed you may want to avoid emotions, but addressing them in a non-judgmental way is useful. Consider journaling or finding ways to create more positive emotions.
- Physical: using your body and being active. getting out of your head and into your body can act as a form of self-care. The examples are endless but may include yoga, running, or working out.
- Social: connecting with others. For example, take the time to make a phone call or meet up with a friend or loved one.

Each of these ideas could be added into your own first-aid kit. Choose what works for you and what you have time for, which may be as simple as a phone call or taking a short walk or something that requires more planning such as meeting up with a friend.

Ideally you will have plenty of time to utilize these skills when they are needed, but there will also be times when you need to employ self-care strategies quickly. Think about what you would include in your first-aid kit that would give you a quick, yet effective, response, i.e. your *go to* strategies. Breathing may be one form of Band Aid, but what is another? For example, if you have had a stressful session with a client, you want to be able to refocus and regroup before the next session or meeting. Scheduling your sessions with 5–10 minutes minimum in between is ideal so that you can take notes, process, and address your self-care needs. Consider what other mental skills will be beneficial in your first-aid kit for these specific times. Be prepared with alternatives in your first-aid kit so that you do not end up ignoring your need for self-care because you were not prepared with an option. Additionally, remember that we want to be using our first-aid kit on an ongoing basis; while there is no shame in needing more than what you can provide yourself, your first-aid kit can hopefully set you up so that you do not need more extreme interventions on a regular basis.

How Do You Begin Implementing Self-Care?

With the challenges of being an intern or professional in the field, you may be questioning if it is realistic to practice self-care regularly. It is, and there are several steps you can take. Use these ideas as jumping off points to come up with your own plan:

1) Commit to the idea that self-care is critical for your own well-being and the work that you will be doing. Put affirmations in your phone that pop up as reminders: "I am committing to me today!" Tell yourself daily that self-care is important. Use the same self-talk that you teach your clients.
2) Take the time to determine what will go in your own first-aid kit. Use the ideas above as a starting point. You can also reflect on anything that feels like it is missing. For example, maybe you used to enjoy playing an instrument but no longer take the time. Make a list of activities that you enjoy. Keep track of how often you are doing these activities or if they have slipped off your radar. If you are struggling for time, maybe you take a 30-minute run instead of an hour. If something makes you happy, find a way to fit it in.
3) Determine the moments you can create to add in these self-care activities. You will likely need to add in self-care spontaneously but planning proactively is ideal. Plan now for how you will make the time. See the sample schedules below for how self-care may fit into a daily routine (self-care activities are noted in bold). Once you make your self-care a priority, it becomes more of a habit.

MONDAY SCHEDULE (Example)

9:00AM-9:50AM	Client A
9:50AM-10:00AM	Notes/Prep for Next Client/**Deep breathing**
10:00AM-10:50AM	Client B
10:50AM-11:00AM	Notes
11:00AM-11:10AM	**Imagery**
11:10AM-12:10PM	Team Meeting/Presentation
12:10PM-12:20PM	**Deep breathing and relaxation**
12:20PM-1:15PM	**Lunch**
1:15PM-4:00PM	Case notes and internship paperwork; homework
4:00PM-4:20PM	Drive to class – **listen to energizing playlist**
4:20PM-4:25PM	Walk to classroom – **practice deep breathing**

4:30PM-7:00PM	Class
7:00PM-7:30PM	Drive home—listen to calm down music
7:30PM-8:30PM	Dinner
8:30PM-9:00PM	Shower, prep for bed
9:00PM-9:30PM	**Deep breathing and relaxing imagery**
9:30PM-10:00PM	Drift off to sleep

WEEKEND SCHEDULE (Sample)

9:00AM-11:00AM	**Short run then farmers' market and breakfast**
11:00AM-1:30PM	Study
1:30PM-2:15PM	**Lunch**
2:15PM-4:30PM	Internship Work (Case Notes, Presentation Work, Prep)
4:30PM-6:00PM	**Shower and get ready to go out; listen to music!**
6:00PM	**Dinner with friends**

The Connection Between Self-Care and Balance

The concepts of self-care and balance are certainly connected. When we are unbalanced, or out of balance, we may need more self-care than when we are experiencing a sense of balance. Keep in mind that self-care should be an ongoing practice in order to help maintain feelings of balance as much as possible.

What Is Balance?

Before you try to create balance in your life it is important to consider what balance means. A simplified understanding of balance is having areas or parts of your life even or equal so that everything feels like it fits well together. Being in balance may feel settled and at peace. However, as you are probably already aware, life is rarely like this. Achieving balance becomes unrealistic when we are aiming for all aspects of life to be equivalent with one another, giving all the same amount of attention. When you give up on this *even and equal* idea of balance, it can be quite freeing. Instead, we encourage you to look at being in balance as a more dynamic process that can change quickly and often.

Many of us look at balance as being even or neatly organized together, much like a pie chart. It may seem that to create balance we take stock of the components of life we need to give time and attention to and then divide up the available time we have amongst those. In this scenario, other than sleep, you may give ¼ of your time to school, ¼ of your time to work, ¼ of your time to family/socializing and ¼ of your time to your internship. However, this is too simple; balance is subtler than this. To create balance, you do want to be aware of the areas of life that need your attention, but then you give those areas of life only the time and attention needed. If it is a light school week, you have more time to socialize. If you have just begun your internship and you have a long commute, you need to take time and attention away from another area. Often it is easy to notice when we are out-of-balance because it can feel stressful; this is likely because the priorities we have are competing against one another. There is not enough time or mental energy, and yet if we don't acknowledge this and make a change, we will be stuck feeling unbalanced.

Both of us are moms and prior to having children we had much more time (and energy!) available for projects and tasks. Now that we have children, and overall have less time for ourselves and our work, balance is a constant goal and an ongoing process for us both.

Balance shifts happen over time, such as during the quarter or semester when your workload slowly increases, but can also happen much more rapidly such as throughout the day. For example, in general you may have work, school, family, and socializing, and a schedule that allows you to address each of those as needed. If your partner or child becomes sick, you may need to shift your focus to caring for them versus studying for school, which may cause some stress as school also requires your time and attention. However, if you attempt to handle everything else while your loved one is requiring more time from you, you will likely feel unbalanced because you are trying to pack everything in. If you allow yourself to shift priorities, then you may feel more in balance with the current situation, even if you would like to put more time toward something else. Part of creating balance is acceptance that not everything may *fit*.

It is also important to know that some days will feel very balanced and other days will not. Though it would be nice to feel balanced day-in and day-out, there is also the overall sense of balance that you likely want to aim for. If you look at one week, for example, there may be some days where you *get it right* – you accomplish the tasks you need related to each of your roles or responsibilities, you handle them without too much stress and you even find time for self-care. The next day, however, may be vastly different: You are running late to your internship because you got a speeding ticket, you feel stressed during your team presentation, and you are distracted during your individual meetings. This tough day leads to a distracted night of studying and feeling like you did not get enough done. Then, the next day begins unbalanced. When this happens, it is easy to push the self-care aside because it seems like the easiest place to take time from.

However, if you are prepared with your self-care first-aid kit, including options that can be done quickly (but are also efficient), you do not need to give up self-care entirely. It is also important to remember that there may be days (or longer) where self-care does get pushed aside, is minimized, or becomes non-existent. Do not let this become a source of guilt; acknowledge what is happening and find ways to improve and work toward better balance and more self-care. Creating more stress over the lack of self-care can create a negative spiral of guilt that can make everything feel more difficult.

To create balance in your life, identify what is most important to you. Journaling may allow you to identify the areas of your life that are most important and what may be getting in the way. Or, you can simply spend some time making a list of what is currently happening in life that requires your time and attention. Depending on how much you have on your list, you may need to edit some items out, or know that you will not be able to spend time daily on a particular hobby or interest that is ideally a part of your self-care first-aid kit. Instead, weekly or monthly may be appropriate at this point in time. Everyone is different in how they manage their priorities, time, and tasks, but consider setting goals, planning out your daily schedule, or creating daily task lists. Remember that flexibility is often a key component of finding and maintaining balance and that ongoing and proactive self-care can help further create feelings of balance.

Another important way to give yourself the best chances of creating and maintaining balance relates to setting boundaries for your work and your time. A strong trainee or consultant is not one who says yes to everything, but rather is one who protects their time and their energy so that they can do their work well in the areas required of them. Starting out in this field, trainees often want to show their value, and providing their time is one way of doing this. However, there are only so many hours in the day and, while you do want to be there for your clients, it is important to know that you cannot make yourself available all of the time. Hall, Lee, Kossek, and Las Heras (2012) studied professionals who reduced their workload over time and found that the individuals who had done very well in their careers by objective indicators, such as pay and promotion, consistently said that having a life outside of work was very important to their sense of success in their career. If we always say "yes" to work, then neglect our self-care and our personal life, we risk facing burnout.

Addressing Burnout

Though burnout feels different for each person, it may include feeling overwhelmed, negative, exhausted, distracted, and just done with the situation. We encourage you, at the end of each day, to check in with yourself and how you're feeling so that you do not hit this point. Reflective practice (see Chapter 5 in this book) and journaling can be useful tools in self-care and may allow you to notice that you are on a path toward burnout before it reaches full impact. If writing at the end of a long day seems unrealistic, consider using a voice recorder to capture your thoughts.

As mentioned earlier, taking a holistic approach to your self-care is important. Check in with yourself somatically and emotionally on a regular basis. When I (Alex) am meeting with clients or students who are struggling, I often pull out an image of Maslow's Hierarchy of Needs. Maslow studied those who were generally happy in life to understand exactly what made them feel happy (Maslow, 1987). He found that these individuals were also more grounded. I know when I am grounded, I can take care of myself much better. Starting at the foundation of the triangle, ask yourself: Are your physiological needs being met? Are you eating, sleeping, and resting well? Work your way up through the top ending with self-actualization. If any of these areas feel off, stop yourself and address the area before you reach a point of feeling burnt out. Use your first aid-kit or other resources to help you return to feeling positive, settled, balanced.

An important point related to avoiding burnout is to be aware that there may come a time where you need to say "no." This may include sticking to your set times for individual meetings with clients; for example, a client is running late or forgets your session and wants to meet later. You may feel that saying yes is the professional choice, but if it leads to more stress for you then you are not in the best mental space for this client or others. In this case, you could say something like, "I'm happy to do a brief session for 20 minutes as that's all the time we'll have. Or, we can reschedule for a full session another day." Another example to consider is if you travel with a team as part of your work. This is a very exciting time and allows you many opportunities to work and engage with your athletes. However, your clients will have more access to you. Saying "no" in this case may look like setting very clear hours as to when they can contact you. For example, proactively telling the team "I'm looking forward to traveling with you and will have an open-door policy from 8:00AM until 8:00PM. Feel free to text me in that time frame as well if you need to check in." You can then remind them of these boundaries if they contact you outside of the designated times. Do not confuse saying "no" with being rigid or inflexible. As professionals in a helping field, we are prone to saying yes and taking on more; we are often inclined to help others which may be why you are in the field. However, constantly saying yes is not a healthy approach. Know your capacity and know when to say no. When we say yes to everything and continue to push, we may find ourselves burnt out. And when this happens we are putting ourselves at risk: our physical health and emotional well-being will both suffer.

Conclusion

With training in the field, we may find ourselves in an interesting dilemma when we know that we can help others, and yet we cannot quite figure it out for ourselves. We may be hesitant to reach out to another professional because we feel like we should be able to handle it on our own. Not only do you need to be able to recognize when your level of need goes beyond your ability to provide self-care and support, but you also need to be willing to reach out. Bringing someone in to help you is a huge step in the right direction. How this looks may be different for each individual. Some of you may seek out individual therapists, others may check in with mentors or a peer support group, and some may consult with their own medical doctors. Regardless of the professional you seek, reaching out for support as needed is a great option.

As a student or trainee, you are not alone. You have your peers, professors, and your supervisors to guide and support you. Your peers are likely experiencing similar challenges and may have great insight into how to implement self-care. They can help keep you accountable in following through with your self-care practice. Your supervisor is also a great resource as well as they have likely been in your shoes before. If you are starting out in the profession, build your network of other professionals who can help you in ways well beyond your self-care need. Never discount the knowledge of others or feel like you need to have all of the answers.

Remember that self-care is an ongoing act, it will look different for everyone, and you can create your own self-care first-aid kit to meet your needs. However, be mindful that some forms of self-care may be considered negative or even detrimental to your work. If you like to drink alcohol to unwind at the end of the day, but the next day you are sluggish, then your self-care methods should likely be re-examined. You are stepping into a helping profession and want to be as close to your best as you can; self-care is a critical piece in being a strong professional no matter where your career takes you.

Lastly, keep in mind that self-care should not be an excuse to not do your work. For example, you may not be feeling your best, so you decide to skip a day at your internship so that you can take care of yourself. Yes, self-care is important, but it also should not be used as an excuse. By building regular self-care into your routine and having quick and effective strategies you can use in the moment, hopefully you can avoid needing to remove yourself from work or school. Remember that feeling stressed is normal and taking care of yourself is important, but balancing this with being professional is key.

A Trainee's Perspective on Being Your Best

Joey Velez, M.A., M.B.A., student at JFKU 2015–2017

After completing an M.A. in Sport Psychology along with an M.B.A, Joey's goals are to open a training facility in Northern California that focuses on the key elements of sport: mental training, physical training, and nutrition. His career pursuits include volunteering his services throughout the area in hopes of gaining entry with various teams and organizations, establishing his own private consulting practice, and applying to major business organizations in hopes of gaining entry with his M.B.A. Joey can be contacted at joeyavelez@yahoo.com.

I never truly understood the importance of self-care until I started my first season-long internship with a high school girls' volleyball team. Prior to this internship, I expected to be able to balance a full school workload, my responsibilities as a volunteer high school basketball coach, a part-time job, and my internship duties, all while continuing to take care of myself. My self-care practices included working out, playing basketball, and sleeping in on weekends, though I never considered those activities important in regard to my well-being.

During my internship, I spent three hours a day, five days a week at my internship site. This is what I thought it would take for it to be a positive experience for myself and the athletes. By the end of the 15-week season, however, I was exhausted and felt burnt out. Even though in supervision we talked about the importance of self-care, I never took it seriously. I didn't understand the amount of work that was involved in working in an internship and I felt that I was capable of handling it all. Had I understood the importance and benefits of self-care during this time, I could have avoided the exhaustion and feelings of burnout that occurred. I would like to say that I made changes before my next internship, but that wasn't the case.

Because I continued to not make self-care a priority, *and* I continued to be over-extended in my daily schedule, things got even worse in my next internship. I was working with a collegiate men's golf team, while once again taking a full course load and volunteering as a basketball coach. This time I felt the exhaustion earlier in the season and I could tell it was adversely affecting my work. I felt a giant weight on my shoulders because I wanted to provide quality work, and I felt that the stress I was experiencing was causing my work to suffer and my emotions to be negatively affected—I wasn't acting like my normal, energetic self. It got to a point where I almost broke down during group supervision class. Thankfully, with the support of my peers and supervisors, I was able to lighten my load during the internship by being more efficient with my time, while also finding time to incorporate much needed self-care.

Because of these two experiences, I realized that self-care allows your mind and body to relax from the daily exertions that are normal for students and interns. Now, for self-care, I take five minutes periodically throughout the day and use deep breathing to help me feel calm and relaxed. Additionally, I meditate for about ten minutes at least every other day, which helps clear my mind. I also read more; this allows me to focus on the content of the material and is a calming activity because it narrows the direction of my thoughts while stimulating my mind, which is important to me. I also changed my workout schedule, moving from 5AM to later in the afternoon, which helps me get more sleep and be more organized. This change helps me manage my time better and allows me to find the time to participate in self-care. Looking back, self-care is something I wish I would have taken more seriously earlier on during my graduate program, but is something I now place as a priority.

Reflective Questions and Activities for You to Consider Before You Proceed

- What mental skills can be a part of your personal self-care first-aid kit?
- What other strategies or steps help you feel at your best that should be included in your kit?
- What are your current priorities? When you are in an internship, what tasks or responsibilities may need to move lower on this list to allow you the time and energy that an internship requires?
- Whose support might you need to help make self-care a priority?

References

APA. (2002). Ethical principles of psychologists and code of conduct. *American Psychologist, 57,* 1060–1073.

Baker, E. K. (2003). *Caring for ourselves: A therapist's guide to personal and professional well-being.* Washington, DC: American Psychological Association.

Baltzell, A. L. (Ed.). (2016). *Mindfulness and performance.* New York, NY: Cambridge University Press.

Barnett, J. E., Baker, E. K., Elman, N. S., & Schoener, G. R. (2007). In pursuit of wellness: The self-care imperative. *Professional Psychology: Research and Practice, 38*(6), 603–612. doi:10.1037/0735-7028.38.6.603

Beauchamp, T. L., & Childress, J. F. (2001). *Principles of biometrics.* (5th ed.). Oxford, UK: Oxford University Press.

Hall, D. T., Lee, M. D., Kossek, E. E., & Las Heras, M. (2012). Pursuing career success while sustaining personal and family well-being: A study of reduced-load professionals over time. *Journal of Social Issues, 68*(4), 742–766.

Markway, B. (2014, March). *Seven types of self-care activities for coping with stress.* Retrieved from www.psychologytoday.com/blog/shyness-is-nice/201403/seven-types-self-care-activities-coping-stress

Maslow, A. H. (1987). *Motivation and personality.* (3rd ed.). New York, NY: Harper & Row.

Norcross, J. C., & Barnett, J. E., (2014). *Self-care as ethical imperative.* Retrieved from https://www.nationalregister.org/pub/the-national-register-report-pub/the-register-report-spring-2008/self-care-as-ethical-imperative/

Richards, K. C., Campenni, C. E., & Muse-Burke, J. L. (2010). Self-care and well-being in mental health professionals: The mediating effects of self-awareness and mindfulness. *Journal of Mental Health Counseling, 32*(3), 247–264.

10 Ethical Quandaries

What Were You Thinking?

Hillary Cauthen and Amber M. Shipherd

No matter how much one prepares, trainees and qualified practitioners will face situations which they were not afforded the luxury of previewing. Many of these situations require a response long before the situation can be discussed with supervisors or peers. While preparing for each and every possible situation is an unachievable goal, developing a decision-making model and practicing the decision-making process can prepare trainees to better handle these potentially stressful scenarios. Through the presentation of various scenarios, as well as information on how one might come to a decision to proceed, trainees will feel better prepared to handle the unexpected.

Background Information on the Authors

Hillary Cauthen is an adjunct faculty member in the Sport Psychology Department at JFKU and an adjunct professor at Texas State University. Dr. Cauthen received her B.A. and B.S. from the University of New Hampshire, a M.S. from Miami University, and an M.A. and Psy.D. from The Chicago School of Professional Psychology, Los Angeles. Dr. Cauthen is a member of AASP and APA, and has been an active member of the AASP Ethics Committee since 2014. Dr. Cauthen is also a licensed Psychologist Associate, and the Director of Performance Services at Texas Optimal Performance & Psychological Services, LLC., a company she co-owns. For more information on her practice visit www.txopps.com, and she can be reached at Hcauthen@jfku.edu.

Amber M. Shipherd is an Assistant Professor and Program Coordinator for Performance Psychology at Texas A&M University–Kingsville, adjunct faculty member in the Sport Psychology Department at JFKU, and owner/mental performance consultant at Next Level Mind Consulting (see www.nlmind.com). She is a member of AASP and APA, is a Certified Consultant with AASP, is a member of the United States Olympic Committee Sport Psychology Registry, and has been an active member of the AASP Ethics Committee since 2011. Dr. Shipherd completed her Ph.D. at Texas Tech University, her Master's Degree at Florida State University, and her Bachelor's Degree from the University of California–Davis. Dr. Shipherd can be reached through her practice website at www.nlmind.com or amber.shipherd@tamuk.edu.

Developing Ethical Awareness in Three Steps

A question often asked by trainees or young professionals is "How will I know that I am even facing a potential ethical dilemma?" The key to developing awareness in the field is first having the knowledge of what an ethical dilemma or concern actually is. An ethical concern is when one faces a problem or feeling that could impact themselves or others negatively, but there is no clear right or wrong decision to be made. Ethical concerns require one to evaluate possible alternatives and then choose an outcome. To assist in increasing your ethical awareness, we developed the three-step model outlined below. Ideally, these steps should be followed prior to even beginning work with clients in the field of sport psychology.

Step One

Increase your knowledge of the relevant ethical code(s) of conduct. These standards are there to provide you with a guideline to best practice. Read them, learn them, and live them. If we embrace our ethical codes, we will in turn work from an established framework that always keeps the best interest of the client in mind. Having this as the foundation of your work is the first step to protecting your client and yourself from harm.

Step Two

Develop an awareness of your emotions, as they are key in identifying ethical dilemmas. If you experience an emotion at any point during a conversation with a client or an observation, pay attention to it. Having awareness of our emotions will provide a warning sign of what you need to explore further.

Step Three

Identify your biggest fear(s) that may come up within the work we do. If we do not address and discuss fears, they cloud our judgement when they arise. Our fears can freeze us and control our ability to focus and perform our best. Explore potential ethical issues you fear or feel unequipped to handle, and talk about them with peers, mentors, and supervisors. Develop your own pre-performance routine to help you be in the best mindset to handle potential ethical situations.

These three steps assist us in our work, and allow us to better develop an awareness of what constitutes an ethical situation. For a trainee or young professional, being unafraid to ask questions and ask for help is key in your professional development and in continuing to develop your ethical and moral compass.

Why Ethics?

Let us illustrate the importance of ethics through the following example. Joe recently graduated with a Master's Degree in Sport and Exercise Psychology and earned his certification through AASP. He initially focuses on developing a social media presence in the hopes that marketing through this means will lead to potential clients. Given his focus is on marketing, he struggles with what to call himself. He makes the decision to describe himself as a sport psychology consultant, believing that the general public will be able to better identify and recognize the services he can provide over other common titles such as mental skills consultant or coach. After developing a presence online, he begins to market his services through meetings and personal connections in the community.

Joe was previously a collegiate runner and is well connected in his local running community. Soon his local running store is asking him to create workshops on mental skills for runners. Several elite collegiate runners and coaches attend one of his workshops, and at the end of the workshop he chats with them briefly and gives them his contact information.

The next day Joe follows up with the runners and coaches he met by tweeting some catchy mental tips on Twitter. Several of the runners and coaches retweet him, and one of his tweets goes viral in the running community. Joe is thrilled, until he receives a private message from a psychologist who saw his tweet. The psychologist congratulates Joe on his viral tweet, but lets him know that, in his state, the term psychology is legally protected and he is breaking the law by referring to himself as a sport psychology consultant. Joe does not possess a license as a psychologist, and the state laws prohibit anyone without a license from using the word psychology in their title in any form. Joe is concerned about the psychologist's message, but brushes it off, thinking that so many of his colleagues also represent themselves as a sport psychology consultant so it must be fine. Joe decides not to respond to the direct message sent to him, nor change information on any of his marketing materials. Several weeks later Joe receives an official notice in the mail from his state's licensing board of psychological examiners, informing him that an official complaint has been filed against him for misrepresenting himself to the public and for incorrect title usage.

While the above vignette may seem extreme, it is a scenario that many trainees and even young sport psychology professionals could find themselves in if they are not careful. Mistakes are bound to happen to any practitioner at any point during their career, and these mistakes are considered an essential part of learning how to practice sport psychology (Andersen, Van Raalte, & Brewer, 2000). However, when the same mistakes become chronic, or when a practitioner attempts to hide or cover up their errors, the real issue may be impairment and potential harm to the client(s), the professional, and/or the profession.

Research has found considerable variation in sport psychology/mental skills practitioners' ethical beliefs, behaviors, and views of what is ethical and unethical (Etzel, Watson, & Zizzi, 2004; Watson & Clement, 2008). Etzel (2014) argues that this is likely due to some sport psychology practitioners having stronger backgrounds in kinesiology or sport science fields, while others come from psychology or counseling backgrounds. Though psychology and counseling programs require that students receive substantial training in ethics, few sport psychology programs contain a formal ethics education (Etzel, 2014). Not having adequate coursework in ethics could affect a sport psychology practitioner's sense of what is right and what is wrong, as most people develop their own ethical compass from observing others, their own personal experiences, and formal academic preparation (Etzel, 2014; Hays, 2006).

In mental health fields, including sport psychology, ethical matters are regulated by both laws and professional codes (Corey, Corey, & Callanan, 1998). Therefore, it is essential that anyone (novice or experienced) in the field of sport psychology be familiar with the laws in their territory and their organization's codes of ethics (e.g. AASP, APA, BASES). Ethical codes serve multiple functions, including outlining the scope of practice, regulating the relationship between a professional and their clients or students, providing guidelines in ambiguous situations, and helping to reinforce proper behaviors and discourage inappropriate ones (Corey et al., 1998; DeSensi & Rosenberg, 2010). While codes of ethics are not meant to provide clear solutions for every situation that practitioners may find themselves in, codes of ethics can nonetheless guide practitioners in determining what is right or wrong in uncertain situations.

Everyone is at risk of engaging in unethical behavior or making poor decisions at some point in their career; new professionals and those lacking adequate ethical training are the most vulnerable (Etzel, 2014; Koocher & Keith-Spiegel, 2008). Although it is unrealistic for a trainee to prepare for and prevent all ethical situations from occurring, it is important for trainees and practitioners to develop and practice using a decision-making model so they are better equipped to respond when they encounter potential ethical situations.

Decision-Making Models

Decision-making models are particularly useful for sport psychology/mental skills practitioners when encountering a few select situations (Knapp & VandeCreek, 2006):

- Identifying situations where ethical or legal standards need to be implemented, such as knowing when and why to break confidentiality.
- Facing an issue that is not addressed in an ethical code or legal standard. For example, many ethical codes do not explicitly address the topic of navigating social media.
- Recognizing circumstances where conflict exists between the law and an ethical code or organizational policy. For example, most ethical codes in mental health professions address the topic of multiple relationships; however, some organizations may require their employees to wear multiple hats and take part in multiple relationships with clients.

There is not one decision-making model that has been created specifically for sport psychology, but it has been recommended that sport psychology/mental skills practitioners utilize decision-making models from other related helping professions (Harris, Visek, & Watson, 2009). Thus, the model outlined below is a compilation of the key points shared by several widely used models (e.g. seven-step model, Hadjistavropoulos & Malloy, 2000; five-step model, Knapp & VandeCreek, 2006).

Using a Decision-Making Model

Most of the major decision-making models recommend: (a) identifying the parameters of the situation and defining any potential ethical issues involved; (b) creating a list of potential courses of action to take; (c) considering all the short- and long-term consequences of each decision, the likelihood of each consequence, and how each decision could potentially impact all stakeholders; (d) determining which potential solution is best and taking action; (e) evaluating the decision and the resulting consequences; and finally (f) determining if any further action is necessary. An example of a sport psychology/mental skills practitioner using these steps in an ethical dilemma is described below.

Tiffany is a graduate student in sport psychology, completing an internship with her university's Varsity men's soccer team. She has been implementing weekly mental skills workshops with the entire team; however, at the start of the internship she discussed the possibility of adding sessions with individual athletes to her workload. About mid-way through the season, some of the athletes begin to meet with her individually on a weekly basis, including Eric, one of the team's captains. After one particularly demanding and mistake-filled practice, the head coach says to Tiffany loudly and within earshot of the athletic trainer and numerous soccer players, "Next time you have one of your meetings with Eric, make sure he understands one of his roles as captain is to get his team in line!" Let's look at how Tiffany could apply the steps of a decision-making model to best respond to the coach's actions.

Step One: Identify the parameters of the situation and define any potential ethical issues involved.

Tiffany is concerned that confidentiality may have been broken. Tiffany has not told the coach that she is seeing Eric, so she wonders if Eric has told the coach, or if the coach is merely speculating. Tiffany is familiar with the AASP Ethics Code and is concerned that her situation may not be explicitly addressed in the code.

Step Two: Create a list of potential courses of action to take.

Using a decision-making model, Tiffany comes up with a list of potential solutions once she has considered all the information and discussed the situation with her supervisor. Among others, her list of courses of action to take with the coach includes approaching the coach and reminding him that her work is confidential and she cannot disclose who she is seeing with him or anyone else. She also generates several courses of action to take with Eric, one of which is to notify Eric in their next individual meeting that others may be aware she is working with him.

Step Three: Consider all the short- and long-term consequences of each decision, the likelihood of each consequence, and how each decision could potentially impact all stakeholders.

Numerous short- and long-term consequences seem to exist in this situation. For example, by approaching the coach she could accidentally reveal that she is seeing Eric if he does not already know, which could tarnish her relationship with Eric, the coach, or the team. She could also possibly lose Eric as an individual client if she notifies him of the incident. Furthermore, if she handles the situation poorly, she could damage her own reputation, which could interfere with her own goal of approaching the coach at the end of the season to explore working with the team the next season after she graduates.

Step Four: Determine which potential solution is best and take action.

Based on Tiffany's evaluation of the potential consequences and the likelihood of each decision, Tiffany decides the best course of action is to tell Eric about the situation and then solicit his input on the necessary steps to take moving forward. Eric tells Tiffany that he had not told his coach he was seeing her, although he believes his coach may have figured it out on his own. He says he does not mind if the coaching staff and some of his teammates know he is seeing her, but he does not want any outsiders to the team finding out. Tiffany informs Eric she will discuss the importance of confidentiality at the next coaches' meeting to remind them all of what she had discussed with them at the beginning of the season. Eric agrees to this course of action and his relationship and work with Tiffany is positively impacted. Tiffany highlights confidentiality, as well as some of the other ethical issues she discussed previously, at the next coaches' meeting. The information and reminders seem to go over well with the coaches.

Step Five: Evaluate the decision and the resulting consequences.

Tiffany determines that she was fortunate in this situation and with the outcome. She is able to continue working with Eric, the coach, and the team as a whole. This situation did open up her eyes to the importance of revisiting topics, such as confidentiality, with the coaching staff and athletes throughout the season. Although she did discuss confidentiality with the coach at the beginning of the season, she believed a well-placed reminder or more concrete examples could have possibly prevented the issue from occurring. Tiffany has now learned information that can make her a better mental skills consultant and she is better prepared for working with her next team or athletes. She also recognizes that taking additional preventative steps may not have completely prevented her situation from occurring.

Step Six: Determine if any further action is necessary.

Tiffany plans to briefly revisit relevant topics once a month with the coaches. Through this process her awareness has improved in regard to establishing and managing boundaries, multiple roles as a mental skills consultant, and continuous exploration of ethical considerations and potential hurdles one may encounter in the field (see Figure 10.1).

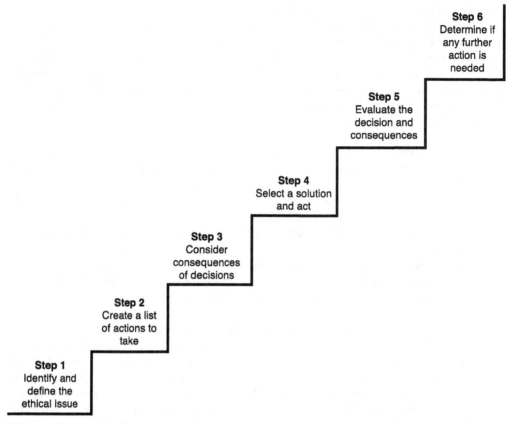

Figure 10.1 Ethical decision-making model. This figure illustrates the steps to take when faced
with an ethical issue.

Potential Ethical Quandaries

When starting out in any new experience there comes an array of feelings. Think about
it—what was the last new thing you tried? What feelings did you have on the first day you
tried it and how did you prepare to be your best self? If you considered your emotions,
you may have felt excited, curious, anxious, apprehensive, and/or calm. All of these
emotions can be difficult to manage when we forget about our core reason for doing
the task we initially signed up for. It is important to remember *why we do what we
do*. The field of sport psychology focuses on providing a service to others, i.e. assisting
them in achieving their goals. In those pursuits we need to make sure we are keeping
our clients' best interests in mind when we make decisions and face situations with no clear
solution.

There are many potential ethical dilemmas that may occur when working in the field.
Although we cannot provide an overview of all ethical situations, we feel it is important to
provide you with the most common ethical situations found in the literature (e.g. Andersen
et al., 2000; Andersen, Van Raalte, & Brewer, 2001) and that other interns and young
professionals have experienced. Our goal for this section is partly to prepare you for how
to handle these situations if they arise in your work, but also to help you understand
how you might approach an ethical situation and apply sound decision-making skills in
these stressful moments.

Who Is Your Client?

As practitioners our work is variable, with an assortment of different client populations. The work may be contracted or conducted in a number of ways, often making the protection of clients' confidentiality difficult. For example, we may work with: individual athletes who pay for their own services; individual athletes whose parents pay for services; an individual athlete and her/his coach; or a team of athletes and coaches, contracted by a sport organization. These multiple relationships can be problematic in regard to identifying who is the client and protecting the client's confidentiality.

We have found it useful to ask ourselves the following questions, to first identify who the client is and then assist in developing best practice to protect client's confidentiality:

- Who are you meeting with and providing mental skills training to?
- How old is the individual you are providing services to?
- Who contacted you to conduct services or set up a session?
- Who is paying you for individual or team services?

These questions are guidelines in helping you understand how to best protect yourself and your client. It is significant to note that the person receiving sport psychology/mental skills services may not be the party paying for the service. For best practice you should hold the person receiving the services as your primary client and protect their information and confidentiality to the highest standard. However, the financial provider may also hold rights to the client's information or work you are providing. For example, a parent paying for services for their child does have the ability to explore information shared in session. You may have ethical concerns in regard to wanting to protect your client's information, but also know that the third party is paying for your services to be conducted. We recommend you develop practice policies and contracts that state who is your client. Within this contract you should also disclose how a third-party payer may receive information, if at all. Discuss confidentiality and the work that is conducted to all members as early as possible. Explain that, while they may have the right to the information, it is not in the minor's best interest to disclose it so you can ask that that aspect is respected, etc.

Where Do You Conduct Your Sessions?

It is common practice to conduct your work in the same setting or venue as the individual trains. There are many benefits to working in the field, including that we make ourselves a part of the athletic environment, relationships and rapport may be established more easily, and we can observe the client(s) behaviors in, and away from, their competitive setting. From a business perspective, you will have lower overhead if you do not have a brick and mortar office. However, one common factor that detracts from all these positive aspects of being in the field is the fact that our work is never truly confidential, and anonymity is lost if we do not have a private setting.

To develop best ethical practices, we find it important for you to consider how to protect your client's confidentiality and yourself when conducting sessions outside of a traditional office. Taking these steps will assist you in providing best ethical practices:

- Establish boundaries and communicate services prior to the work beginning.
- Consult with supervisors, mentors, colleagues, and/or legal assistance to aid in the development of practice policies and informed consent forms that discuss services provided, location of services, financial fees, etc.

What Do You Call Yourself?

Due to legality and training, title usage can be different for each region and country. Please note the below examples are based on American titles and practice. For further information and best practice, always refer to your state or country/region's requirements and laws. Currently, there is not one set title that all professionals working in the field of sport psychology in the U.S. utilize or agree upon. With that being said, the field of sport psychology is in agreement that misrepresentation of oneself is problematic. Etzel et al. (2004) conducted a web-based survey about AASP members' personal ethical beliefs and practices relevant to the practice of applied sport psychology. The participants in the study unanimously agreed that, if someone misrepresents themselves by affiliations falsely implying sponsorship or certification, this behavior is unacceptable and unethical.

Applied professionals, educators, and students in the field can assist in preventing misrepresentation through guidance on best ethical practices by referencing the AASP ethical code. Principle B: Integrity reads, "When describing or reporting their qualifications, services, products, fees, research, or teaching, [AASP Members] do not make statements that are false, misleading, or deceptive" (Association of Applied Sport Psychology [AASP], 2011, paragraph 9). Although the ethical code addresses the importance of proper title use and representation in the field, we have seen many unethical practices in regard to title use.

When deciding on your title, you should first look at what stage you are at in your professional development. If you are currently a student, you must state this when you are conducting your work while at an internship—both verbally and on any written documentation you provide. Students and young professionals working under supervision must also state this and include their supervisor's contact information on any documentation provided to clients. When moving to the next phase of your professional development, post-graduate, it is necessary to develop a working title. Given there is not one set title that all practitioners in sport psychology utilize, we recommend you research common titles that are used, as well as best ethical representation. As highlighted in the example earlier, a common ethical problem is individuals not credentialed as psychologist utilizing any form of the term psychology in their title. In many states in the U.S., and countries around the world, the term psychologist or any form of the word psychology is protected and can only be used by someone who has obtained their doctorate in psychology and/or is licensed by the appropriate authorities. Given that misrepresentation of oneself is a common ethical pitfall, we are providing some examples to guide you on your journey. To ensure you are using the best ethical working title, seek guidance from mentors, supervisors, peers, and familiarize yourself with organization, state, and/or regional laws. It is especially important you understand the state and regional laws on title use so you do not misrepresent yourself and your work to the public. These examples are generally representative of an American perspective, due to our training and expertise:

Student:

• Master's student in sport psychology, Eastern Tech University, supervised by: Julie Gonzalez, Ph.D. CC-AASP

Post-Graduate:

• John Smith, M.A., Mental Skills Coach, supervised by: Sarah Clark, Ph.D. CC-AASP
• Sally Jenson, Psy.D., post-doctoral fellow, supervised by: Billy Bob, Psy.D. CC-AASP

Master's Trained:

- Jimmy John, M.A., CC-AASP, Performance Coach

Doctoral Trained:

- Jenny Baker, Psy.D., CC-AASP, Licensed Psychologist #55463
- Henry Park, Ph.D., CC-AASP, Mental Skills Coach

How Do You Manage Personal and Professional Social Media Accounts?

Social media is an ever growing and changing venue that has become increasingly impactful for socialization, business marketing, and the latest news and events (Watson & Halbrook, 2014; see Chapter 15 in this book for more information on social media). Social media may blur private and/or public boundaries when an individual's personal information, opinions, and values enter a public realm through the use of social media platforms (Institute of Business Ethics [IBE], 2011). The unique characteristics and benefits of these social media platforms pose many ethical challenges.

One potential ethical hurdle that trainees and young professionals face is what to do if a client or previous client wants to follow their personal social media account. The first step in protecting your confidentiality is making sure you are aware of the privacy settings on your personal accounts and adjusting these settings to ensure your comfort. Given the interconnectedness of social media, some people still may have access to your personal accounts despite your best efforts to make your sites private. Keep in mind best ethical practices and be mindful of information you place on your personal social media accounts; as we stated before, boundaries and misconceptions can ensue and cause potential harm to your clients if they misinterpret information you post. To assist in developing best ethical practices when utilizing social media, consider taking the following steps:

- Having a social media policy on your informed consent is important for your private social media accounts, as well as your professional accounts. Inform clients about the purpose of your business accounts and that you cannot guarantee confidentiality if the client chooses to follow you on specific social media accounts, as they are public domains.
- Your title should be the proper ethical representation of yourself; do not state services or titles on your sites that you do not provide or that are not fitting to your education and training.
- You should not follow or befriend your clients without their permission, and if you do choose to follow or befriend your clients, explore why you feel this is necessary to your work.
- Do not post pictures or information about your clients without their consent. If they do consent, keep documentation of their consent in your files.

How Much Information Can You Share in Peer Case Consultation or Supervision?

Trainees and young professionals should engage in case consultation and supervision on a regular basis. With that being said, a common ethical hurdle that occurs is disclosing too much information in case consultation, or sharing case consultations of others in your individual supervision.

The purpose of peer case consultation is for you to share information in a setting of peers or colleagues with the goal being assistance from the group in case conceptualization, or to learn of new interventions that may assist your work. It is important to remember that when you are sharing information in a peer consultation group or group supervision you should do so in the following way:

- Do not disclose the identity of the client, or the specific team.
- Keep information broad; the group should not be able to identify the location of the athlete, the team the athlete is on, or other identifying information.
- Ask specific questions you need assistance with, this will help to keep the consultation on how you can better assist the client instead of sharing too much information about the client.

We suggest keeping in mind the following:

- Do not share who said what from peer supervision to your individual supervisor.
- Your individual supervisor should not be able to identify other peers' cases or clients.

Conclusion

We can only prepare and predict so much in the work we are doing. Given we are working with a variable population, we cannot control or account for all possibilities that may arise. Knowledge, practice, and experience are the best ways to feel confident when addressing situations in the field. Having a developed ethical framework is one of the best ways to assist you in preparing for an ethical situation that was not planned or previewed.

If you are a trainee, utilize your supervisor and ask how to handle a situation. As young professionals, we encourage you to continue to have supervision, mentorship, or peer consultation while working in the field. It is helpful to continue to have a network of professionals to assist you in these times. If you are unsure if you are dealing with an ethical situation, or do not know how to manage the situation, *refer to the ethical codes, utilize our decision-making model from the beginning of this chapter, and ask for help from trusted colleagues!*

A Trainee's Perspective on Ethical Quandaries

Lindsay Jones, M.A., student at JFKU 2013–2015

Since graduating from JFKU, Lindsay has opened her own practice in Southern California and has worked with the United States Army as a Cognitive Performance Coach. While working in this role, Lindsay discovered her passion for teaching and tailoring performance enhancement skills to fit various populations, skill levels, and performances. Lindsay's future goals include: earning a Ph.D. with a specialization in injury recovery, further building her private practice, and continuing to use her teaching skills in the field of performance enhancement. Lindsay can be contacted at ljones@email.jfku.edu.

As graduate students, we are prepared to enter the applied world with a tool bag filled with theories, research-based techniques, interpersonal communication skills, and an eagerness to help athletes and other performers. Our professional expectations require us to have concern for others' welfare and dignity, as well as to have integrity. As we grow in the field, we build upon these expectations and develop our own personal code of ethics that guides our work along with applicable professional ethics codes (e.g. APA, AASP). Through first-hand experience, I've learned the importance of upholding both professional and personal values.

While completing an internship with a high school team, rapport was built quickly with the young players and parents. As I began to meet frequently with the players on an individual and group basis, the head coach began to pressure me for the information divulged during these sessions. I politely reminded her of the confidentiality portion of our internship contract, but the request quickly turned to a demand. The coach explained that, by knowing the content of the sessions, she could decide "whose head is in the game" and who "deserves" a starting position. Immediately, I could see the ethical issue arising.

As the coach continued to pressure me for information, the players noticed; rapport decreased and sessions became superficial. I was faced with an ethical issue: Do I divulge information about my sessions, information I had promised to keep confidential, in order to keep the gatekeeper happy? Or do I continue to politely decline and remind her of our confidentiality agreement, hopefully improving the relationship with my clients, but most likely lose any chance of being hired upon graduation? As I pondered this decision, I began to feel conflicted. I knew that, by giving this information to the coach, my clients would feel betrayed or angry, which would greatly affect our relationship. I also knew that standing firmly against the coach's request could cause friction between her and me, which would inevitably affect the team. I immediately turned to trusted colleagues during group supervision for advice and to discuss a plan of action. While using the Five Step Model of Decision-Making (Knapp & VandeCreek, 2006), it became clear that the best course of action aligned with not only my professional responsibility but with my personal ethics as well.

My plan of action included a meeting with the head coach where I would voice my concerns while remaining strong in my beliefs to uphold confidentiality. As I began to firmly state my core values as a mental skills coach and how breaking confidentiality directly goes against what I stand for, the conversation took an interesting turn. She began to open up about her coaching values and how she has shifted her focus away from the team's welfare. As she became more successful in her career as an Athletic Director, the less her coaching values aligned with her own. She began to identify this dissonance; her coaching philosophy had shifted from an environment focused around skill improvement and enjoyment to peer comparison and winning. As she and I began to work as a cohesive team, the wall that was built between the two of us seemed to immediately crumble, rapport began to rebuild, and a level of respect was established between us. After going through this situation, I discovered the importance of remaining steadfast in the ethical values taught to us during our graduate level training, and having a decision-making model in place to help make these difficult decisions.

Reflective Questions and Activities for You to Consider Before You Proceed

- Look up and become familiar with the ethical code for your appropriate professional organization(s).
- Brainstorm independently or with someone else some potential situations you could find yourself in as you read through the code.
- Ask yourself: What does a competent trainee look like to you?

- Identify your biggest fear(s) about working with clients as well as your own strengths and weaknesses as a practitioner.
- Generate a list of faculty members, professionals, or peers in the field that you trust and that can help you when you face potential ethical quandaries.
- Consider the population/site you are working with or would like to work with. Brainstorm as many potential ethical situations and ways to either prevent or resolve the situation as you can, and ask a colleague to do the same. Exchange ideas. Were their solutions different from yours? Do you feel you should make any revisions to your ideas now after hearing what your colleague came up with?

References

AASP. (2011). Ethics code: AASP principles and standards. Retrieved from www.appliedsportpsych. org/about/ethics/ethics-code/

Andersen, M., Van Raalte, J., & Brewer, B. (2000). When sport psychology consultants and graduate students are impaired: Ethical and legal issues in training and supervision. *Journal of Applied Sport Psychology, 12*(2), 134–150.

Andersen, M., Van Raalte, J., & Brewer, B. (2001). Sport psychology delivery: Staying ethical while keeping loose. *Professional Psychology: Research and Practice, 32*(1), 12–18.

Corey, G., Corey, M. S., & Callanan, P. (1998). *Issues and ethics in the helping professions.* (5th ed.). Pacific Grove, CA: Brooks/Cole Publishing Company.

DeSensi, J. T., & Rosenberg, D. (2010). *Ethics and morality in sports management.* (3rd ed.). Morgantown, WV: Fitness Information Technology.

Etzel, E. (2014). Some impressions on ethics in sport and exercise psychology. In E. Etzel & J. C. Watson (Eds.), *Ethical issues in sport, exercise, and performance psychology* (pp. 3–11). Morgantown, WV: Fitness Information Technology.

Etzel, E., Watson, J., & Zizzi, S. (2004). A web-based survey of AAASP members' ethical beliefs and behaviors in the new millennium. *Journal of Applied Sport Psychology, 16*(3), 236–250.

Hadjistavropoulos, T., & Malloy, D. C. (2000). Making ethical choices: A comprehensive decision-making model for Canadian Psychologists. *Canadian Psychology/Psychologie Canadienne, 41*(2), 14–115.

Harris, B. S., Visek, A. J., & Watson, J. C. (2009). Ethical decision-making in sport psychology: Issues and implications for professional practice. In R. Schinke (Ed.), *Contemporary sport psychology* (pp. 217–232). Hauppauge, NY: Nova Science Publishers.

Hays, K. (2006). Being fit: The ethics of practice diversification in performance psychology. *Professional Psychology: Research and Practice, 37*(3), 223–232.

Institute of Business Ethics [IBE]. (2011). The ethical challenges of social media. *Business Ethics Briefing, 22*, 1–4.

Knapp, S. J., & VandeCreek, L. D. (2006). *Practical ethics for psychologists: A positive approach.* Washington, DC: American Psychological Association.

Koocher, G. P., & Keith-Spiegel, P. (2008). *Ethics in psychology and the mental health professions.* (3rd ed.). New York, NY: Oxford University Press.

Watson, J., & Clement, D. (2008). Ethical and practical issues related to multiple role relationships in sport psychology. *Athletic Insight, 10*, 1–13.

Watson, J. C., & Halbrook, M. (2014). Incorporating technology into practice: A service delivery approach. In J. G. Cremades & L. Tashman (Eds.), *Becoming a sport, exercise, and performance psychology professional: A global perspective* (pp. 152–159). New York, NY: Psychology Press.

11 Handling Referrals

What If Your Clients Need More?

C.A. Gajus-Ramsay and Michael-Thomas Wilson

During the course of a trainee's internship experience, it is highly possible that a red flag or clinical issue may arise while working with a client. It is imperative for the trainee to have the awareness to initially identify the red flag, the confidence to assess the issue, and the support to handle a potential referral, if necessary, from beginning to end. There are key steps to making this process a successful experience for both the trainee and the client. The relationship between the supervisor and trainee is critical during this time, as the need to make a referral can provoke anxiety for the trainee. The supervisor is instrumental in providing a safe, supportive, and quality learning experience for the trainee during this process. This chapter will help readers identify when a referral is needed as well as the best practices for making the referral.

Background Information on the Authors

C.A. Gajus-Ramsay (C.A.) received her Master's Degree in Sport Psychology from JFKU. She has been core faculty, taught performance enhancement courses in the program, and been Director of the Life Enhancement through Athletic Participation (LEAP) Program. LEAP works with underserved youth and teaches life skills through mental skills training activities. C.A. has supervised JFKU sport psychology interns and worked in applied sport psychology for the last 20 years. C.A. also holds a Master's Degree in Counseling Psychology from JFKU and is currently in private practice as a psychotherapist. Her focus is clinical; however, she works with some athletes for a blend of performance and counseling within this practice. C.A. supervised the second author (Mike) for one of his internships, and during his internship an athlete referral was necessary. Through a collaborative and supportive dialogue, they followed the referral process outlined in this chapter. Mike felt confident going through the process and the athlete benefitted from a compassionate, caring, and competent referral. C.A. can be contacted at ca@caramsaytherapy.com.

Michael-Thomas (Mike) Wilson also received his Master's Degree in Sport Psychology from JFKU. Since graduating, Mike founded and is currently the director of a private consulting firm, Evolving Concepts, which specializes in mental performance training programs for elite levels of competition. After winning the National Championship with his collegiate soccer team, he began to understand the relationship between psychological and physical performance. His passion is working intently with elite athletes, coaches, and organizations from Southern California to the Pacific Northwest. Mike can be contacted at mike@evolvingconcepts.net.

Introduction

During the course of the internship experience, our trainees may find themselves in situations where they can't provide the appropriate ongoing service to their athlete/client. The trainee must be ready and prepared for this scenario at all times during their internship. A referral may be given for a myriad of different issues and may include various types of referral resources. These may include a psychologist, nutritionist, physical therapist, sports medicine expert, and many more. A referral means putting people in touch with other professional services that have the resources to help them achieve their goals. When making a referral, you are basically sending a person to another professional who specializes in working with particular needs or problems (New South Wales Department of Education and Training, 2009).

A referral for counseling/psychotherapy should be considered when the athlete's problems go beyond the trainee's own experience and expertise, or when the trainee may feel uncomfortable helping the athlete with some psychological issue that has arisen. A referral may be made because of the way the athlete's problems are interfering with their sport, academic work or their general functioning in life. Referrals may happen at any point in the trainee-athlete relationship and so it is important that the trainee is prepared and equipped with the necessary tools and support to make any kind of referral. The trainee should realize that acknowledging they don't have the necessary skills is not a sign of failure but rather an ongoing commitment to always put the client's needs first. How successful the referral process is can be greatly influenced by how the referral is discussed and presented to the athlete (Bobele & Conran, 1988). This chapter will outline the process and steps for making a successful referral.

First Steps for Referral Success in Supervision

From our experience, we feel it is essential for a trainee to be aware, when working with an athlete, that there will always be some sort of crossover between personal life and issues and performance. This does not mean there will be a need for a clinical referral; it simply means that, when treating the athlete as a whole person, life issues may come up in the trainee-athlete relationship. The foundation of referral success occurs when the supervisor talks about the referral process from the very beginning of the trainee-supervisor relationship. From our experience, it's helpful when the supervisor shares personal accounts of referral experiences in their own practice and while supervising. During this conversation, the supervisor has the opportunity to evaluate the trainee's experience, if any, with referrals, and how to implement educational strategies for the trainee. This open-dialogue conversation from the very beginning prepares the trainee to handle a referral with confidence.

Scope of Practice

We feel it's important here to talk about scope of practice for a trainee working with an athlete on performance enhancement issues. For a trainee in the JFKU Sport Psychology Master's Program, there are clear guidelines in determining what is inside and outside their scope of practice. Examples of what a trainee can work with include performance enhancement issues and interventions such as goal setting, concentration, visualization, relaxation, and self-talk, and concepts such as motivation, self-confidence, and team cohesion. Examples of what a trainee would need to refer out to a qualified mental health expert (also known as red flag issues) include depression, anxiety, trauma, relationship issues, anger management, substance abuse, and eating disorders. Tod and Andersen (2010) state that problems in performance are related to issues like competition anxiety, motivational problems, poor self-talk, and lapses in concentration, but other (often clinical) factors may also be involved. There are always interrelated issues between the personal and the performance. Getting athletes to talk about their lives can lead to understanding their performance or motivational problems, as well as the whole person.

It is also important to highlight here that making a referral is not limited to clinical issues regarding mental health. A referral may also be made for nutritional, spiritual, social, cultural, and physical concerns. For example, while assessing the client's diet in relation to their performance, it is revealed they are not getting adequate nutrition specific to their needs. The athlete has shared information that may be negatively impacting their performance. Since it is not within our scope of practice to advise on such matters, it is paramount the client be referred to a registered dietician for proper diagnosis and/or education.

First Session with Athlete

In the first session, it's important for the trainee to be clear about their scope of practice, specifically what they are trained to work on and what they are not. This preparation should begin at the first meeting with the athlete. There is no one way to make the perfect referral, but *do* prepare the client-athletes for the referral. Athletes should be informed that, during the course of their work with the mental skills coach (trainee), referral to other practitioners is possible (Van Raalte & Andersen, 1996). That way, if a clinical issue that warrants a referral does come up during the internship, the trainee will have laid the groundwork for a professional and caring referral. It will not come as a shock to the client and is designed to set the trainee and athlete up in the best possible way for the referral process. It is the foundation which the trainee can go back to and utilize when beginning the referral process.

How to Talk about Confidentiality

AASP states in their ethical code that we have a primary obligation to uphold and take reasonable precautions to respect the confidentiality rights of those with whom we work or consult (Association for Applied Sport Psychology [AASP], 2011). Confidentiality is the cornerstone of any successful consulting relationship as it creates a safe environment for an athlete to share issues that are impacting their performance and/or life. The athlete can share their challenges with the freedom, trust, and security that what they disclose is strictly between the trainee and themselves. There are of course some exceptions to confidentiality. A trainee can disclose private information without consent in order to protect the athlete or the public from serious harm if, for example, the athlete discusses plans to attempt suicide or harm another person. Under the *Tarasoff* rule, California law now provides that a psychotherapist has a duty to protect or warn a third party only if the therapist actually believes or predicts that the patient poses a serious risk of inflicting serious bodily injury upon a reasonably identifiable victim (Ewing, 2005). It should be noted that, even without this rule, it is ethically appropriate to break confidentiality to protect the client in this situation. Other reasons confidentiality should be broken include suspicion of abuse or neglect of children, the elderly, or people with disabilities.

In my (C.A.'s) experience in supervising trainees, whether in a first or fourth (final) internship, a common thread I see is their anxiety and discomfort in talking to athletes about confidentiality. The JFKU trainee has a written consent form that they give their clients that does include information about confidentiality and its limitations. This is a great start to the process; however, we have found that it is most beneficial when the trainee and supervisor have role-played and talked through the form so when the trainee shares it with the athlete they have practiced and already feel confident about sharing the information. This should happen in the first trainee-supervisor meeting, which takes place before the trainee has begun seeing clients. The supervisor should emphasize the importance of athlete confidentiality and its limitations. This means knowing what to include, how to word it, and how not to diminish the fact that at some point in the consultant relationship there may be a need for a referral.

Often when trainees explain confidentiality they describe breaking it as something that rarely happens and this can impact the athlete-trainee relationship right from the very beginning. An example we see consistently with trainees explaining confidentiality is to tell their athlete "clinical or referral issues never happen." If an athlete was going to share about personal aspects affecting their performance and they hear the consultant say "clinical issues never happen," the athlete may not open up about these issues and the trainee loses an opportunity to help the athlete.

When talking about the limits of confidentiality and why a trainee would break it, it is imperative for the trainee to be able to tell the athlete what this would look like and what the process would be if they did. This way there are no surprises and the athlete knows what to expect if a referral is necessary during the consulting relationship. The importance of being able to discuss confidentiality and its limitations with ease and confidence is the beginning of building trust with the athlete. It also builds the foundation for the trainee to reference if they need to make a referral.

Although there is always potential for a "red flag" concern to come up when talking to the athlete about life outside of sport that they may feel is out of their scope of competence, we still encourage trainees to work with and treat the athlete as a whole person. For the trainee and the athlete this means openly sharing about any issues in life that may be impacting their performance. When the trainee is aware and prepared that this may include a referral, they will hopefully feel comfortable and confident talking about all aspects of the athlete's life. This continues to reflect why feeling grounded and at ease with the referral process is so important as part of the trainee-athlete relationship.

Assessment and Follow-Up

Assessment is how we get to know our athlete. When doing broad assessments in the beginning of the consulting relationship, the trainee is asking the athlete to share about their life, both sporting and personal. This opens up the possibility of something more personal emerging that may need to be assessed more fully. During the assessment process, the supervisor can play an instrumental role in supporting the trainee. The supervisor can do this by encouraging and supporting the trainee to feel comfortable and confident doing further assessment around red flag issues. In our supervisory experience, what we have witnessed is that trainees often miss a potential red flag concern. Many trainees have shared that they are scared for anything too personal to come up in sessions because they are not comfortable or confident with navigating a potential clinical issue. The process of the supervisor talking about red flags and referrals from the very beginning of supervision helps prepare the trainee to be less scared when they hear potential *out of scope* issues.

This collaborative experience is where the supervisor can be instrumental in helping the trainee grow and develop a stronger skill set when faced with potential referral issues. The supervisor can help the trainee develop questions to ask to further assess if there is a more personal or clinical issue involved. These questions should be open-ended and give room for the client to share more information. We have provided some sample questions that are appropriate for a trainee to ask when doing follow up assessment on a possible red flag issue. For example:

- Can you tell me more about . . .?
- Can you share with me a little more detail about this . . .?
- What feelings are coming up for you around this issue . . .?
- How often are you feeling this way . . .?
- How long have you been experiencing this situation . . .?
- Are there other aspects of your life that are being impacted by . . .?
- What kind of support system do you have . . .?

Assessment is not restricted to what the athlete is saying—it also includes observation of the athlete's mood and behavior. This can also give a subtle indication that a clinical issue may warrant assessment. For example, in the therapeutic relationship between client and psychotherapist, non-verbal communication can be a powerful source of insight in therapy. A therapist who is attuned with a client's non-verbal expressions, while also taking in the words actually spoken by the client, is more easily able to recognize when body language and speech don't match. These kinds of cues help the therapist and client identify and access deeper emotional issues of which they may not consciously be aware (Foley & Gentile, 2010). The supervisor can still help a non-clinical trainee delve into this more by having them pay attention to non-verbal cues, or the way the client connects with the trainee. Paying attention to the athlete's affect, eye contact, and body language and whether this matches what the athlete is sharing with the trainee is a critical part of assessment. What is the athlete's mood and behavior like in sessions and when practicing or competing? Is this mood and behavior aligned with the experience? All these pieces are imperative to pay attention to when assessing for a potential clinical issue. By talking about this in supervision and preparing for these kinds of experiences, we help equip the trainee with the necessary tools to assess a potential clinical issue and have the support and confidence to refer, if necessary.

Identifying When a Referral Is Needed

A trainee should be aware that the identification of a referral-based issue can come up at any time during the consulting experience. However, the identification process for the referral has usually begun during the assessment phase. The supervisor has encouraged the trainee to follow up on something the athlete has shared that may be outside their scope of practice. We have outlined an example of what this might look like for a trainee. During a session, the athlete has shared something with the intern that feels more personal and warrants further assessment to determine if it is a clinical problem. The next step is for the trainee to do further assessment around what the athlete has shared. The trainee will ask open-ended assessment questions to gather more information about the potential issue. The trainee is simply gathering information to understand the extent and nature of the problem. Unless the athlete is in crisis, the trainee is not expected to do any kind of intervention. The trainee is assessing to determine: 1) the severity of the issue, 2) how long the issue has existed, 3) how often it has been happening, and 4) the impact on the athlete's life functioning. The trainee must also be alert for subtle factors that might signal the need to extend the focus beyond performance enhancement, like unusual emotional reactions or mood changes and how effective more traditional performance enhancement interventions are in solving and/or presenting problems (Brewer, 2000). Once the trainee determines the issue is outside their scope of practice, the third step is to talk to the athlete about a referral.

Finding Appropriate Referrals

Prior to beginning the fieldwork experience, the trainee should research local specialists for each potential referral subject. With guidance from their supervisor they will create a solid resource base to include professionals from mental health, nutrition, biomechanics, sports medicine, and the like. When looking for appropriate and qualified resources, the trainee can look on professional websites for each different category. For example, if a trainee in the U.S. was looking for a licensed psychotherapist for their athlete, a good place to look is either www.psychologytoday.com or www.goodtherapy.org. The professionals listed on these sites have been verified, reviewed, and approved by the appropriate professional associations.

Making a Referral

After finding potential referrals, the trainee would follow up with a call and interview the referral expert to see if this professional would be a good fit for their practice (for general referrals) and any particular athlete who needed one. It would be even more beneficial if the trainee could meet the professional in person. One key factor when looking for a clinical referral is that the professional is licensed—for example, a licensed psychologist or a licensed marriage and family therapist (LMFT) rather than a life coach or other non-licensed professional. Other factors that would be important are their experience working with people in sports, performance, and/or creative arenas, depending on the specifics of your client. The modality the therapist uses is also important when determining a good fit. For example, from our perspective, Cognitive Behavioral Therapy (CBT) is often not a good fit when working with potentially deeper problems such as depression, anxiety, trauma, or other mental health issues. In California, for example, licensing laws only allow a LMFT trained in California to work with clients in California, and similar rules apply to therapists and psychologists to work in other states in which their license is issued. These legal factors in regard to licensed professionals are important when determining an appropriate referral for the athlete. The underlying goal here is for the trainee to establish contact with a potential referral source and begin to build rapport; this helps create reliable relationships, whether or not referrals are made, and allows for open lines of communication with other professionals.

Making a referral can be daunting for both the trainee and the athlete, so it's imperative that it's done with confidence, compassion, and collaboration. In our experience, this is the process that enables it to happen. When making a referral the trainee will initially talk to the athlete about the beginning of the consulting relationship. They will re-emphasize the conversation around scope of practice and what the trainee is and is not qualified to work with. This conversation begins the referral process.

Next, the trainee validates the athlete for opening up and sharing this issue. By using empathy and compassion, the trainee has provided a safe space for the athlete and this is the foundation for making the referral. Empathy is the ability to recognize and relate to other people's emotions and thoughts. Rogers (1959) defined empathy as the

> perception of the internal frame of reference of another with accuracy and with the emotional components and meanings with pertain thereto as if one were the person, but without ever losing "as if" condition.
>
> (pp. 210–211)

This is why empathy and compassion are cornerstones of any therapeutic relationship.

The trainee will then talk to the athlete about the issue being outside their scope of practice and that the athlete would be best supported by a professional who has experience and training to deal with these kinds of issues. A referral is most effective when the trainee explains their role in the referral process clearly and how they will support the athlete through it.

The trainee will then have the athlete sign a "release of information" form that will allow the trainee to break confidentiality and consult with the appropriate referral resource. They will have their list of specialists with whom they have already built a professional relationship and should feel confident about who they are referring their athlete to. Next, the trainee will give the athlete the name and number of the professional referral and then this may also include helping the athlete set the first session, going with the athlete to the first session, consulting with the clinician or other specialist on an ongoing basis, and utilizing a team approach. The trainee then connects the athlete with the appropriate resource.

There are times when an athlete may not want the referral the trainee has provided. If this is the case, it is important for the trainee to monitor the issue consistently and to continue to gently encourage the athlete to utilize the referral. This may include providing more education and information about how the referral would be beneficial, offering to set up and/or go to the first meeting with the athlete, and continuing to assess the extent to which the issue is impairing client functioning. This does not apply if the client issue falls under any of the limitations of confidentiality (as above).

Follow-up

When the trainee gives the athlete a referral, the process does not end here. It is important, appropriate, and necessary for the trainee to check in with the athlete about following through on the referral and how the athlete is feeling about the process. The trainee should have ongoing conversations around how they can continue to support the athlete with this additional part of their performance/treatment plan. A team approach, whereby all professionals involved with the athlete collaborate in the treatment plan and have the advantage of being convenient for the athlete, helps to alleviate some of the client's fears that if they pursue the referral they will be abandoned by their consultant (in this case, the trainee).

Tips for Making Good Referrals

- Prepare athletes for the possibility of referral from the beginning of the work.
- Use assessment tools to identify if referral is needed.
- Explain why you are making the referral if one is necessary (Bobele & Conran, 1988).
- Describe to the athletes what is generally involved in working with a mental health or other practitioner (Heil, 1993).
- Be sensitive to athlete concerns in the referral process (Heyman, 1993).
- Get written consent from athletes to share information with the referral source if necessary.
- Give the athlete necessary information to schedule an appointment at the time the referral is made, or schedule an appointment for the athlete at that time.
- If the athlete decides not to follow through, discuss alternative strategies. Do not hesitate to reintroduce the idea of referral (Heil, 1993).
- Consult with your supervisor throughout the referral process.

Additional Considerations

An additional consideration in the referral process is working with youth athletes. Working with minors, who are under the age of 18, brings a new complex dimension to the referral process. The trainee working with youth athletes is often considered a mandated reporter and must learn how to manage breaking confidentiality with the parents and/or guardians if any kind of referral situation arises as part of the consultation. For example, in California, mandated reporters are defined as individuals who are mandated by the law to report known or suspected child maltreatment. They are primarily people who have contact with children through their employment. California state law requires mandated reporters to report all known or suspected cases of child abuse or neglect. It is not the job of the mandated reporter to determine whether the allegations are valid. If child abuse or neglect is reasonably suspected, or if a minor shares information with a mandated reporter leading them to believe abuse or neglect has taken place, the report has to be made (California Penal Code, Section 11165.7). It is imperative for the trainee and supervisor to be aligned in this process, as the supervisor may need to step in and aid the trainee in making the report. Our goal as supervisors in the field of sport psychology is to teach our trainees in real life practices when concerning overriding client welfare.

Gender is another important consideration to take into account when thinking about the referral process. The difference in gender of a trainee and athlete may have an impact on how to present the need for a referral to the opposite sex. Awareness of the multi-cultural implications, such as whether the trainee is a male or female, helps determine the trainee's verbal and non-verbal approach and presentation of the referral conversation. Similar implications are also present for other multi-cultural considerations, such as ethnicity, sexual orientation, and religion.

Potential Hurdles

In our experience, as both supervisor and supervisee, we have found that when faced with a potential referral situation the trainee is forced to examine their own assumptions, biases, and personal experiences in relation to the issue at hand. If the trainee lacks self-awareness, they may debate with themselves the very reality of the situation. Their self-talk may include trying to determine whether the situation is *that* serious, if my supervisor *really* knows what they are talking about, or maybe *I'm* overreacting. Whatever the rationalization, this hesitation can result in a myriad of challenges for both the trainee and the client. The trainee may experience fear around being in an uncomfortable situation and anxiety around talking about it with their supervisor. This can often lead to not addressing the issue and is a detriment to the client, as well as the trainee. This is where the supervisor-trainee relationship is integral to the process. If they have built a solid, trusting and collaborative relationship, the trainee will feel confident asking for help and support and use the guidance to better serve their client. As supervisors at JFKU, we emphasize the importance of our trainees being aware of their own personal belief system and experience, and understand how this may impact their work with the client. We have conversations around what could come up in a session that would be uncomfortable or scary and then role-play how to work with it within a session. We also encourage the trainee to debrief and process their feelings with their supervisor.

Lack of experience is another factor when considering potential hurdles. The less time spent learning how to identify red flags, the less confident the trainee will be when the time comes to refer. Trainees beginning a first internship are new at everything and this is where the supervisor can be instrumental in educating and helping the trainee become comfortable with the idea they may need to refer. Even trainees who are in their final internship can feel they lack experience with referring. The more the referral process is talked about and practiced in supervision, the more comfortable and confident the trainee will feel if there is a need to refer. Therefore, we believe it is imperative for the trainee to routinely practice mock referral situations to develop their self-efficacy with the required skills in the art of referring.

Fear of negative repercussions or impact on personal standing with the individual and/ or organization is a valid and understandable reality. While using any ethical modality, there is still an element of the unknown in the athlete's response to your recommendation. There are numerous factors that could potentially result in negative repercussions. For example, depending on the quality and integrity of your rapport with the athlete, your referral suggestion may be met with acceptance, jovial misunderstanding, rejection, or feelings of offense. Whatever the response, there is always the potential for the termination of your relationship. Still, another factor could be the role which the athlete has within the organization, club, or team. For example, the trainee is working with an all-star player exhibiting signs of legal or illegal substance abuse. Although the nature of your relationship is protected by confidentiality, if word were to get out that "so-and-so" is abusing substances, there could be a negative effect on the coach's, administration's, or teammates' perception of not only that athlete but also of the trainee's involvement. This highlights the importance of the trainee speaking transparently with their supervisor about the multi-faceted process of making referrals and collaboratively coming up with a plan to address these potential issues successfully.

Ways to Handle These Hurdles

Supervisors and trainees take responsibility upon themselves to routinely perform mock red-flag situations or select a specific topic to address during the supervision sessions. This content can be related to current events, a supervisor's example from previous or current experience, or random selection. From beginning to end the trainee must represent and present the referral as an integral aspect of high performance, not just in athletics but also in life.

Maintaining transparency with the organization and staff concerning your scope of practice and role will help facilitate the referral process. As a trainee you may be faced with hesitation, apprehension, and even confusion from members of the training or medical staff or members of the organization when faced with making a referral. These reactions arise when there is a lack of clarity on the role of the trainee or the purpose of a referral. When possible, we advocate a team approach when making a referral and, if the client is alright with other members of the staff knowing, it is often wise to include them in the treatment approach. This is so that everyone can be clear about the referral process and be able to discuss concerns, if warranted, with the other members of the athlete's treatment team.

The trainee must take the initiative to debrief with their supervisor to attempt to clarify and articulate the professional rationale for the referral. This dialogue will help the trainee examine the nature of the potential hurdle, such as culture or competitive level at the internship site. This conversation will provide the trainee with solutions to articulate and clarify the purpose of making a referral along with their professional reasoning.

Self-awareness is important in any consultant-client relationship. It is essential for the trainee to be doing ongoing personal reflection and work. The more self-aware a trainee is the better equipped they are to work with both their supervisor and their client. In our internship program at JFKU, our trainees are often expected to do daily self-reflection journals. This is a way for them to assess their work with their clients and review their strengths, challenges, and areas of growth. They are also asked to work on self-awareness around personal biases, understanding how their own personal history and experience may impact how they relate to and work with a client, including giving a referral. See Chapter 5 for more information about the importance of self-awareness.

Ethical Issues

There are numerous ethical considerations in the process of the supervisor-trainee relationship which can impact the outcome of making a successful referral. We have included some of the ethical issues that we have encountered when doing this work, as well as others that might exist. Ethical issues are subjective moral dilemmas that typically involve conflicting choices between desirable and undesirable alternatives. Although we have ethical guidelines from both the APA and AASP, the trainee may or may not find a universal solution for a very specific dilemma. The following sections will address ethical issues that we have identified in our experience.

Trainee

One ethical consideration we see consistently in the referral process includes the trainee missing red flags or avoiding dealing with potential clinical issues because they are scared or don't feel competent enough to assess and refer. This can potentially put the athlete's well-being at risk. Further education in identifying red flags and assessing potential referral issues and ongoing support, practice, and conversations within the supervisory experience will help with this issue. We feel it is the responsibility of the supervisor to instill confidence in the trainee to handle red flag issues. This will hopefully result in the trainee feeling less or no anxiety addressing these often difficult issues. The supervisor can also encourage the trainee to do further research and/or specific coursework related to clinical issues and referral practices.

Another ethical issue is when the trainee is not self-aware and is unable to track or assess potential red flag issues, specifically when the trainee is unaware of their own personal history, issues, and biases they may have about mental health and the impact this has on the consulting relationship and their capacity to address and make referrals. Another aspect of this is around the trainee not being aware of countertransference and transference issues that come up as part of the consulting relationship, and therefore they are unable to address this dynamic within the session. Countertransference, which occurs when a therapist or consultant transfers emotions to a client, is often a reaction to transference, a phenomenon in which the person in treatment redirects feelings for others onto the therapist or consultant (Murphy, 2013).

It is not enough for the trainee to just give a name to the client and feel like they have gone through the process of making a referral. Ethical issues occur when a name is given to the athlete for a referral and there is no follow up at all with the athlete about whether they utilized the referral, and no mention of the red flag issue again as part of the consulting process. This, in fact, is not helpful at all to the athlete or the trainee. Referrals require a team approach with extensive communication and follow-up on an ongoing basis between the trainee and other professional resources.

As mentioned earlier, it is necessary for a trainee to find appropriate clinical and exercise-related referrals for their internship. Ethical issues arise when the trainee has not done the due diligence needed to find these resources, and therefore does not really know the capabilities of individuals to whom they are referring. This has the potential to jeopardize the trainee's relationship with the athlete. It is therefore imperative that strong relationships have been established with the professionals being used for referrals.

Supervisor

Supervisors who have no clinical training or experience may be less prepared to help the trainee with a red flag issue and referral process due to their own lack of training. They may err on the side of not dealing with the issue if they don't feel competent themselves in helping the trainee navigate the process. Supervisors with insufficient clinical experience should have resources within their own group consultation, other supervisors or meta-supervisors to help them feel more capable of handling the process in the most appropriate way for the trainee, and in turn for the athlete. Continuing education and training is an ideal way to gain more experience and competence within these areas. Supervisors must be aware of the potential liability issues that come with working with a trainee's consulting style. Ethically, they have a duty to take red flag issues and any referrals (but specifically clinical referrals) seriously. It is of paramount importance that, if a supervisor finds that a trainee is dealing with an issue that is outside their scope of experience and practice, they should get the necessary support to address the issue and help the trainee appropriately.

Conclusion

We believe that the relationship between the supervisor and trainee is the key aspect in helping the trainee feel confident when navigating a referral situation. In our experience, the quality of this relationship is paramount for cultivating a partnership that is built on trust and respect and develops the foundation for making a referral if needed. We feel it is imperative for these conversations to be part of the first supervisor-trainee meeting, prior to the internship beginning, and as the work evolves. The more information, education, and awareness a trainee has in regard to red flags, the better equipped they are to handle a referral situation. It is important for the supervisor to help the trainee feel confident and qualified to be able to assess any potential *out of scope* issue and to give a compassionate and competent referral. By using this overview, we feel strongly that the trainee will be ready to navigate these kinds of situations that may come up in their consultation experience.

A Trainee's Perspective on Referrals

Martin Rasumoff, M.A., student at JFKU 2014–2016

Originally from Argentina, Martin moved to California to study at JFKU. Martin would like to work with a college or a professional team and in a few years start his own practice. He would also like to supervise interns as a way to give back what he got from JFKU. He can be contacted at mrasumoff@email.jfku.edu.

Referring clients is definitely one of the most challenging parts of being an intern. I never had to do it, but in case I had needed to I prepared and previewed referrals carefully. There are a lot of things to consider, such as how I am going to tell my client, their reaction, the discussion with my supervisor, how to choose my referral, and—probably the most critical part—how the relationship between me and my client is going to be after the referral.

Though a formal referral was not made, in one of my internships I had to discuss referring a client (or not) with my supervisor and group supervision class. I was doing my internship at a high school with a girls' tennis team and was having a session with two young ladies at the same time. One of them shared that three years earlier her grandmother died and after that she felt depressed, had suicidal thoughts, and actually had some attempts by cutting her forearm. She added that she had been feeling well for at least a year prior to this, so I recognized she was not in any immediate crisis. The moment, however, was uncomfortable for me, especially as there was another girl in the conversation and it happened at the very end of the session. I decided to finish that meeting and follow up with her the next time, in which I confirmed she was currently fine. Also, I wanted to talk with my supervisor and my group to have extra support on any decision I might have to make with regard to a potential referral.

That was probably the first time that I realized how important the support of others is, especially when you are just starting out and do not have a lot of experience. My supervisor told me that there was no need to refer, especially because the thoughts and behaviors happened a long time ago, she had been clear of symptoms, and teenagers sometimes have those reactions to death. I agreed and I followed up with her soon afterwards, making sure that she was still fine. This was a valuable lesson for me.

Another challenge regarding the possibility of referring athletes is where I draw the line with my scope of practice. I am from Argentina and was trained to deal with clinical issues, but here in the U.S. as a Master's student studying sport psychology I am not allowed to address clinical concerns. Because of my training, I feel comfortable talking to athletes about things that are not necessarily related to sports, but at the same time I have to be aware of when I need to take a step aside and recommend the athlete talk to a professional trained in clinical or counseling psychology.

I have found a good way to solve this dilemma is by asking myself, or more importantly, the athlete, if what's bothering them is affecting their performance. If this is the case then I feel competent to work with the athlete to figure out how to not let the issue impact their performance. However, when that issue starts to take over the whole session and sport seems to be secondary, I believe it is time to refer.

Reflective Questions for You to Consider

- How will I manage the anxiety or fear that comes up around making a referral?
- What kind of support is important from my supervisor during this process?
- How do I go about finding professionals to refer to in my network?
- What could be some potential psychosocial biases for me making a referral?

References

AASP. (2011). *Ethics code: AASP ethical principles and standards.* Retrieved from www. appliedsportpsych.org/about/ethics/ethics-code

Bobele, M., & Conran, T. J. (1988). Referrals for family therapy: Pitfalls and guidelines. *Elementary School Guidance, 22*, 192–198.

Brewer, B. W. (2000). Doing sport psychology in the coaching role. In M. B. Andersen (Ed.), *Doing Sport Psychology* (pp. 237–247). Champaign, IL: Human Kinetics.

Ewing, C. P. (2005). Tarasoff reconsidered. *APA Monitor on Psychology, 36*(7), 112.

Foley, G. N., & Gentile, J. P. (2010). Nonverbal communication in psychotherapy. *Psychiatry (Edgmont), 7*(6), 38.

Heil, J. (1993). *Psychology of sport injury.* Champaign, IL: Human Kinetics.

Heyman, S. R. (1993). When to refer athletes for counseling of psychotherapy. In J. Williams (Ed.), *Applied sport psychology: Personal growth to peak performance* (pp. 299–308). Palo Alto, CA: Mayfield.

Murphy, S. (2013). Attending to Countertransference. Retrieved from http://ct.counseling.org/2013/09/attending-to-countertransference/

New South Wales Department of Education and Training. (2009). *School Counselling Services.* Retrieved from http://www.schools.nsw.edu.au/gotoschool/a-z/counselservice.php

Rogers, C. R. (1959). A theory of therapy, personality, and interpersonal relationships as developed in the client-centered framework. In S. Koch, (Ed.), *Psychology: A study of a science (Vol. 3, Formulations of the person and the social context)* (pp. 184–256). New York, NY: McGraw Hill.

Tod, D. A., & Andersen, M. B. (2010). When to refer athletes for counseling or psychotherapy. In J. Williams (Ed.), *Applied Sport Psychology: Personal Growth to Peak Performance.* (6th ed.). (pp. 405–420). New York, NY: McGraw-Hill.

Van Raalte, J. L., & Andersen, M. B. (1996). Referral processes in sport psychology. In J. L. Van Raalte (Ed.), *Exploring Sport and Exercise Psychology* (pp. 275–284). Washington, DC: APA.

12 Evaluation

You Think You're Good, but Do You Really Have Any Idea?

Sean J. Fitzpatrick and Spencer Ingels

Ideally, evaluation is an ongoing practice in consulting work. Evaluation is considered before a consulting relationship begins, is conducted continually during the work, and is utilized again at the end of the working relationship. Assessing effectiveness at all points of the consulting process is a critical step for growth as a trainee and professional in the field of sport psychology. Both formal and informal evaluation lead to a better understanding of a trainee's or professional's strengths and areas of improvement, and how to tailor the work to best meet the needs of clients. This chapter surveys the literature on evaluating the effectiveness of sport psychology professionals, with specific attention paid to a case study approach, and also outlines a novel means of assessing work with clients through the utilization of a revised version of Bloom's Taxonomy of Learning Objectives (Krathwohl, 2002).

Background Information on the Authors

Sean J. Fitzpatrick is currently an Assistant Professor and Program Director for the Exercise and Sport Science Program at Marian University in Fond du Lac, WI. Previously he was an Assistant Professor and the Research Director within the Sport Psychology Master's Department at JFKU. Sean has experience working with athletes at the national, collegiate, and youth levels. He received his Ph.D. in Sport and Exercise Psychology from West Virginia University. In addition to his training in Sport and Exercise Psychology, Sean has begun to develop an expertise in higher education learning assessment, accreditation, and curriculum design. He can be reached at sjfitzpatrick02@marianuniversity.edu.

Spencer Ingels is currently a Sport and Exercise Psychology doctoral student at West Virginia University in Morgantown, WV. He completed his Sport Psychology Master's from JFKU in 2012. Spencer has worked as a consultant with athletes and clients in a weight loss setting, coaching his clients to improve health through lifestyle change. Exploring how to evaluate progress and effectiveness plays a large role in this work. Almost all clients focused on losing weight gauge their success based solely on whether the scale went down. Unfortunately, this focus misses opportunities to learn and improve, thus part of his work focuses on developing effective measures of progress that help his clients achieve their goals. Spencer can be reached at spencer.ingels@gmail.com.

Frank has served as an intern for an entire season with a college basketball team. He worked hard to prepare team sessions that built cohesion by running team building activities. He also taught sport psychology skills and led engaging discussions about topics of interest to the team. Frank made the extra effort to be present at as many practices, workouts, and competitions as possible to get to know the players and to be able to provide impromptu consulting. This effort led to working with several of the players one-on-one, including some of the team leaders. As the season is wrapping up, the team has officially been eliminated from the playoffs, despite fighting to reach them, and Frank finds himself doubting whether the work he did had a positive impact. The team had high hopes for the season, and Frank feels that he let them down.

Francine, like Frank, has been interning in applied sport psychology with a collegiate soccer team during their season. She completed the same types of activities, working to build a strong, cohesive team. She too put in many hours at practice and competitions to get to know the players, and to be available for short, spontaneous consultations. This led to her working with several of the players on the team, and she felt these sessions were successful in helping the players perform better throughout the season. The year ends with the team having one of their most successful seasons, leaving Francine feeling quite good about her work; she cannot help but feel responsible for some of their success since they were not working with anyone on their mental skills last season.

Francine and Frank are two interns who conducted similar work but are ending their internships with different perceptions of their effectiveness with their teams. Evaluating our effectiveness is difficult as many variables impact performance, yet we often determine our success based on how the team or individual performs. In Frank's case, it could have been that the team was struggling with injuries, a bad coach, or simply lacked the talent compared with other teams in their league. Francine, on the other hand, could have joined a team that had the talent, leadership, and commitment to succeed. However, we cannot merely look at the outcomes our clients achieve as the standard by which we measure our effectiveness. Pulling apart all these variables to understand the impact we have can be a challenge, but this is a challenge we all need to tackle.

If we don't spend time thinking about what successful work will look like, we open ourselves up to falling into the trap of feeling our self-worth is connected to how the team or individual performs. There is a LOT more to evaluating how we are doing than simply examining winning or losing. Hopefully you can agree about the importance of being clear on your effectiveness, but what makes professionals in applied sport psychology effective? Several research projects have asked this question to coaches, players, and professionals to understand their perspectives of successful sport psychology consultation. The results have identified several important themes that we can use to inform our work and to find ways of monitoring our effectiveness with our clients.

What Do Effective Professionals in Sport Psychology Look Like?

Interviews with athletes (Anderson, Miles, Robinson, & Mahoney, 2004; Sharp & Hodge, 2014), coaches (Sharp & Hodge, 2013), and professionals (Sharp & Hodge, 2011) have identified a myriad of characteristics that contribute to effective sport psychology consulting. The findings from these studies can be divided into four broad categories: creating connection, counseling skills, service delivery, and being professional. These categories will be explored in the following sections and are presented here to expand our understanding of what effective sport psychology professionals look like. These then become areas for us to pay attention to as we evaluate our own effectiveness.

Creating Connection

No consulting work, let alone effective work, will get done without first establishing a connection with those you work with. Athletes and coaches have reported that effective professionals were easy to talk to, good listeners, and personable. Effective professionals made the time to get to know athletes at practice and competitions without pressure to work with them one-on-one. It is important for professionals to fit in with the team culture and be both accessible and approachable. For example, if we are present at practices and competitions (accessible), but are always next to the coach, athletes are unlikely to view us as approachable. This may be because we are seen as being too close with the coach, leading the athletes to question if what they tell us will stay confidential. Finally, effective practitioners build strong connections and relationships that lead to providing constructive feedback in an engaging but non-intrusive manner.

Counseling Skills

This category encompasses skills and characteristics of effective professionals who, after creating a connection, are now working individually with a client. Athletes and coaches emphasized the importance of having a trusting, honest, and respectful relationship between client and practitioner. Effective work entails engaging the athletes in the session and creating a collaborative effort to determine how to help the athlete with whatever may be most pertinent. This often includes serving as a sounding board for clients to vent or unload concerns that may be unrelated to performance. It is also important for consultants to notice athletes' moods or reactions, both in session and during practice and competitions, and to reflect these back to the athlete. Reflecting client's reactions and moods helps clients build awareness that can take our work to another level. Utilizing counseling skills effectively will help to further the relationship you are building with your clients while creating a solid foundation from which to address sport psychology skills and techniques.

Service Delivery

Two themes emerged within the service delivery category from these four studies: being athlete-centered and possessing confidence in teaching mental skills. First, effective professionals tailor their sessions to fit the specific needs of each athlete so that the skill being taught is based on what the client needs in that moment and for the given situation. It is important for professionals to understand the dynamics of the sport, but they do not need to be experts in it. They do, however, need to possess expert knowledge of sport psychology skills so they can teach these skills confidently and in an engaging manner. Athletes want a professional who will make learning the skills fun and engaging through use of multiple teaching tools. Athletes also want practitioners who provide flexible sessions: Some may be short and take place at practice, while others are longer and take place in an office or quiet corner. Finally, effective professionals create a positive change through their work; identifying how to measure if this has been done, and to what degree, will be addressed later.

Professionalism

The last category highlighted in the research encompasses many characteristics that are critical to effectiveness overall but do not expressly fit into the other areas. First, it is important for effective professionals to set and maintain clear boundaries. They stay in their role and take steps to both communicate and maintain this role clearly with coaches and athletes. For example, if the professional is with the team to work with the athletes, it is vital that they maintain a neutral role with the coaches so that athletes feel comfortable approaching and working with them. While it is important to be friendly and create connections, effective practitioners make it clear that they are not friends with their clients; they are able to create informal consulting relationships with clear boundaries. Informal in this case means that much of the work will take place at practice or competition, yet our role (and that we're not a coach, player, or peer) is clear. Finally, effective professionals make their clients feel safe by creating an environment where confidentiality is not questioned. Players need to feel that what they say will stay within that relationship and not get back to their coach.

Clearly, providing effective consulting is complicated. Therefore, future professionals need to seek out supervised internship opportunities so they can practice and improve how they deliver their sport psychology skills. Supervision is not only a best practice, but also a requirement for most certification and training programs. Perhaps of even greater importance is the opportunity internships provide trainees in learning the soft skills of consulting work: building relationships, navigating boundaries, and being comfortable within an ever-changing environment in which sessions could last from 5 to 50 minutes (or more if on a playing field). Such a dynamic environment makes evaluating our effectiveness that much harder, but without evaluation we do not know if and how we are succeeding, or how we can improve. Increased knowledge of our strengths and weaknesses can help us continue to grow as professionals, and ensure that we continue to provide the best possible services to our clients. The challenge, however, is determining how and when to evaluate our work with clients.

Due to the dynamic nature of our work, adopting a flexible approach is necessary. One such method is the case study approach as outlined by Anderson, Mahoney, Miles, and Robinson (2002).

Using a Case Study Approach to Evaluate Effectiveness

There are multiple ways to evaluate our effectiveness as consultants, from standardized questionnaires to relying on our gut feelings. The complex and dynamic nature of performance makes using only a standardized tool ineffective as it does not allow the flexibility needed to evaluate the unique characteristics of each situation. Our gut reactions to our work can easily adapt to each situation, but it is likely that there are indicators of our success, or lack thereof, that we fail to notice or appreciate. Conversely, standardized measures can provide a bevy of information across multiple domains, but may be limited in their flexibility. The case study approach fills the shortcomings of both methods by providing structure while still being adaptable to each unique situation.

The case study approach compares an individual or team performance with itself instead of a standardized score; this allows effectiveness to measured based on improvement from an earlier time. Gardner and Moore (2005) emphasize using a case study approach to gauge effectiveness based on the distinct needs of each situation, and to tailor interventions based on the needs of each client. When used correctly, a case study approach will provide structure to measure effectiveness and progress, as well as inform the content or focus of our work. This is ideal because the needs of our clients will vary greatly; we need an approach to evaluation that we can tailor to fit the situation. For example, if a client wants help with nerves before competition, then figuring out a way to measure nerves in a clear way (e.g. body tension, rating of thoughts) becomes an important indicator for the impact of the work we are doing together. Our intervention should naturally develop from our assessment of the needs of our client and our chosen measures of progress. So, if we are having the athlete self-report body tension during critical moments of competition, we will want to first assess their current level of tension (e.g. *1 = no tension, 10 = super tense*) to understand a baseline, then teach them a skill to reduce tension (e.g. deep breathing).

We will then continue to monitor body tension to assess if this skill was effective and, if so, we will see a decrease in self-reported tension, or perhaps we will see a decrease in tension but performance does not improve. If the latter occurs, we now know that the skill was learned, but it did not target the right area since performance did not improve; this is a sign that we can now shift focus to another mental skill. In this instance, a standardized instrument may lack the precision needed to measure tension in the way the athlete experiences it, leading to potential frustration on both the part of the athlete and professional.

Creating a systematic evaluation strategy that is not situation-specific can lead to a rigid process that does not accurately capture or highlight the impact (or lack thereof) of our work. A case study approach is ideal for applied sport psychology as it involves collecting data before we begin our work and at regular intervals throughout our work, all the while tailoring the evaluation to the client(s). In the above example, the athlete's perception of tension would be gathered prior to teaching a skill, collected regularly while they employed the skill, and then any reflection of change will be used as an indicator of the skill's impact. The case study approach is a practical tool for the applied setting as it gives both the professional and the client feedback on whether our work is helping, and allows for ongoing evaluation.

We are responsible for implementing an evaluation procedure that fits the specific goals of a team or client. It is important that data be collected in a systematic manner—in that data is collected with enough regularity that effectiveness can be assessed over time. For example, ahead of the season a consultant met with the coach and together they decided that the athletes' use of mental skills may serve as an indicator of the consultant's effectiveness. This could be measured by giving a standardized pre- and post-questionnaire, such as the Athletic Coping Skills Inventory (Smith, Shutz, Smoll, & Ptacek, 1995). Additionally, both the coach and the consultant would like to collect information on athletes' use of skills during the season, so the coach agrees that she will ask the athletes about what skills they are using and how they are using them during her regular meetings with players throughout the season. She agrees to share this information with the consultant and they will also meet regularly to plan which skills to teach during the team sessions led by the consultant. At the end of the season the consultant and coach have a meeting and share their impressions of what worked well, and what did not.

We also need to ensure that the evaluation will provide useful information, both for our own improvement and to gauge the effectiveness of our work. Anderson et al. (2002) describe four broad effectiveness indicators that we should focus on when evaluating our work:

1. Quality of support.

    a. Methods to assess: ongoing verbal feedback from clients; standardized feedback forms (e.g. Consultant Evaluation Form, Partington & Orlick, 1987); self-monitoring or self-reflection on our practice (for more on self-reflection, see Chapter 5).

2. Psychological skills and client well-being.

    a. Methods to assess: psychometric tools; informally (e.g. chatting with clients); well-being scales (e.g. Profile of Mood States, Shacham, 1983).

3. Athlete responses to support.

    a. Methods to assess: client self-report; coach, teammate, parent/guardian report; observation of behavior during practice or competition; personal reflection on client attitude in session; questionnaires regarding the use of mental skills, such as the Test of Performance Strategies (TOPS, Thomas, Murphy, & Hardy, 1999).

4. Performance.

    a. Methods to assess: client's subjective judgments of performance (e.g. Performance Profile, Butler & Hardy, 1992); performance statistics (e.g. shot percentage, batting average, or average number of digs per match).

The case study approach is ideal as it can be applied to the multiple areas of effectiveness reviewed earlier (creating a connection, counseling skills, service delivery, and being professional) and can be tailored to the specific goals of our clients. The goals of our work and the nature of the situation influence how we use formal (e.g. questionnaires, forms) and informal (e.g. our reflection, clients' perceptions) measures to assess our effectiveness. How we assess our effectiveness in the four areas laid out by Andersen et al. (2002) or other personally constructed areas will vary across team or individual work. For example, a professional who is hired to lead four pre-season team building sessions might set performance goals to improve communication, explore team values, and create a team identity. They could assess their effectiveness by self-reflection (How am I supporting this team? How is this effective? What other ways could I support the team?), self-report (asking the team members to fill out pre- and post- forms or questionnaires on communication, well-being, and other relevant topics), and with client reflection (regular check-in with the coach to determine what changes they are seeing). A systematic evaluation through case study allows the gathering of multiple sources of information to improve our work, while being flexible enough to fit the dynamic environments in which we will work.

So far, we have covered various components of effective work in applied sport psychology and why using a case study approach to evaluate effectiveness is often ideal. Next, we will explore how different models and tools from the teaching world can be applied within a case study approach to further evaluate our effectiveness in the ongoing process of working with clients.

Thinking of Our Work as Teaching

As we have discussed, applied sport psychology is complex. There are many frameworks with which to understand and conceptualize the work we do in our field. Though our work takes many forms, we would argue that our work is often grounded in teaching. This is not a unique view and others have made this connection as well (e.g. Danish & Hale, 1981). Our work classically includes the teaching of various mental skills to athletes. Additionally, we may be teaching coaches how to better connect with their players. We might also teach parents or other gatekeepers about what sport psychology is and why athletes will benefit from working with us. Though our work looks starkly different from that of a teacher in a classroom, our end goal is often the same: to provide skills and knowledge that our clients (i.e. learners) can later apply. If we conceptualize our work in this manner it allows us to look to educational research for insight into the learning process and identify indicators that we are indeed teaching our clients well.

There are numerous ways to assess learning, but many do not translate well to the sport psychology setting. Quizzes, tests, and other traditional means of assessing learning are not great tools in our line of work as they can conjure up feelings and attitudes about school for our clients, which may or may not be positive. Nonetheless, if we can find ways to assess how well our clients are learning this can help to ensure that we are teaching them effectively. One useful means to do this is to apply a taxonomy of learning to our work. A learning taxonomy is simply a scheme for categorizing different types of learning. The most well-known learning taxonomy is by Bloom, created in 1956 (Granello, 2000). Bloom's

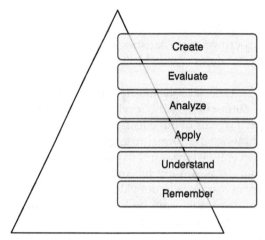

Figure 12.1 Revised version of Bloom's taxonomy. The higher the placement of an outcome, the more advanced it is.

Based on Krathwohl (2002).

taxonomy, as it is commonly referred to, lays out six levels of learning in a hierarchal fashion. The most basic level is *knowledge*, or simply being able to recall or recognize information. *Knowledge* is followed by *comprehension*, the ability to grasp meaning, and then *application*, the ability to use learned material. The next two levels are *analysis* and *synthesis*, the ability to break down material into its component parts and the ability to put these parts back together in new ways, respectively. Bloom believed that the highest of learning was *evaluation*, the ability to judge the value of material for a given purpose. This framework has long been applied in many domains, and has shaped learning curricula at an array of levels.

As we continue to gain insight into the learning process, individuals have modified Bloom's work. The revised version of Bloom's taxonomy by Krathwohl (2002; Figure 12.1) is the framework that we expand upon as a model for assessing our work with athletes and teams. This revised taxonomy is very similar to the original, with modifications being the relabeling of each section as verbs, and the reordering of the top two levels. There is more complexity to the model than just the simple hierarchy of these six learning dimensions but, for our purposes, investigating these dimensions can help us to assess our work with clients. We will explore each section in more detail to further illustrate how evaluation may happen in your work.

Remember

The lowest level of learning is simply being able to retrieve information from memory. This dimension could also be titled recall, and individuals can display their learning within this dimension by being able to recite learned terms, facts, or methods. For example, revisiting our case studies from earlier, perhaps Frank has led a session on goal setting with his basketball team. During practice a few days later, Frank asks a group of players to recite the different types of goals they went over. If they can recall this information, then they have shown that at the very least their learning on the subject has reached this level. Though this level is the lowest in the framework, it should not be undervalued. Learning the terms and processes of skills and techniques is a vital foundation for athletes. This dimension is also one of the simplest to assess, both formally and informally. Formally, just like Frank, asking clients to recall the information that was previously taught to them is an easy assessment technique for this level of learning. Paying attention and noticing when clients begin to use the language shared with them from our sessions is an informal display of learning that can be very telling of their ability to remember or recall.

Understand

Individuals highlight their understanding by interpreting new material, explaining concepts, and summarizing what they have been taught. Understanding, or being able to determine the meaning of material that is learned, is the next level within this taxonomy. Without reaching this dimension, individuals cannot move on to higher levels of learning. Identifying ways to assess whether our clients understand the skills, concepts, and techniques is a skill that all professionals need to develop. Let's look at an example. Francine is working with an athlete on concentration. This athlete, a goalkeeper, has found that her focus often lapses when her team has the ball at the other end of the field. At its worst, these moments lead her to have trouble identifying the ball when her opponent wins back possession. Francine and the athlete discuss attention and the need to be able to switch between narrow and broad attention during the match. The athlete can provide examples of both broad and narrow attention, signaling to Francine that she grasps the concepts. Francine could gauge her client's understanding by asking for examples of different types of attention. Few things will cause more frustration for an athlete than feeling like they do not understand what is being taught to them.

Apply

Being able to carry out and execute new learning represents this next dimension. For many professionals, having their clients reach this level is often the goal of their work. They teach their athletes and teams new skills and techniques to employ in their performances. Perhaps Francine taught her athletes a calming technique to utilize before penalty kicks—a deep, complete breath followed by the cognitive recital of a confidence-boosting phrase. Taking note of an athlete who pauses during a late game penalty kick to employ this routine would be a signal to Francine that the athlete has applied the technique. Looking for cues of the application of the work we do is an observational skill we all should develop. Additionally, asking athletes for examples of when and how they applied their skills should be routine follow-up questions in our work. The Test of Performance Strategies (TOPS, Thomas et al., 1999) is a popular instrument that assesses the various skills we teach within this domain, and can shed light on athletes' utilization of various mental skills. Without implementation, mental skills do not positively impact our clients' performance.

Analyze

Analyzing is the next dimension of learning, which is being able to break material down into its basic parts, and identify how these parts relate to each other. Important abilities within this dimension are being able to differentiate and organize components, as well as attribute causes, effects, and outcomes of various components of material. For example, Frank has been working with the coach of the basketball team he was assigned to for his internship. He and the coach have had many discussions on how to best motivate the various athletes on the team. The coach has tried several new strategies throughout the season. In a late season discussion, he tells Frank how he has come to realize that, when he first compliments his starting point guard on an aspect of his game, the player then becomes more responsive to critical feedback. The coach explained,

> I told him that I was proud of his hustle on defense, and I then shared that I thought he could make better decisions with the ball in our half-court set. Normally he rolls his eyes, and shuffles back to the game. But this time he asked for suggestions on how to avoid getting trapped at the elbow. I really think that he needed that initial boost to be able to think critically about his game.

The coach's realization shows the beginning of an ability to analyze the approaches he and Frank have discussed. The coach broke his interaction with his player into individual components and attributed the player's responsiveness to his initial praise. Though this may seem simple and somewhat logical, this is a dimension of learning that many do not reach. To deepen our athletes' learning and hence their use of skills, we can ask their thoughts on how or why the skills seem to be working, or not working. These conversations force athletes to analyze the skills, and can thus ingrain their importance and utility.

Evaluate

At first glance, this dimension may seem synonymous with the previous. While there is overlap, to evaluate is to be able to make judgments on the value of material based on internal or external criteria and standards. This is a slightly deeper level of learning than analyzing material. Critiquing material and evaluating its value can be realized in many ways in our work. For example, Francine had worked hard to prepare a team presentation on accountability. She had conceptualized an exercise where athletes would pair off and then each set of teammates would share their goals for practice prior to reaching the pitch each day. When she shared this idea with her team, she sensed a hesitation from the players who nonetheless agreed to try out the idea. Later that day she was approached by one of the captains who shared that she did not believe that this process would lead to increased accountability among the team. The captain explained that, while she agreed that the team needed to be more accountable with one another, she was worried that they were placing too much responsibility on the freshmen and sophomores who may not have the courage to call out their more senior peers. Though Francine was initially discouraged that her idea was not being lauded, she understood the captain's position and appreciated the feedback. The captain's ability to see that the potential gains in accountability did not outweigh the potential negative costs highlights her ability to weigh multiple criteria and decide based on her assessment of the situation at hand. This dimension of learning can be difficult to observe and/or assess. Many clients may not want to disagree or critique our ideas. However, developing relationships that allow for such conversations can help to improve the clients' learning tremendously and are a sign of a strong relationship, which is another sign of effective consulting!

Create

The last and most complex dimension of learning is create—the ability to put various elements together to form new products. Athletes who reach this level of learning with their mental skills can face new challenges and obstacles with a heightened sense of self-reliance. This self-reliance can greatly increase efficacy and provide the athlete with the evidence needed to know that they will be able to overcome unforeseen hurdles in the future. While a hardworking professional will do everything she/he can to help the athletes grow, there will be innumerous times when the athlete is called to be self-sufficient. For instance, Frank had been working on pre-game nervousness with the center on the team. The athlete would find himself jittery, nauseous, and tense before games. Together, he and Frank developed a pre-game routine that included progressive muscle relaxation and self-affirming thoughts. He would begin the routine while getting dressed and continue right until tip-off. Frank was worried about the player during a holiday tournament that the team would compete in. Frank knew that the tournament atmosphere could lead to unpredictable starting times, and he was unable to meet with the athlete before he left. When the athlete returned, Frank was pleasantly surprised to hear that the client had put together a new, shorter routine that included deep breathing and positive imagery, two skills Frank had taught in team sessions but not in individual sessions with the athlete. Though the athlete had previously reported that the pre-game routine that he and Frank had created was working, he possessed an increased level of confidence upon returning from the tournament. This resulted from creating and employing his own solution to a new problem: a shortened pre-game time. It is ultimately this level of complexity and creativity that we are looking to reach with our athletes. The more self-reliant they can become, the greater chance of success they will have.

This learning taxonomy represents just one of many ways to conceptualize the effectiveness of our work. Considering the growth of clients along this hierarchy provides us with an understanding of how clients' skills and abilities might grow, and can provide an understanding of where there are shortcomings. If an athlete is simply executing their skills (i.e. apply) for instance, but has reached a perceived plateau, it might be due to their inability to analyze the skills they are using. Similarly, if a professional feels that her/his client cannot interpret or summarize what they are learning (i.e. understand), the professional will want to be patient and continue to work at this level prior to having the athlete employ the skill, technique, or approach. Continually assessing the level of learning among clients, both formally and informally, can help to ensure our effectiveness.

Moving Forward

As we have discussed, there are many ways to approach and evaluate your effectiveness. When your work is ending, you may want to consider implementing an evaluation form to gather the perceptions of the athletes that you worked with. You could use Partington and Orlick's (1987) Sport Psychology Consultant form to gather information. Conversely, you can create your own evaluation form. In doing so, consider what to include; adopting a competency-based approach can be useful. Identify and articulate the competencies that you believe are important to your work and ask for feedback in these areas. You can ask for both quantitative feedback (e.g. rating items: How well was the goal setting workshop run, 1–10) and qualitative feedback (e.g. what did you enjoy most/least about the goal setting workshop). Hutter, Pijpers, and Oudejans (2016) provide a survey of the relevant literature related to sport psychology competencies in their study's introduction. Reading this information may help you better understand how the field views professional competence.

Conclusion: Frank and Francine Revisited

Let's return to the two case studies that we introduced at the start of chapter. We can see now that evaluating Frank and Francine's effectiveness would require *a lot* more information than simply knowing how their teams performed at the end of the season. Just because Frank's team did not make the playoffs does *not* mean he was ineffective. Likewise, just because Francine's team had one of their best seasons does not mean she *was* effective. Without building in evaluation throughout our work we will not know if we are effective, and this is critical information. A case study approach allows us to know what we do well, where we can improve, and what works with certain individuals or teams. The case study approach allows us to measure our effectiveness, monitor our improvement, and collect valuable data on our client outcomes. Formulating our work around a case study approach provides ready to use information for our current and future clients. It gives us a strong answer to the client's question "how can you help me?" You can answer by confidently explaining how you implemented an approach in a similar situation and then discuss the results you achieved. When we use evaluation effectively, we become better practitioners and more confident advocates for our services.

A Trainee's Perspective on Evaluation

Damon Valentino, M.A., student at JFKU 2012–2015

Damon works as a Performance Coach in the San Francisco Bay Area. He has a private consulting practice in San Francisco and is the co-founder of FlowSport, which offers an online mental training program that is geared toward high school and college performers. FlowSport offers workshops for athletes, parents, and coaches. Damon can be contacted at damon.valentino@gmail.com.

The first day of my internship with a high school basketball team was an awkward experience. For most of my working life, I had been either a coach or a teacher. What was once a familiar and comfortable space—the court—became foreign to me, as I was unsure exactly where to be or what to do in my new role. I had so many thoughts swirling in my head that I forgot to smile and say hello to the players. That initial experience was humbling, but as I would come to understand over four internships, not unusual.

As my sport psychology knowledge increased, so did my confidence. I was more comfortable in my role as a mental skills intern. I grew to know how to establish a connection, utilize appropriate counseling skills, link theory and service delivery in a cogent manner, and accomplish these tasks in a professional way. In my mind, I was well on my way. Upon sharing this information with my supervisor, she snapped a quick smile my way and said, "You're right where you need to be." It was her way of reminding me to reflect on the goals I set, and assess my progress up to this point. The reflection process re-focused me on my central goal, which was to help athletes improve their performance.

It is not as if I did not know that my work would ultimately be judged by how well my client performed. After all, I wanted to enter the field of sport psychology to help athletes and performers become more successful. However, as I reflect upon it, I was focused on my actions with the assumption that, if I made the right decisions, my clients would benefit. There are several methods that JFKU incorporated to highlight this crucial lesson and understanding. During my hour-long individual supervision sessions each week, my supervisor would always conclude our time by asking me to list the takeaways from the session. She was modeling a great technique to check what I learned from our time together. This gave her a better understanding of what I was taking with me, which in turn provided her with an assessment to measure my progress.

In my work, I began to expand my performance assessment with athletes to include more than just results. With this wider scope, I came to realize that, often, a gap existed between my assumption of what I thought my client understood and what they *actually* understood. I began to discover that assessment tools can provide a baseline of data about an athlete that can include cognitive, emotional, and physical information. The appropriate assessment tools can provide a more holistic picture of an athlete, as well as create a forum for the athlete to drill deeper into their own relationship with performance and the variables surrounding it. If done properly, this can provide insight into what the athlete values and where they see their strengths and challenges. Improvement becomes more objective, and I could evaluate my effectiveness (and their improvement) based on actual data. Collecting this information was crucial but, without observation, it did not provide the whole picture. I was encouraged to triangulate my data by observing athletes in practices and games. This allowed me to gain a deeper understanding of change and progress, particularly as it related to the data I collected from the assessment process.

Much like my own learning, my athletes were also processing and learning information in a nonlinear way. Some lessons would stick immediately while others needed much more attention. Some lessons were solidified in memory, but were not able to be translated in real-life situations. My assessment processes now included a myriad of factors that considered much more than performance results. As my training furthered, I came to understand the complexities that I bring with me to the work, as well as those that my athletes also possess. Improvement is the ultimate goal, but now I am much more aware of what that might mean. By establishing a wide-ranging baseline of assessment data at the onset, I am able to tailor my work based on the data, and I can plot their progress in a way that is tangible and rooted in evidence-based methods.

Reflective Questions and Activities for You to Consider Before You Proceed

- What are three characteristics that you think all effective professionals must possess?

  o How might you measure these characteristics in your own work? Who can provide you with information regarding your performance in these areas?

- Which of the four broad areas—creating a connection, counseling skills, service delivery, and professionalism—do you think is your strength? Your weakness?

  o What signs can you notice within each area that will show your growth?

- If you were to employ the case study approach to better understand your effectiveness during your internship, how would you select what to evaluate?
- Are you more comfortable with formal or informal evaluation methods? Why?
- Which of the levels of learning do you think most of your clients will/do reach? How might you reach higher levels?
- What types of methods would you use to assess the levels of learning that your athletes achieve?

References

Anderson, A. G., Mahoney, C., Miles, A., & Robinson, P. (2002). Evaluating the effectiveness of applied sport psychology practice: Making the case for a case study approach. *Sport Psychologist*, *16*(4), 432.

Anderson, A. G., Miles, A., Robinson, P., & Mahoney, C. (2004). Evaluating the athlete's perception of the sport psychologist's effectiveness: What should we be assessing? *Psychology of Sport and Exercise*, *5*(3), 255–277. http://doi.org/10.1016/S1469-0292(03)00005-0

Butler, R. J., & Hardy, L. (1992). The performance profile: Theory and application. *The Sport Psychologist, 6*, 253–264.

Danish, S. J., & Hale, B. D. (1981). Toward an understanding of the practice of sport psychology. *Journal of Sport Psychology, 3*, 90–99.

Gardner, F. L., & Moore, Z. E. (2005). Using a case formulation approach in sport psychology consulting. *Sport Psychologist, 19*(4), 430.

Granello, D. H. (2000). Encouraging the cognitive development of supervisees: Using Bloom's taxonomy in supervision. *Counselor Education and Supervision, 40*, 31–46.

Hutter, R. I., Pijpers, J. R., & Oudejans, R. R. D. (2016). Assessing competence in sport psychology: An action research account. *Journal of Sport Psychology in Action, 7*, 80–97. doi: 10.1080/21520704.2016.1167150

Krathwohl, D. R. (2002). A revision of Bloom's taxonomy: An overview. *Theory into Practice, 41*, 212–218.

Partington, J., & Orlick, T. (1987). The sport psychology consultant evaluation form. *Sport Psychologist, 1*(4), 309–317.

Shacham, S. (1983). A shortened version of the Profile of Mood States. *Journal of Personality Assessment, 47*, 305–306.

Sharp, L.-A., & Hodge, K. (2011). Sport psychology consulting effectiveness: The sport psychology consultant's perspective. *Journal of Applied Sport Psychology, 23*(3), 360–376. http://doi.org/10.1080/10413200.2011.583619

Sharp, L.-A., & Hodge, K. (2013). Effective sport psychology consulting relationships: Two coach case studies. *Sport Psychologist, 27*(4), 313–324.

Sharp, L.-A., & Hodge, K. (2014). Sport psychology consulting effectiveness: The athlete's perspective. *International Journal of Sport and Exercise Psychology, 12*(2), 91–105. http://doi.org/10.1080/1612197X.2013.804285

Smith, R. E., Schutz, R. W., Smoll, F. L., & Ptacek, J. T. (1995). Development and validation of a multidimensional measure of sport-specific psychological skills: The Athletic Coping Skills Inventory-28. *Journal of Sport & Exercise Psychology, 17*, 379–398.

Thomas, P. R., Murphy, S. M., & Hardy, L. (1999). Test of performance strategies?: Development and preliminary validation of a comprehensive measure of athletes' psychological skills. *Journal of Sport Sciences, 17*, 697–711.

13 Reaching the Finish Line

That's It . . . What Do You Do Now?

Michelle Cleere and Elizabeth I.R. Hunter

At the end of each internship experience, using a closure or wrap-up strategy is helpful for all parties involved: trainee, clients, coach, supervisor, etc. A sense of psychological closure is useful for the trainee and clients to allow each to move on from the experience with a sense of growth, and so that both parties understand the boundaries of the relationship going forward. For closure to be successful, various strategies may be helpful such as doing assessment or evaluation of the work via performer and coach feedback, leaving the clients with a packet of information that may include worksheets on topics and skills covered, referral information for future use (e.g. clinicians, nutritionists, biomechanists, etc.), information on the country's main sport psychology organization (if applicable), and how to know if someone else in the field is a credible and qualified consultant.

Finishing internships is also a time for the trainee to reflect with his/her supervisor, get paperwork completed and handed in, and discuss what happens next. Other points to consider include determining if the clients want to continue the work and start to pay for it, how to transition into another internship, and how to turn the current internship into a potential future job.

Background Information on the Authors

In addition to personal coaching, **Michelle Cleere**, Elite Performance Expert, takes on many roles—a best-selling author, athlete, and teacher. Dr. Michelle's best-selling book series, *Beating the Demons*, helps clients develop practical skills to gain more control over competitive environments and mitigate the interruption in play to overcome intense odds and defeat adversity. She has been involved in many different sports and understands the stress and demands to perform at the top. As a 15-year USAT Coach, she developed simple and effective tools to mentally train her athletes, and these tools are used by coaches around the world. She has been an adjunct professor and intern supervisor at JFKU for the past 12 years, helping students and supervisees focus on applying the essential skills to become professional mental skills consultants. You can read more about Dr. Michelle and her work by visiting her website, www.drmichellecleere.com, and reach her via email at mcleere@jfku.edu.

Elizabeth I.R. Hunter, M.A., has worked in sports for nearly three decades. During her coaching career, Ms. Hunter recognized that sports provided valuable life skills for the athletes which led to her to pursue her Master's Degree in Sport Psychology at JFKU. Her work in mental skills training began over 20 years ago, when she was asked to develop, implement, and then administer the JFKU LEAP (Life Enhancement through Athletic Participation) program. Beginning with LEAP interns, she began supervising for JFKU and has continued since then. She took a brief sabbatical (2005–2009) from JFKU to establish her own sporting goods product and returned to supervision following the closing of her business. Ms. Hunter is also on the LEAP Advisory Board and can be reached via email at ehunter@jfku.edu.

All internships have a beginning and an end, even though each internship and its timing is unique. For example, clients may be participating in a year-round sport that has no competition while you are working with them. Your start and end dates are insignificant to this type of team or group since you are basically there in the off-season. However, if your internship is during a competition season, the end of the internship could depend on any post-season play.

This chapter aims to help you understand the importance of closure as an essential part of an internship. We will help you plan closure even if the exact end date is unknown, and understand how to successfully move beyond the internship experience. You should plan to conduct closure with all your clients: individuals and the team if both were part of your work. It's also beneficial to wrap up with the coaches, other support staff, and your supervisor. Closure can be achieved emotionally, mentally, and practically. As you wrap up your work, you should also consider what your next steps are, both with the current site and in the bigger picture of your professional work. These points and more will be discussed in this chapter.

What Is Closure?

Closure is the opportunity to reflect on all you have accomplished and all that has transpired in the internship. Although your work did not take place in a classroom, your work has included a lot of teaching. Closure is an important bookend, formally wrapping up this period of learning. In a mental skills internship, closure encompasses what you taught, what the client found helpful and useful, and how these skills will be used moving forward.

Closure not only allows you to wrap up and reflect on the internship, but an important piece of it is being able to move on from the experience. In supervising hundreds of interns over the last 25 years, we have found that closure is as important for you as the trainee as it is for the clients with whom you have worked. Closure is especially important when you have worked with clients over a period of time and have built strong relationships, and is often much more than just saying "thanks and good-bye" (Poczwardowski, Sherman, & Henschen, 1998), as you will learn in this chapter.

Planning the Timing of Your Closure Session

There is no hard and fast rule as to when you should begin to prepare for closure with a client. An overly simplified answer is that closure should take as long as it takes. That decision is yours, but should be based on your estimation of how much time you think you need to have productive closure with each client. Before you can determine when to begin closure, you need to be clear on when your time with the team or site officially ends. In working with interns for a number of years, we have found that interns need to give themselves approximately three weeks before the *official* end of the internship.

Deciding When to Start the Closure Process

Once you have determined the official end date of your internship (as best as possible), you can plan accordingly for the process of closure. You will also want to be sure to communicate with the clients that the work will be wrapping up and when. Occasionally, upon learning that your work with them will soon be coming to an end, clients suddenly decide they need your help in a new situation. You need to determine if there is enough time to address the new topic or if time will not allow for it. Here are a few points to consider to help you determine how much time you need to complete the closure process:

- *How many topics have you discussed with your client?* If you have covered many you may need more time to wrap up than if you have only focused on a few ideas.
- *Is the client effectively utilizing the skills learned, or are there some details that need attention; for example, a revised script for imagery?* If your client needs more time on a particular topic, you'll want to make sure you have time for this before you shift to wrapping up.
- *Have you helped the client establish practices to continue to utilize the mental skills?* If you have not already discussed how these skills can be used moving forward, then you may need more time at the end to discuss this.
- *Have you informed the client that your time together is coming to an end?* If not, then you may need to wait a bit longer to begin wrapping up if you feel this will come as a surprise to your client.

As you are planning for your closure sessions(s), keep in mind how difficult or easy it has been to schedule a meeting with each client, and take this into consideration when planning. For example, if someone tends to cancel sessions, you may want to start scheduling with this client extra early if you typically have to reschedule.

When Is Your Finish Line?

When you approach an internship professionally you will be aware of when you begin your work and when it's contracted to end. However, as the end of the season nears the team may become eligible to compete in playoffs or post-season. Playoffs can add days or weeks to the internship. By all means, you should stay and work with the team until their season concludes in order to support the athletes and maintain your working relationship. Though you had a specific end date planned, if possible, work with the team until the season is completely over.

A different scenario to consider is that internships may end earlier than your anticipated end date; many high school and club teams do not continue to meet once they have been eliminated from the playoffs. Your internship can come to a very abrupt halt. Prior to either scenario occurring, it would be useful to talk to the coach about what happens at the end of the season regarding practices and your meetings so that you can be as prepared as possible and to plan when you should begin closure meetings.

In other situations, you may be working with clients who have no competition during your internship and so it is likely that you will meet with them for the duration of the contract. In this situation, you have a clear end date. However, in all situations clients may come and go. For example, athletes may move away, drop off the team, or transition to a different level of team (e.g. from Junior Varsity to Varsity). All of this influences your work and how you will wrap up. There will be times where you don't get to wrap up if a client leaves unexpectedly. However, in as many situations as you can, thoughtfully plan for how to create closure. Additionally, as much as you are aware of your contracted time frame, there will be times where your work with an individual has been completed before the end of your contract. For whatever reason, you may work with some individuals for a brief period of time. These situations also have opportunities for closure. As best as you can, try to wrap up your working relationships, even if they are brief within your longer-term internship experience.

Preparing for Closure with Your Clients

Several weeks before the end of the season, you will want to begin preparing for your wrap-up meetings. One of the best ways to begin to prepare is to review your case notes. Keeping strong case notes throughout the internship is essential when you have worked with a half dozen or more clients over the course of a couple months. In order to thoroughly prepare for your final meetings with your clients, it helps to begin by methodically reviewing your case notes on each client and, if appropriate, with the team. You want to start to think about closure several weeks before the end of the internship experience.

Reviewing your notes provides you with an in-depth summary of the work you accomplished. Beyond general information, your notes might include your assessment, suggested interventions, and outcomes (Luepker, 2010). Additionally, review your handouts and notes you made on their effectiveness. Consider the skills you taught and how well they were (or not) implemented.

A similar review of all notes on group presentations to the team is also helpful. Look back on notes for team meetings that were educational, but also ones that were not; where you helped the team discuss what was *going on* and how to make improvements. Review your personal journal as well. The purpose of this review is to remind you of the details of your work and to help you prepare for effective closure meetings.

What to Include in the Closure Meeting(s)

How you handle closure with a team or individual will vary from one situation to the next, as your work with clients varies. However, there are some common points you will want to consider covering during these sessions.

Review of Content

Closure is an opportunity to review your work with your clients, to remind them of all that you did together, and to allow them to review and plan for what is to come. Your clients may not remember all the topics you addressed, nor what they accomplished as you worked together. In addition to reviewing each topic discussed, reinforce basic concepts of mental skills, including how to use the skill and what to keep in mind or remember when using this skill in the future. Ideally, you can also review situations where the client utilized the skills and the positive impact of those skills. This discussion helps to reinforce what was done and encourages ongoing use of the mental skills they have learned.

Within the closure meetings you also help the client plan how to utilize the skills in the future. This is one of the most critical steps in wrapping up. Your client may have enthusiastically embraced and utilized your ideas and skills while you worked together, but what's next? How have you encouraged clients to continue utilizing the techniques and skills? If you have not talked about ongoing use of skills already, closure is the opportunity to develop a plan with your client about how to continue to practice the techniques and incorporate them into his or her daily routine.

For individual clients, teams, and coaches, you can leave a packet of information when the internship ends. The packet may include copies of all handouts you distributed, including the edits you may have made after noting how the clients responded to the handout. You can include articles you may have referenced, research, supplemental reading links, referrals for other professionals including personal trainers or nutritionists, as well as how and where they can locate qualified mental skills consultants in the future. If your country has a professional organization, include this information as well.

Getting Feedback About Your Work

During your closure meetings, we suggest you take time to gather feedback from your clients. Learning what you did well, what the client found helpful, or areas to improve on provides insight into your consulting skills and contributes to your development as a professional in the field. Feedback can inform you of your strengths and weaknesses. Chapter 12 addresses evaluation so that at the conclusion of your work you have a clearer idea of how effective you have been.

Feedback can be gathered verbally in a final session, or you can prepare a handout asking clients for their comments. Allowing your athletes to share anonymously may allow them to be more honest with feedback, which is helpful in your learning. Limit your feedback sheet to one page so as not to overwhelm the client or have them speed through to complete it. The feedback sheet can be anything you would like, but with our interns we have found it helpful to list the topics covered, each skill you addressed, and have a place for the client to rate the effectiveness or how helpful each topic was. You can ask for qualitative feedback such as what they thought you did well and what they liked or disliked about your work. Be sure to provide pencils for them and an envelope in which clients can place their evaluation of your work, so they can remain anonymous.

Keep in mind that the coach with whom you have worked is also a possible resource for feedback. Perhaps you met weekly with the coach and s/he has provided feedback all season. It could be helpful for your professional development to know how the coach feels about each mental skills topic, your style, what you did that worked well, as well as areas you could focus on for improvement.

From these sources of feedback, you can obtain a breadth of information on how effective you were. With this information, you can create your personal growth goals for your next internship or your time as an early professional. All of this can also be discussed in supervision to further reflect on the feedback you have received; your supervisor might require that as part of their closure with you. Knowing your strengths and weaknesses will help make you a better consultant. If you respond favorably to constructive criticism, this reflects well on you. This sends a message of wanting to improve and a willingness to learn, which we consider desirable traits for professionals in the field.

Closure with a Team

If you work with a team, it can be a little difficult to determine when to hold the final team meeting. You should work with them as long as they are competing, including into the playoffs. Typically, a team continues until they are eliminated from the playoffs or win it all. Either way, the season can come to an abrupt halt. Once the season is over it can be difficult to have all the players return for a final meeting. Therefore, it often makes sense to have a final formal team meeting at the conclusion of the regular season. Final meetings should consist of reviewing your work with the team, discussing how they might use the techniques going forward, and asking for their feedback on your skills as a consultant. If the team is in the playoffs, such a review would be a valuable reminder of the skills they can utilize during the final games of the season, where they may feel more pressure to perform.

Having a closure meeting with the team at the end of the regular season does not mean you are no longer available to them. You still may be asked during the playoffs to provide some words of encouragement to the team, or to remind them of and review the techniques they have utilized in the season, like remaining positive, or how to stay focused. Individuals may request meetings with you to help them utilize the techniques you taught. Sometimes your work during playoffs may simply be your presence and silent encouragement. Talk with the coach and athletes about what they would find most helpful and what time is available to you (if any) to conduct additional check-ins or meetings in the post-season.

Maintaining Boundaries as a Part of Closure

During your consulting relationship, you have likely developed warm and genuine working relationships with your clients. As a trainee or professional in sport psychology, your ability to develop relationships is critical to your success. However, as noted in the AASP Ethical Principals & Standards (Association of Applied Sport Psychology [AASP], 2011), due to your teaching role you have a responsibility to not develop an additional relationship with clients. At JFKU, interns agree to abide by these guidelines even though they are not yet officially AASP certified. We find that having clear guiding principles is important for students to maintain boundaries throughout their work, and at the end of an internship. JFKU considers learning about AASP guidelines, and adapting behaviors to be in line with those guidelines, are important elements in a student's education.

The information the client has shared by working with you is unlike information shared in a social relationship. Hopefully you have been clear about the nature of your professional relationship throughout your work with your actions and words. Additionally, your relationship beyond the internship should also be clarified at the conclusion of the internship. Even though you are wrapping up, it's possible you may work again with these clients in a different setting. Maintaining an appropriate relationship allows you to preserve your professional stature with clients even if you are not actively working with them, leaving the door open for future work.

Closure with Your Supervisor

If you are a student or early trainee working with a supervisor, you should have a closure process with your supervisor similar to the closure you have with clients, which is what happens at JFKU. Within supervision, your closure will likely be focusing on the work that you have done, reviewing and receiving feedback, and your next steps. As you wrap up with your supervisor, you will want to review your work, your progress on your internship's goals, and how to take what you learned and apply it in the future. Your supervisor can help you identify your strengths and areas where you had challenges and may need improvement. Reflecting on your work should become a self-care practice that can help you grow and improve throughout your career (Poczwardowski et al., 1998). Each internship can help you become closer to your vision of an ideal consultant.

Receiving Feedback and Evaluation of Your Work from Your Supervisor

Some applied programs, such as at JFKU, have identified Program Learning Outcomes (PLOs, see the list in Chapter 1 of this book) and, if the program does have PLOs or similar criteria, you will likely be evaluated by your supervisor on the extent to which you have achieved these outcomes. For example, you may be evaluated on your ability to assess clients' needs, or your ability to teach appropriate techniques. As you and your supervisor discuss your progress in the various areas, the supervisor may also discuss and suggest goals for your next internship or work in the field. Your supervisor may have additional ideas for how to conclude your time together, including reflection of your work and perhaps discussion of the site itself.

Your supervisor will want you to move on in a positive way, whether that is into another internship, further into your career, or perhaps into additional studying and preparation. You are encouraged to utilize the suggestions of your supervisor as they have worked with you, and in the field, and therefore have insight on how you can improve. It is the supervisor's job to help you become the best you can be in the field. As part of the closure process, when reviewing areas of improvement, supervisors may provide suggestions for additional work or other ideas to help you develop, such as taking some time off for personal growth or doing some additional reading and training in a particular area. Remember that these suggestions come from someone who wants to see you succeed, and they recognize the areas in which you will benefit from more training.

Additionally, supervisors may provide suggestions such as what type of site you should pursue for your next internship that would provide you the greatest growth opportunity. For example, you may have had an internship in one of your favorite sports and you thoroughly enjoyed what you did, leading to your realization that this is what you want to do for your career. But for your personal growth and benefit, your supervisor might suggest you work with clients who are completely out of your comfort zone, such as working with the opposite gender or in a sport in which you are totally out of your element to further your growth.

Continuing with Supervision and Boundaries

Early professionals may need additional supervision beyond their experiences as a trainee (for example for AASP or BASES accreditation). This is a point to discuss within the supervision process to determine if both parties want to move forward with additional supervision or mentorship. If so, what would it look like? Both the trainee and supervisor can give thought to this topic before the conversation happens.

For the supervisor, if you are not comfortable with this or are too busy to continue to act as a mentor, what does your relationship look like with this trainee when you are done? For example, consider if they can they use you as a reference or email you with questions. Be clear if you are available for more than that and, if not, set clear boundaries for the conclusion of your work. Just as your trainees need to wrap up work with their clients and set clear boundaries for the future, you need to do the same with your supervisees.

Other Topics for Closure with Supervisors

Supervisors and programs are also encouraged to gather feedback from trainees about their experience at the internship site. It is helpful for the educational programs and other students to be aware of thoughts about the site, including if the coach and staff were supportive of you and the work, and if your access to the clients met your expectations and needs. One way to evaluate an internship site is to ask yourself if you would suggest this site to a friend or not, and why.

Lastly, supervisors are encouraged to get feedback directly from the trainees with whom they work. Ask the students what you as a supervisor did that the trainee found particularly helpful and if there was something you could have done differently. Additionally, discuss if there was anything you could have done to help the trainee learn more than they did. Much like asking clients what they would like you to do differently next time, supervisors should be given the same feedback, which will allow you to grow as a supervisor. You are even encouraged to do a mid-internship check in to see how you can further support your intern.

Goal Setting to Gain Employment

Within the process of closure in supervision, if this is your final, or only, internship, it might be beneficial to spend some time preparing for the next steps after the internship. Supervisors can help trainees prepare for entry into professional work, and provide some guidance on "Now what do you do?" as they move from trainee to proficient professional.

As the internship ends, supervisors and trainees can work together to develop daily short-term goals that will help the trainee meet their larger employment goals, as goals drive our actions. When writing goals, take into consideration how many resources, contacts, and face-to-face interactions you will need each week or month with people or employers in your network. As you set measurable goals such as these, it is important to evaluate and re-evaluate progress. Short-term process goals are what will help you get to your long-term goals (Whitmore, 2010). You can't get to the finish line without being focused on the necessary steps to get there. Daily goals will help you stay organized and allow you to use your time effectively. Goals should be created for the job search but also include your professional development.

Write your goals down and continue to share them with others such as peers, a mentor, or your supervisor who can help keep you accountable and make improvements as you continue to search for work. Supervisors can share about how to use goal setting to assist in your professional career.

Transitioning from Trainee to Paid Professional

Both prior to and during your final internship, it is important for trainees to start thinking about entering the job market. Many supervisors ask trainees at their first meeting what the trainee's goals are, and how do they plan to use their education. Regardless of the type of setting in which a trainee might want to work, there are many steps you can start working on prior to ending your last internship. Trainees and supervisors can work together not only in the context of the current internship, but also planning and preparing the knowledge and tools necessary to move onto professional life. Although supervision should be mostly focused on the current setting and the work with the clients, some time can be spent on preparing the trainee for their time after the internship. We both enjoy this part of the work with interns who are getting ready to transition into professionals. For individuals who are not completing an internship through an academic program, these ideas can still be applied to prepare you for entry into the field.

Transitioning from a Trainee to a Paid Professional at Your Internship Site

Ideally your internship is with a team or in a setting where you have interest working when you finish the internship. Once you have done unpaid work with a site, you have credibility and experience and have started to build relationships in that school, organization, or team. All of this is important and can help lead to employment at that site. Even if you don't see yourself working at the site long-term, there may be a benefit to pursuing paid work as you already have an existing relationship with the site and team. Acting professionally, doing effective work, and building strong relationships is important regardless of if you work with your current site after the internship is over. This site can act as a reference for other sites you may want to work with, so do not underestimate the importance of the current experience. Keep in mind that both the athletes and the coaches with whom you work will move onto other teams and could be interested in working with you in the future.

How to Approach the Organization

As you are nearing the end of the internship, if you are ready to pursue working in the field and want to continue working with the same team or site, consider putting together a proposal for future work. This could address what you have already accomplished with the team, observations of areas that still need work, and how you can specifically address those needs in a paid capacity.

As you prepare to provide closure to the team, this is also a good time to let the coach know that you are finishing up as a student and are going to be working as a professional. Directly ask the coach if they are interested in having you continue to work with the team. If the coach can't pay you to stay and you are willing to do some pro-bono work (working for no fee), consider presenting this idea. Trainees can begin by offering a set amount of sessions at no cost for the team. This can be a good opportunity to get further experience, help to build your resume, and allow you to continue to hone your skills. Pro-bono work with a site you have already worked with will help you continue to build the relationship with the organization, athletes, and parents, and deepen the work you have already done. Being committed to the team or organization in this way may open you up to a potential paid position later. Pro-bono work will be discussed in more detail in the next chapter.

Other ways to increase the likelihood of being hired at your internship site may include:

- Getting to know the school or organization on a larger level, not just the team with whom you work.
- Building relationships with people who work there, particularly the gatekeepers.
- Being conscientious about the work that gets done. Providing consistent, high-level work may mean gainful employment, while average or mediocre work probably means no employment.

For Trainees Interested in Being Hired by a School or with an Organization

If a trainee is not interested in starting their own private practice, there are other business-related tools to focus on when seeking a paid position in applied sport psychology. It's worth noting that those of you who want to go into private practice may still benefit from these tools, which include having a strong resume or CV, being able to write a convincing cover letter, and developing your interviewing skills. As part of supervision, if time permits, these items can be reviewed, or mock interviews can be conducted.

Keep in mind these and other tools are forever being edited and adjusted as a person grows and matures both personally and professionally. Though there may not be time within supervision to address this topic, we have found it best practice that interns have some knowledge of what needs to get done so that they can start moving in that direction. Trainees are encouraged to discuss these topics with supervisors rather than wait for supervisors to address them. For supervisors, if these areas are outside your scope of knowledge, try to have resources or referrals available.

Emotional Aspects of Creating Closure as a Trainee

When you move from your internship to being a working professional, there is a mind shift that must take place. One minute you are unpaid, with one set of expectations and experience, and the next you are having to think about starting a practice or finding a job. What is important about this mind shift is not only that you find confidence in your abilities, but that you also realize your value (Taylor & Herzog, 2015). Handling emotions and feelings should be directly discussed as the internship and supervisory relationship concludes.

Dealing with Fear

If you experience fear or nerves as you enter the field, this is quite common (Orlick, 2008) and is something to talk about and work through within the supervisory relationship. Fear exists in many shapes and forms, and it is how you deal with it that is important. Completing an internship and moving from an unpaid to a paid position can invoke anxiety as you must provide a service worth paying for. As a trainee, you may not yet be aware of any fear related to taking on a paid position, but it is an important conversation to have with your supervisor or peer group. Supervisors know how fear can impede any process and experiencing fear may lead to self-sabotage which makes it incredibly difficult to land, or keep, a job. To give yourself the best chance of finding the job(s) you want, you are encouraged to preview how you will feel as you enter the *real world* of applied sport psychology.

Building Confidence

Confidence is believing you can handle the task at hand. As a trainee, you may feel that you can do the job when there is no payment, but receiving payment raises the stakes. Beginning to be paid for your work can add pressure and impact your ability to continue to be confident about your work. Mugford, Hesse, Morgan, and Taylor (2015) discuss what you need to be an entrepreneur: necessary qualities, developmental steps, key competencies, credibility, and how you differentiate yourself. Confidence can be increased when trainees realize that the skills learned in an unpaid position are often the same skills used when being paid. Supervisors can help trainees figure out how to develop more confidence. They can also help trainees recognize the skills and knowledge they have developed in the internship (e.g. their sport psychology skills, counseling skills, business skills, etc.) and how these directly translate to their paid positions. Understanding areas for growth and the steps needed for how to get there can also help to increase confidence, and should be a part of the closure process.

Have Realistic Expectations for This Transition

Trainees should have a realistic mindset as they start looking for clients and applying for jobs. You will most likely need to work your way up to your ideal status or position, and even the ideal amount of money you want to make. While professional success is attainable, it does not come all at once. During your education, you have gained skills that will provide many opportunities for success, but with a limited amount of work experience it takes time to build a career and high levels of pay. Supervisors can share with trainees expectations and experiences about beginning a career in the field, to help create understanding for the new professional about the time and dedication this work can take.

Conclusion

A trainee should go into an internship thinking about the experience as if it were a job. You should do your best to treat it as if you are getting paid, because an internship is practice for the real world. Your early applied experiences are the start of building some very important relationships and skills and provide great opportunities to evaluate what you need to do to continue to grow. Wrapping up your internship and creating closure with clients is one of the many ways that you can establish yourself as a professional. Supervisors should always be thinking about supporting interns throughout the internship and helping prepare their trainees for the importance of the closure process.

A Trainee's Perspective on Reaching the Finish Line

Julian Coffman, M.A., student at JFKU 2013–2015

As a consultant and mental performance coach, Julian works with the United States Ski & Snowboard Association, the Utah Lacrosse Association, multiple winter sport clubs, team sport organizations, and athletes all over the world. He helps to improve systems that promote psychological and physical skill acquisition and execution. Find out more about Julian at juliancoffman.com or contact him at Julian@juliancoffman.com.

My final internship at JFKU was with an organization I knew I would like to have a professional relationship with once the internship finished. With that in mind, throughout the internship I aimed to be on top of my game at all times while engaging with the athletes, coaches, and managers. This meant exhibiting a high level of professionalism and showing long-term commitment.

Professionalism takes many forms and is critical when cultivating relationships with the gatekeepers of the organization for whom you want to work. I made sure to demonstrate my value by collaborating with the administrators and managers on redefining and strengthening the organization's mission, vision, and core values. Working with the organization on these foundational measures helped guide how I wanted to finish out the internship with my clients, and hopefully helped to set the stage for continuing in a professional capacity after the conclusion of the season.

Having three internships under my belt prior to my last, I knew that working with athletes during the internship experience can be very challenging. This can largely be due to the fact that they don't always have a desire to immerse themselves in mental skills training. On the one hand you as the trainee have certain requirements to achieve as a student (e.g. fulfilling all PLO requirements and hours), and on the other hand you may have athletes whose current direction does not exactly match up with the student requirements. When this happened in my final internship, we were able to fall back on the mission, vision, and core values of the athlete's program and work from there. We were able to frame the work between the athletes and myself as a commitment to the organization, rather than a commitment to my trainee requirements.

Also, during this final internship, the relationship between my supervisor and myself became a balancing act between meeting student requirements and setting me up for future professional success. A central matter of importance as we neared the end of supervision was preparing me to create closure with my clients. My supervisor and I discussed how I would be sure that all parties involved comprehended the work that was done, as well as understood the changes that would ensue. During the closure meetings with the athletes, they were reminded of the insights, skills, and tactics they obtained from working with me.

Coaches were asked to reflect on any changes witnessed in their athletes, and for themselves if they were someone I spent extra time working with individually. Managers were provided a brief rundown of services provided without compromising confidentiality. It was important for me to review feedback from anyone I developed a professional relationship with to assist my personal reflections and continued growth. Additionally, within supervision we spent time reviewing challenges and successes of the experience.

Beyond finding closure to the internship experience, it was equally as important for me to transition my mindset into truly believing in my professional abilities and value. This did not come easily to me, as I am very critical of myself and felt increased expectations to do great work at every moment if I was getting paid for it. Being able to discuss these points with my supervisor helped to prime the transition into becoming a professional in the field.

Reflective Questions and Activities for You to Consider Before You Proceed

- When you think of creating closure with clients, how might you effectively wrap up your working relationship?
- At the conclusion of an internship, from whom do you want to gather feedback and how will you gather that information?
- When wrapping up an internship, how will you know that your competencies have improved and what areas you need to continue to work on?
- What does "professionalism" mean in both paid and non-paid situations? If you want to continue working at your site in a paid capacity, how can you prepare to present this to the site and what considerations might you need to make (e.g. ethical considerations, learning from your time as a trainee, etc.)?

References

AASP. (2011). *Ethics code: AASP principles and standards*. Retrieved from www.appliedsportpsych. org/about/ethics/ethics-code/

Luepker, E. (2010). Ethical practice in sport psychology. In S. J. Hanrahan, & M. B. Andersen (Eds.), *Routledge handbook of applied sport psychology: A comprehensive guide for students and practitioners* (pp. 51–54). London: Routledge.

Mugford, A., Hesse, D., Morgan, T, & Taylor, J. (2015). Now what do you do? How to develop your consulting business. In J. Taylor (Ed.), *Practice development in sport and performance psychology (*pp. 59–80). Morgantown, WV: Fitness Information Technology.

Orlick, T. (2008). *In pursuit of excellence: How to win in sport and life through mental training*. Champaign, IL: Human Kinetics.

Poczwardowski, A., Sherman, C. P., & Henschen, K. P. (1998). A sport psychology service delivery heuristic: Building on theory and practice. *Sport Psychologist, 12*(2), 201–202.

Taylor, J. & Herzog, T. (2015). "What's your thing?" Creating your unique value proposition. In J. Taylor (Ed.), *Practice development in sport and performance psychology* (pp. 21–26). Morgantown, WV: Fitness Information Technology.

Whitmore, J. (2010). *Coaching for performance: Growing people, performance and purpose*. (4th ed.). Boston, MA: Nicholas Brealey Publishing.

14 Securing Work

Will Anyone Pay You?

Carrie Jackson Cheadle and Fernando Lopez

There may be a variety of career goals that individuals have when beginning their studies in sport psychology; this chapter focuses on those who want to do applied work with clients and provides ideas for how to secure work. Consulting is quite different from a "typical" 9am–5pm job. In this work, though an individual is his or her own boss, ultimately the aim is to be hired by clients who become empowered, i.e. they become the boss. As a consultant, one is often working with several (to many) clients at any given time. With the large number of athletes and other professionals who can benefit from performance enhancement services, there are endless opportunities for work, but this also creates the need to be professional, organized, and timely in all aspects of one's career. Professionals must also consider whether to focus their work in a particular niche of clients/environments, or branch out further.

As part of finding employment in the field, new professionals will need to understand how to leverage their existing networks, create new connections, and become comfortable with rejection. When going into conversations about potential work, a consultant needs to be able to articulate what work will be done once hired as well as be clear on rates for service. This chapter will guide new professionals in determining their worth, provide ideas for how to have the conversation about rates with individuals and groups, and touch on resources for developing business plans. Additionally, there will be times when pro-bono work is a strong choice for a new professional, as it can help to grow an individual's business; knowing when and how much pro-bono work to do will be discussed. Finding work is often an ongoing process for professionals in the field, which can be exciting and/or daunting. This chapter will help to address some of the nuances of gaining and maintaining employment as a consultant.

Background Information on the Authors

Carrie Jackson Cheadle lives in Northern California and is a Mental Skills Coach and CC-AASP. She is author of the book *On Top of Your Game: Mental Skills to Maximize Your Athletic Performance*. A popular source for media, Carrie has been interviewed for publications such as *Men's Fitness, Women's Health, Outside Magazine, Shape Magazine, Runner's World, Bicycling Magazine,* and *Huffington Post*.

Carrie received her Bachelor's Degree in Psychology at Sonoma State University, California, and her Master's Degree in Sport Psychology at JFKU, and has been teaching and supervising students in the JFKU Sport Psychology Department since 2006. She consults with high school and collegiate athletes, as well as elite and professional athletes competing at national and international levels. She is one of the foremost experts specializing in Mental Skills Training for athletes and exercisers with Type 1 diabetes and is the head of the Mental Skills Training Program for Diabetes Training Camp. Carrie can be reached at carrie@carriecheadle.com and at www.carriecheadle.com.

Fernando Lopez is a core faculty member at JFKU and currently the only core member who is also an alumnus of the program. After graduating with his Master's from JFKU he worked with a variety of populations, including Olympic athletes, the U.S. Army, and non-profit organizations. Fernando's most recent position was with the U.S. Army's Comprehensive Soldier and Family Fitness (CSF2) program, where he had the privilege of working alongside Army Soldiers across the United States. His work included working with medics, infantry, and Special Forces Recruiting. He was part of the 2015 CSF2 Warrior Games team, where he offered resilience and performance enhancement skills to wounded, ill, and injured service members. He also proudly reached the highest level of the Master Resilience Training program, becoming a Primary Instructor.

Fernando has also worked with performers outside of the military, including the USA Olympic and Paralympic Archery teams. In his work with USA Archery, Fernando has had the honor of presenting at the USA Archery Coaching Symposium in 2012, 2013, 2015, and 2017. Fernando can be reached at flopez1@jfku.edu and at www.mentalcomponent.com.

Will Anyone Pay Me for Applied Sport Psychology Work?

Congratulations and welcome to the professional world of sport psychology/mental skills training. Now it's time to get paid for your work, but where do you start? After graduation, a sport psychology professional can attain employment in three main areas: teaching, research, or applied sport psychology (Aoyagi, Portenga, Poczwardowski, Cohen, & Statler, 2012; Fitzpatrick, Monda, & Butters Wooding, 2015; Kornspan & Duve, 2006; Winter & Collins, 2016). For this chapter, we will be focusing on applied sport psychology, which can be defined as "the application of psychological techniques and strategies that are aimed at aiding athletes in achieving greater performance" (Roper, 2002, p. 53). Fortunately, there are many areas in which one can practice applied sport psychology, including university athletic departments, Olympic training centers, university counseling centers, private practice, professional sport organizations, sport clubs, high school athletics, and military programs (Kornspan & Duve, 2006).

Upon graduating or completing your post-degree internship, you likely have a wealth of sport psychology knowledge and even some applied training. However, an area you might be unfamiliar with is the business side of consulting and how to find clients. Fortunately, the field of sport psychology is growing and so is the need for sport psychology practitioners (Kornspan & Duve, 2006; Connole et al., 2014; Weinberg & Gould, 2015). Unfortunately, the process of acquiring work as a consultant is not as easy as submitting a résumé to a company. The nature of consulting in and of itself is complex, and in this chapter we will help illuminate strategies to familiarize yourself with finding clients, getting paid for your work, and creating a business plan.

The wonderful part of being a consultant is you have freedom to choose your own path and be your own boss. With many benefits of practicing applied sport psychology, there is also the reality of needing to find clients and pay the bills. Determining how much to charge, getting comfortable with asking for payment, and the possibility of working for free will all be discussed. For now, let's focus on the demands and realities of being a consultant.

As a consultant in applied sport psychology your possibilities for work are vast. For a moment consider all the different types of sports, and then consider how many people play those sports. This should help you understand there are many athletes you could possibly work with. The challenge lies in finding or creating these opportunities, which takes a lot of effort and time. One reality for consultants in applied sport psychology is the unique opportunities to work in extraordinary locations with extraordinary athletes. Another reality is experiencing the frustration of clients canceling on you. Consulting is not like a regular 9 *to* 5 job; you'll work weekends, early mornings, evenings, and sometimes miss important life events because you might be traveling with a team or athlete. There is some control over when you meet with your clients, but a large part of scheduling depends on when the athlete is available and how much help they need. As you progress in your career, your learning will be based on the experiences you go through in trying to navigate your way through the consulting world. You will find what works and what doesn't. You will get into a groove and find a population which suits your passion. Nevertheless, having a foundation of where to start and how to maintain momentum in your career is extremely valuable. This chapter will start building your foundation in regard to identifying your clients, networking, pricing models, and creating a business plan. Please keep in mind this information will not guarantee payment, nor does it guarantee you clients. You will need to navigate some areas on your own to decide what is best.

What Value Do I Provide?

Before we dive in and start the conversation about finding work, we need to discuss an important notion many early professionals need to learn: What can I provide and what am I worth? After your internship experience(s) you probably have a good idea of what you can offer to athletes and teams (e.g. performance enhancement skills, objective perspective, helpful advice, and lessons to increase team cohesion). The harder question to answer is what is the worth of what you offer? What value can you provide to an athlete's life? How confident are you in delivering what you say you can offer? These questions should work as a springboard to help you reflect on your own perceived value as an applied sport psychology practitioner. The key is being aware of what we can and cannot offer as well as producing what we say we can do. The truth is you probably are able to offer a lot to your clients. You simply need to identify what it is and what value it can produce.

Knowing what you can offer and the value it can produce is certainly a good start, but what might your athletes be looking for? Researchers found that an advanced degree and interpersonal skills were the top two qualities athletes preferred in a sport psychology practitioner (Lubker, Visek, Watson, & Singpurwalla, 2012). Knowing the material as well as your ability to care, empathize, and relate to the athletes are qualities which provide value and increase your worth. Lubker et al. (2012) also mentioned athletes prefer a sport psychology practitioner who has knowledge of their sport and can communicate about the unique demands specific to it. The more we can meet the needs of the athlete, such as knowing the language and challenges of their sport, the more worth we are seen to have.

Knowing what you offer and the value of what you offer are the first steps in finding work. To help you begin identifying what you bring to the table, consider the internships you completed, the education you have gained, the mentorship and supervision you received, as well as your experience with sports, coaching, and teaching. From this reflection, identify your strengths and weaknesses as a sport psychology practitioner and create a measurement for how effective you are in the specific areas you listed. In essence, create a performance profile for yourself and rate your abilities. Several areas to consider could be assessment of individual and team needs, confidence in delivering content, connection with athletes and coaches, and understanding of their sport. Use the feedback you were given from teachers, athletes, and coaches to help you identify your effectiveness in each area. You can also compare your feedback to the grades you received in your classes and with the feedback from supervisors. Having a clear breakdown of your strengths and weaknesses will help you begin to formulate your worth as a consultant in a more objective way and give you the beginnings of a strong foundation to your consulting practice.

Who Will Pay You?

When entering the field, it can be easy to think "I want to work with everyone!" or "I can do it all!", but this type of thinking actually limits your chances of acquiring clients. Rather than trying to work with every athlete you come across, narrowing your target market (and having a niche) will typically be more advantageous. There are several reasons behind this idea. One reason is it will make you more marketable and credible if people consider you an expert on a topic. Another reason is that, if you are working with a population you love and are knowledgeable about, you will be more energized and more likely to put in your best work. In approaching your work this way you are offering higher value to those athletes. As mentioned before, the more you can offer athletes, in this case high energy and investment, the more worth you have. As Michael Port mentions in his book *Book Yourself Solid* (2011), "Choose your clients as carefully as you choose your friends" (p. 4). What is meant by this statement is you want to be surrounded by people you want to work with. Simply working with an athlete because you need money isn't best for you or the athlete. If you don't like working with your client you will be less invested in helping them, and they will not be getting what they need. By working within a specific market or a specific population, your clients will likely be more willing to talk about you and your work. They will recognize the value you offer as well as what exactly it is you do and the type of clients you work with. This type of information will spread through word of mouth. The more people talk about the good work you do, the more your worth increases, as does your client base. Keep in mind as an early professional that you may not always be clear on your niche and you may be well served to work outside of your target market. We'll touch on that shortly, but first let's clarify who your ideal clients are. Use these questions to help you to determine your target population and niche:

- What population would you love to work with? Think age, gender, sport, competitive level, and location. What is it about the population(s) that brings the passion out of you?
- What qualities, values, or characteristics would you want your ideal client to have? Are they optimistic and outgoing, what do they talk about, who do they associate with, and how do they impact your own life?
- Who are those clients which suck your energy and leave you feeling empty? Who do they associate with, how do they impact your life, and what specific personal characteristics do you want to avoid?
- What do you offer? What problems can you help solve? How do you solve them? What challenges will get in your way to solving these problems?
- What resources do you have to make yourself competitive? Think of education, mentors, technology, sport familiarity, and ability to travel to meet clients.

The more detailed your answers, the easier it will be to identify your ideal target population and begin networking to obtain work within that niche. Remember, the idea here is to be clear with who you want to work with and what specifically you can offer them.

When first starting off, your answers to the questions above may seem broad and general, which is okay. As you gain more experience doing applied sport psychology, you will start to notice which populations you like to work with the most as well as what specific offerings you provide that are your favorites. For example, when I (Fernando) first started trying to find clients I went to tennis, golf, soccer, basketball, baseball, swimming, and a variety of other sport clubs. I also went to local gyms and fitness centers. I didn't know who I wanted to work with, just that I wanted to work and thus I shared my information everywhere. I soon came to realize this method of trying to find clients was not effective for two reasons: first, I wasn't specific with who I wanted to work with, and second, the information I offered was too general. It wasn't until I started to narrow my field of potential clients *and* my services that I started to gain traction. I focused on youth athletes and team building, and with time my niche led me to working with the USA Archery team. What is important to know about my work with USA Archery is that it started because I was invited by someone in my network, who knew my niche was team building, to present a team building segment during a USA Archery coaching symposium. When others in your network know who or what you want to specialize in it enables you to market better and get more referrals. We'll cover more of this in the networking section.

Ideally you will be busy working with only your preferred clients: those who allow you to feel passion and enthusiasm. However, when first starting off, chances are you will not have enough clientele to be busy with only *ideal* clients. In your first few years you will work with a variety of athletes, all of whom have their own beliefs and values, and each with their own unique personality. By working with a range of individuals and teams you will find out you love working with some more than others. When it comes to the clients that drain your energy and frustrate you, Port (2011) says to dump them! What he means by *dumping* your clients is to end your working relationship with them in a professional way or to help them find another consultant to work with. It can be tempting at first to keep all clients, especially if you are starving for work, but working with clients who you do not like to work with can cause more frustration than satisfaction. This then could lead to you not doing your best work and thus reduce the value you can offer. Having clear criteria for those you want to work with not only benefits you, it also benefits your client. It is our intention to offer the highest value possible, and one way to do this is by working with those individuals who we have the greatest passion for and those we can offer our best work too.

Gaining Clients Through Networking

Networking can be an effective way to gain access to the populations that you want to work with (Fifer, Henschen, Gould, & Ravizza, 2008). Networking is the act of meeting and connecting with people to form business relationships and provide potential business opportunities. The idea of networking often fills people with dread. It immediately conjures up visions of uncomfortable networking events: getting cornered by someone that wants to give you his or her canned sales pitch and force a business card into your hand. Many people make the mistake of thinking that networking is all about approaching someone to find out "What can you do for me? How can you bring me clients and make me money?"

Networking is *not* about selling (that comes later!) and this self-serving approach to networking is not only uncomfortable, it's ineffective. Networking is not about telling somebody how great you are and schmoozing them with your sales pitch. Networking is about building relationships. The real goal of networking is to create connections with people (Port, 2011). You may have already started networking as you pursued your internships as outlined in Chapter 2 of this book, but if not then now is a good time to start. To start your networking strategy, start by creating these three lists:

- Old connections: Make a list of all the people you already know (e.g. family, friends, acquaintances, colleagues, coaches you've worked with, etc.).
- New connections: Make a list of all the people you would like to know (e.g. potential clients, coaches, training facilities, people that work with the population you want to work with, etc.).
- Networking events: Make a list of formal networking events you could attend (e.g. conferences, meetup.com, chamber of commerce events, etc.).

Don't censor yourself during this stage; write everything and everyone that comes to mind. When creating the lists, you will want to stay broad (you will be amazed at the connections your family and friends have that you may not have known about). Once you have your lists, it is time to set some networking goals and this is where you want to narrow; think about the niche you are creating and be sure to spend time networking there. For example, a networking goal could be to contact at least one old and one new connection each week and attend one networking event per month. To get even more specific with your goal setting, when you contact these people, think about how you can share information and/ or resources with them. What does this person need and how can you help them meet their needs? Maybe you know a great sports nutritionist to recommend as a guest speaker, or you came across a great book or research article that could benefit someone. Remember that you are interested in building the relationship—it's not just about selling yourself and your services.

Related to selling your services, another common question that comes up when you're just starting out is whether or not you should provide your services for free. This is called pro-bono work and choosing to do it can be a great way to build connections and get your name out there when you are just getting started. Not only is it an opportunity to get in front of potential clients, but it is also an opportunity to demonstrate your work and your worth. Before you decide whether or not you want to provide any pro-bono work as part of your networking strategy, consider asking yourself the following questions:

- Am I excited about this opportunity?
- Will this workshop/project strengthen my connection to this person or organization?
- Could this experience lead to potential clients?

Whether it is writing a guest blog post or providing a free workshop, it's okay to ask yourself "What will the return on this investment be?" Making the choice to provide your services at no charge is a deliberate choice in service of making connections and building relationships. It's important to understand that you are providing a service and that service has value—whether you choose to charge for it or not. Just because you are at the beginning of your career does not mean you have to work for free (Blann, Shelley, & Gates, 2011). However, offering a free workshop as part of your networking strategy can certainly be beneficial. Your time is worth something, but the value you get in return for the time invested might come back ten-fold. On the other hand, you don't want to be known as the person who will do anything for anyone. Saying *no* also establishes your value and worth.

Getting Paid

Like any good goal-setting plan, you want to know both where you are going and how you will get there. Part of understanding the business you are creating is becoming clear about what income you want to make, what services you need to provide, and how many clients you need in order to make that income. In the beginning, you can get so excited about getting paid you might not give any thought to how much to charge. It is important to look at the bigger picture and give some thought to what you want your business to look like. Consider both who you would like to work with and what kind of money you would like to make in order to price your services.

One way to do this is to think about how much money you would like to make in the next year, the next three years, and the next five years. Then for each of those salaries, you can break down what percentage of your income would come from each service you provide (e.g. individual sessions, teams, speaking engagements, products, etc.). Maybe in the beginning you need a part-time job that fills 20 percent of your salary. Maybe in your five-year plan you want to have published two books that will fulfill 5 percent of your salary via "passive income" (income that comes in after you have created the product). Breaking this down to see the real numbers will give you a clear idea of what you are working toward.

Another good option for this is to create a business plan. A business plan is basically a written document mapping out the future of your business. This plan can help you figure out what your objectives are, your strategies for growth, and your plans for how to make it happen. There are as many formulas for creating a business plan as there are businesses. If you are new to this idea, a great place to start is with Jim Horan's (2015) book *The One Page Business Plan for the Creative Entrepreneur.*

Once you figure out how much you want to make, you need to figure out how you will be getting paid. This entails deciding what you want to charge for your services, accepting payments, and creating contracts.

Getting Paid: Establishing Fees

When deciding what to charge, it is important to research other consultants in your area or consultants that are specializing in the same population as you, and see what they are charging for their services (Blann et al., 2011). If you specialize in a certain sport, you can also research what athletes are paying specialization coaches for their services in your geographical area. All of this will give you a basic idea of what you may want to charge. Keep in mind that your education, training, and experience will also influence your fees.

When establishing fees, you not only need to consider the work you will be doing but also the costs you will incur. Let us start with fixed costs. Fixed costs are those costs which remain the same from month-to-month or year-to-year. For example, this could be the monthly charge to run your website, the rent on your office, your cell phone bill, or an annual subscription to a professional organization. Fixed costs typically stay constant and consistent regardless of how much business you get. This is to say, the cost to rent your office will stay the same regardless of how many times you use it.

The costs that do change are called variable costs and they are dependent on the services or products you provide or utilize. For example, handouts, travel expenses, team building materials, and apparel are all considered variable costs because they depend on the specific services you are offering. Handouts for a seminar of 20 people might cost you $5, but if you have 50 people the cost changes to $12.50. Typically, as you increase your services and products this will also increase your variable costs. If you increase your client base and have to travel more because of it, then your gas cost will increase. When formulating a price to charge a client, you need to consider both variable and fixed costs in your amount. Doing this will give you a more accurate range of what you need to charge.

To best prepare yourself, make a list of your fixed costs and variable costs. Once written out, create an estimate of how much money you will spend monthly and annually to run your consulting practice. Compare this information to what you want to make in a year and calculate the amount of money you need to make to reach your desired salary.

Making enough money to cover just your expenses is not enough; you need to also make a profit so that you can continue to grow your consulting practice. Ideally, we would want the highest percentage as profit, but this could make us quite expensive and people may not want to work with us. While we cannot give you a set percentage, because everyone's costs, needs, and demographics will be different, consider the following three pricing strategies, which can help you decide how to price your services.

1. *Low-cost pricing*

   The low-cost pricing strategy is based on offering your services or products at the lowest price. Stores which sell large quantities of product at a low price, such as Walmart, follow this pricing model. Due to the prices being so low, a high volume of sales is needed to make a profit. How this looks in the sport psychology world is through seminars/workshops and packages. Let's say you want to run a two-hour mental skills training seminar for athletes and plan to charge $100 per person. If only five people show up you make $500, but if you lower your price more people might show up because it is more affordable. If you charge $30 rather than $100 and 50 people sign up, you just made $1,500. The low-cost pricing model is beneficial when you can get high volume.

2. *Responsiveness pricing*

   Some consultants limit their availability to their clients and limit communication through text and email only. Others do the opposite and follow the responsiveness pricing strategy by always being available. In this second scenario they might show up to games to observe, are available at all times through text and email, and even travel with the athlete. The more available you are to the athlete the more you can charge. When formulating a fee for a client you can add this premium into your price, because offering great, consistent service might not be what others do. This model is effective when you have the time to dedicate to your clients.

3. *Luxury pricing*

   Luxury pricing is about selling a high-quality product at a high price. Keep in mind, high quality is relative to what you are offering. For example, the two-hour seminar you are holding is only going over basics. This could be considered low quality because you are not offering as much value to the athlete. Compare that to holding a two-day mental skills workshop with several guest speakers; the value sky rockets. One would not expect to charge the same amount because what you are offering is worth more. This pricing strategy is effective when the value you offer is of high quality and worth.

Keep in mind these three strategies do not need to be used independently; pricing models can be mixed together to fit your needs. As you gain more experience you will notice that the low-cost pricing might work great for one service you offer while the luxury pricing works well for other services. Take a look at what you can offer a client and which pricing strategies would work best for that specific service. This will help you identify how best to charge your client for your services.

Identifying our fixed and variable costs as well as selecting a pricing strategy are very important steps when considering how much to charge. Another suggestion is to talk with the client about what it is they want. Perhaps they want your luxury services but can't afford it. What do you do in that instance? Perhaps you lower your price, or do you offer fewer services? These are questions you will need to reflect on as you progress. Just remember you have financial responsibilities to manage.

Another point you will need to decide on as you determine fees is whether you want to charge an hourly rate or create packages. Some consultants will have packages (e.g. six-session package, ten-session package, etc.) that provide a price break per session for the client depending on how many sessions they sign on for. For example, you might provide a 5% discount if they sign on for a six-session package and a 10% discount if they sign on for a ten-session package. The thought is that you now have a certain amount of guaranteed income from your client and that might be worth lowering the hourly rate per session. Keep in mind there isn't one right way to do it. You have to figure out what works for your style of services and for your market, and be ready to make adjustments along the way.

Getting Paid: Accepting Payment and Developing Contracts

Once you figure out what to charge, it's time to figure out how to get paid. With the development of new technology, online merchant services like PayPal and Square make it easier than ever to accept debit and credit card payments. These merchants provide services such as allowing you to send invoices to your clients, providing you with a mobile card reader, and options for website payment integration; in exchange, they charge a small percentage per transaction. You can also choose to accept payments in cash or check form as well. Remember that when you are self-employed in the U.S. you are subject to self-employment tax, which means you need to be keeping track of your income (and expenses) and pay estimated taxes to the Internal Revenue Service (IRS) quarterly. Be sure to be aware of applicable tax laws for your state, province, or country related to income, reporting, and payment of taxes.

Once you have decided what you want to charge and how you will take payment, it's time to develop your contract. In short, your contract is a legal agreement between you and your client that outlines the exchange of money for your consulting services. It outlines the expectations between the service provider and the customer so that there are no misunderstandings. Like business plans, there are many templates for contracts. Do some research on what to include in contracts, draft your first version, and get feedback from trusted legal counsel, mentors, and colleagues in the field.

Continuing to Get Paid

With fluctuations of gaining and losing clients, consulting can feel a bit tumultuous and you may even encounter your own performance slump. One of the attributes of long-lasting companies is the fact that they are able to adjust to the needs of their customers. In the book *Built to Last*, author Jim Collins (2004) states that visionary companies try many new things and are adept at understanding and keeping what works while quickly getting rid of what doesn't. As you become established in the field, you should take the time to assess and evaluate your business on a regular basis. Once you understand how your business looks (e.g. how you are spending your time, which parts of your business are creating the most income, etc.) you can start applying the 80/20 principle, which will help you identify the best use of your time and resources (Koch, 2008). The general rule of the 80/20 principle is that 80% of the consequences come from 20% of the causes and 20% of the work and effort will lead to 80% of the result and reward. For example, you want to know:

- What 20% of your services/customers are providing you with 80% of your income?
- What 20% of your marketing efforts are providing you with 80% of your clients?

An effective way to ensure you continue getting paid is to work *smarter* and not harder. Understanding these aspects of your business will help you do just that.

If you find yourself in a bit of a slow period, sometimes the best thing to do is to go back to the basics. Revisit your networking list and goals, get in touch with past clients, do a free workshop, or revamp your business plan; go back to whatever it was that was effective for you in the beginning. Slower times can also be a good time to explore your opportunities for growth and look for new avenues for income. What is a new service or product you could sell to your target market? What other ideas for gaining clients have you not acted on?

Another important point to note is that the most effective way to increase the amount of money you make, and continue to be compensated with a competitive salary, is to give yourself a raise by increasing your fees. When you are an employee, your boss decides both when and by how much you will get a pay raise, usually based on your performance and the average annual pay raise for your industry and location. When you are your own boss, *you* are the one who has to decide this for yourself. You should also consider raising your fee as you gain more experience, get further training, become a published author, etc. Additionally, anytime you have a full load of clients, it's time to consider increasing your fees.

Conclusion

Your business exists only if you have customers willing to pay for your services. Like any new business, it might take some time before you become solvent. When you follow the principles outlined in this chapter and take on a paying client, this can be an incredibly exciting moment in your business. The first time you exchange money for services means you are now a professional in the field of applied sport psychology. Reflect on what allowed you to secure this first client, and repeat; watch your business grow and continue to build from there.

A Trainee's Perspective on Securing Work

Nicholas Kalustian, M.A., M.B.A., student at JFKU 2014–2017

Nicholas's goal is to start a mental training and performance consulting firm with colleagues in the San Francisco Bay Area. In addition to consulting, his career pursuits include coaching in men's volleyball at the elite and collegiate levels. Nicholas plans to focus his work with volleyball, golf, and basketball athletes and coaches. Nicholas can be reached at nkalustian13@gmail.com.

As I complete my graduate degrees, I realize there is much to consider as my entrepreneurial career begins. I have learned that as a businessperson it is imperative that you understand the market you are involved in and how that market can shift, not only day-to-day, but over a longer period of time as well. The way I perceive the business side of consulting is as a puzzle, and taking the time to put together the puzzle correctly is key to success. If a new consultant rushes in and throws the puzzle together, they will constantly be trying to squeeze pieces into the picture and it may not work out well. Taking the time to find the right pieces, putting them together thoughtfully, and creating the business you want to with the right values and ideals you believe in is important to achieving success as a new consultant.

Consulting means running your own practice and handling the business side of being an entrepreneur. Prior to opening your doors, you need to preview the business model, costs, pricing, and where you will find your clients. These can be daunting tasks. My coursework at JFKU allowed me to understand some of these aspects, such as how to value your worth and how business models vary across private practices. Just the thought of the many moving pieces that go into running a business, along with your actual client work, can seem like a lot.

One of my biggest challenges, and a main piece of consulting, is finding, securing, and charging clients. Networking can help get entrepreneurs started in building their business. People who have similar interests to you, or who are involved in a niche that you want to work in, can become stepping stones to securing work. I have connections in the sport of volleyball due to my coaching experience, and using those has allowed me to create opportunities for myself and my peers. For example, I was able to use my network to get a colleague in touch with a local volleyball team for an internship opportunity, which led to an ongoing working relationship. Not only did this networking benefit a colleague, but it was able to showcase the quality people in my network to the volleyball coach. This may encourage the coaches and my colleague to think of me for opportunities they may come across that I would be a good fit for. By supporting those in my network and building relationships, hopefully they will support me.

Another piece to the puzzle I've found important is staying organized, especially since consulting is not a typical *9 to 5* job. During my time as a student in the Sport Psychology Department, I became more aware that organization was not my number one quality. Through the support of colleagues, other professionals, supervisors, and my own research I have utilized my time to try different programs such as Google calendars, Evernote, and Mile IQ. By trying these out as a student, I am able to discover which are most beneficial so that I can be a prepared and organized professional who people want to hire.

Securing work in applied sport psychology is a big task. Students and young professionals must be aware of their own puzzle pieces to create a successful business. From there, they can work on those pieces with peer and professional support.

Reflective Questions and Activities for You to Consider Before You Proceed

- What excites you the most when thinking about working in the field of applied sport psychology?
- What questions do you still have and who can you reach out to for support and guidance?
- What values and beliefs hold you back from being comfortable accepting payment?
- How will you engage a client who doesn't have enough money, but really wants to contract your services?
- In three years' time, what do you want to be most known for in the field of applied sport psychology?

References

Aoyagi, M. W., Portenga, S. T., Poczwardowski, A., Cohen, A. B., & Statler, T. (2012). Reflections and directions: The profession of sport psychology past, present, and future. *Professional Psychology: Research and Practice, 43*(1), 32–38.

Blann, F. W., Shelley, G., & Gates, S. C. (2011). Marketing sport psychology consulting services. *Journal of Sport Psychology in Action, 2*(1), 33–52.

Collins, J. (2004). *Built to last: Successful habits of visionary companies.* New York, NY: Harper Collins.

Connole, I. J., Shannon, V. R., Watson II, J. C., Wrisberg, C., Etzel, E., & Schimmel, C. (2014). NCAA athletic administrators' preferred characteristics for sport psychology positions: A consumer market analysis. *Sport Psychologist, 28*(4), 406–417.

Fifer, A., Henschen, K., Gould, D., & Ravizza, K. (2008). What works when working with athletes. *The Sport Psychologist, 22*(3), 356–377.

Fitzpatrick, S. J., Monda, S. J., & Butters Wooding, C. (2015). Great expectations: Career planning and training experiences of graduate students in sport and exercise psychology. *Journal of Applied Sport Psychology, 28*, 14–27.

Horan, J. (2015). *The one page business plan for the creative entrepreneur.* Berkeley, CA: The One Page Business Plan Company.

Koch, R. (2008). *The 80/20 Principle: The secret to achieving more with less.* New York: Crown Business.

Kornspan, A. S., & Duve, M. A. (2006). A niche and a need: A summary of the need for sport psychology consultants in collegiate sports. *Annals of the American Psychotherapy Association, 9*(1), 19–25.

Lubker, J. R., Visek, A. J., Watson, J. C., & Singpurwalla, D. (2012). Athletes' preferred characteristics and qualifications of sport psychology practitioners: A consumer market analysis. *Journal of Applied Sport Psychology, 24*(4), 465–480.

Port, M. (2011). *Book yourself solid: The fastest, easiest, and most reliable system for getting more clients than you can handle even if you hate marketing and sales.* Hoboken, New Jersey: John Wiley and Sons, Inc.

Roper, E. A. (2002). Women working in the applied domain: Examining the gender bias in applied sport psychology. *Journal of Applied Sport Psychology, 14*, 53–66.

Weinberg, R. S., & Gould, D. (2015). *Foundations of sport and exercise psychology.* (6th ed.). Champaign, IL: Human Kinetics.

Winter, S., & Collins, D. J. (2016). Applied sport psychology: A profession? *Sport Psychologist, 30*(1), 89–96.

15 Marketing Yourself

How Do You Tell the World How Good You Are?

Brian Baxter and Rebecca Smith

When working as a consultant, contacting individuals and teams about being hired for work is only one way to approach marketing; it is also critical to find additional ways to promote oneself and one's services. Creating and maintaining a professional website is an important tool, as perusing practitioners' websites is one way that potential clients will determine if they will hire someone; the website is a first glimpse at what it might be like to work with a particular consultant. Social media is another tool that can allow a consultant to grow his or her name in the field. Twitter, Facebook, Instagram, and LinkedIn are examples of social media sites that professionals in the field are using. Tips for creating a presence and utilizing social media appropriately will be addressed. While a website and social media platforms will not guarantee that a professional gains clientele, when utilized well, these can be important marketing tools to take advantage of. Additional ways to market oneself as a consultant will be addressed, including newsletters, writing for publications, and placing ads in locations/publications most likely to reach the intended market. This chapter will help individuals decide which marketing strategies might be most effective for their business plan and goals.

Background Information on the Authors

Brian Baxter graduated with his MA in Sport Psychology from JFKU in 2004, and has been working in applied sport psychology ever since. He has a National C level coaching license from the United States Soccer Federation and has been coaching for over 20 years. He currently runs BaxterSports Summer Camps (www.baxtersports.com) as well as the Sport Psychology Institute Northwest (www.spinw.com) in Portland, OR. He is the author of "The Sports Mindset Gameplan: An Athlete's Guide to Building and Maintaining Confidence," and creator of the visualization program "Sports Mindset Audio." He can be contacted at brian@spinw.com.

Rebecca Smith also received her Master's Degree in Sport Psychology from JFKU. She is the Director of Complete Performance Coaching (www.completeperformance coaching.com) and the founder of PerformHappy. Rebecca specializes in mindset and performance coaching for youth athletes and teams. She has a background as a real estate broker, sales trainer, and gymnastics coach. She can be contacted at Rebecca@completeperformancecoaching.com.

Setting a Strong Foundation for Marketing

Before we go into detail about the *how tos* of marketing, there are some key elements that must be in place. It is imperative that a consultant have clarity around his or her ideal client before creating a marketing strategy. Who you will be marketing to? What are your offerings? How much will you charge? For the purpose of this chapter, we will assume that you are clear on who your ideal client is, as well as your goals, and you have a business plan (for more information on all of these topics, see Chapter 14). If not, please take some time to decide who you will be targeting with your marketing efforts, and what type of business you are looking to create. Renowned seller and motivator Zig Ziglar (2003) says, "I don't care how much power, brilliance or energy you have, if you don't harness it and focus it on a specific target and hold it there, you're never going to accomplish as much as your ability warrants" (p. 166).

Some consultants choose to cast a wide net, while some have a narrow focus on their niche. There are benefits and drawbacks to each approach. Whichever strategy you choose to adopt in our profession, it is important to meet the client where they are. In order to build a successful practice, your focus must be on the client (Kralj, 1994). What are their needs? What is their biggest problem that you are uniquely equipped to solve? What keeps them awake at night? When you understand the goals and needs of your ideal client, you can make effective choices about where to invest time and money into marketing. It is more important for you to understand the client than to tell them all about yourself and your academic degrees.

There are two main types of marketing: we will call them *active marketing* and *passive marketing*. Active marketing consists of networking, leveraging your existing relationships, and initiating direct contact with your ideal client. This is the process of going to your ideal client, letting them know you exist, and demonstrating how you can solve their problems. Active marketing requires energy, determination, and resilience. Passive marketing, on the other hand, is the process of building a presence that allows your ideal client to find you. This also requires resilience and determination. Good use of passive marketing tools will inspire athletes and teams to contact you or purchase your products. The downside of this type of strategy is the investment of time and money. In order to build a successful practice, both active and passive marketing should be built into your marketing strategy. Although the upcoming ideas would typically be employed when you're working as a consultant (not a trainee), you can be working on some of these pieces as you complete your degree and prepare to enter the field.

Chellie Campbell uses ships as a metaphor for marketing (Campbell, 2002) in the following passage:

> In the nineteenth century, the merchants in London built grand, tall-masted sailing ships. It would take many months, sometimes years, to build them. Then they would hire a crew, outfit the ship, and store provisions for the long sea voyage. One fine day, the ship would weigh anchor, hoist her sails, and sail out of London harbor, on her way to visit foreign ports, and trade for gold, jewels, silks, and spices. The trip would take many months—often years—and there were no communication lines open then: no ship-to-shore radio, no telegraph, no cellular telephones. Once the ship had sailed, the merchant could do nothing more; only wait for that future day when the ship would return, sailing into London harbor laden with treasure. On that day, the merchant's fortune was made. And that's where the expression "I'm waiting for my ship to come in" comes from.
>
> (p. 8)

Following the metaphor, by building great ships and sending new ones out consistently, you increase your chances of having a few of them come back to you full of gold. You never know when active or passive marketing efforts will pay off. The key is to create valuable content, and be consistent in getting the message out.

It is important to consider that, while active marketing techniques may not change significantly over time, passive marketing will continue to evolve as technology and society grow and change. If we were writing this book in 1987, we might tell you to take out an ad in the phonebook or the Yellow Pages. In 1997 we might briefly mention the wonders of the Internet if you had a modem. In 2007, a website was the way to go. In 2017 we are talking mobile optimization, and marketing your smartphone app or virtual courses. In 2027, who knows? Keeping that in mind, we will discuss the benefits of different social media platforms and ways to increase your visibility within your target market, as well as top tips and ethical considerations to be aware of. First, we will discuss the cornerstone of all online marketing efforts: the professional website.

As you read this chapter, notice these key themes and considerations that will come up frequently: 1) time vs. money vs. expertise. Your business plan will help you decide what to do yourself and what to delegate; 2) As technology changes, be sure to change with it. Successful business professionals are constantly evolving and keeping content fresh and up to date; 3) Use a combination of active and passive marketing tools to connect with your ideal client and build your practice.

Passive Marketing Tools

Website

Of all passive marketing tools at your disposal, a website is the cornerstone and most crucial for success. This is especially true for those of us in the service industry. We don't have a brick and mortar store, and we're not in the mall. So mental skills coaches are not getting any walk up business. Not only that, but people, by-and-large, are not yet 100% familiar with sport psychology and its benefits. So having a website is a versatile tool to show professionalism, credibility, and the quality of your work.

A good website will cover everything, from educating the public about sport psychology, to promoting your services and products, offering information about you, and ultimately getting people to hire you or purchase your products. In this section we will outline the benefits of having a website, tips on building and maintaining a website, must-have information, and extras to consider.

One of the great advantages of a solid website is that it provides great value for a relatively low investment. Whether you just have the basics, use it to sell your products, or even create an interactive online community, you have to start somewhere. For this chapter's purposes, we will assume you have a name for your business (whether it is your name or some creative company name), a logo, and graphic design work already done.

Considerations

When creating your website, here are a few questions for you to answer:

- How much time and money do you have to spend on *creating* your website?
- How much time and money do you have to spend to *maintain* your website?
- Do you have web building/maintaining skills, or will you hire someone to do it?

With the answers to those questions in mind, the first thing is to get a domain name and hosting service. There are currently several services out there, and this step is fairly easy. Just search for "best web hosting services" or something similar, and find one that will meet your needs.

The next step is web design; that is creating a website that is easy to use, attractive, and interesting with valuable content. There are several companies that can give you the tools to create your own. Websitesetup.org reports that about half of websites are created on WordPress, which is a platform for managing web content. Please note, we recommend using WordPress.org over WordPress.com. Generally, there are fewer costs and more control associated with WordPress.org. Both Brian's websites (www.spinw.com and www.baxtersports.com) and Rebecca's site (www.completeperformancecoaching.com) are on WordPress, and in our personal experience it is relatively easy to use.

If your budget allows, you can hire a professional to design, set up and/or maintain your site. Working with an expert who is knowledgeable about the latest trends and current programming information may save you money in the long run. Remember, you want the website to portray professionalism, credibility, trust, and quality; first impressions are important.

With your website structure in place, what should go on your site? Now that you have got your domain name and your logo, and your look and feel, let's talk content. Again, before you start filling your site with content, you must know your audience, your clientele, and the people who you want to hire you. Here are some general guidelines and ideas for how a good website is laid out. Most websites include a home page, about page, offerings/services page, blog, testimonials page, and contact page.

Home Page

As the old saying goes, you never get a second chance to make a first impression. The home page is your virtual elevator pitch. Let your prospective client know who you are and the benefits of the field of sport psychology. A dentist does not need to explain that they clean teeth, because everyone knows that. However, we have found that many people do not know exactly what sport psychology is, so it is important to explain the field, what you do, and how you can help clients succeed. The home page is a good place for photos, videos, current topics, and a *call to action*. The call to action offers a way for the reader to engage with you through the website. A couple of examples are: register for a workshop, schedule a session, opt-in to e-mail newsletter in exchange for free downloads, free e-book, etc.

About Page

This is the page on your website for biographical information about yourself. It explains more in-depth who you are and what do you do, with clear information about your qualifications, your credentials, professional memberships, and philosophy. In can also include your specialty, who you work with, and your motivation for being involved in the field of sport psychology.

Offerings/Services Page

This page lays out your methods and how you can help the athlete, team, coach, etc. Again, it is very important to know your clientele and provide clear options for your services. Common offerings are individual consulting sessions, workshops, team or group sessions, and more. Considerations are: How long are your sessions? Do you have a minimum number of sessions or a package of sessions? Do you meet in person, or by phone or video call? Are you going to post your rates?

Blog

Blog, as you may know, is short for web log. Many consultants write and keep a blog to showcase their writing and programs. This is your place to be the expert and relate current topics that are relevant to what you do and can be a part of your website. Writing frequent and interesting articles and opinions creates familiarity and trust with the reader. Writing a blog post can then be used to share on social media, or sent out in e-mail newsletters. One great benefit of blogging is that your articles are online and accessible through search engines like Google. For example, I (Brian) have had a couple of people reach out to me asking questions about an article I'd written and posted several years ago. Sometimes articles get interest, and sometimes they do not. Writing is a practice! Just like you will be telling your athletes, you will have success and you will have failures, just keep at it. In keeping with our themes, stay current and evolve over time.

Testimonials Page

Let your clients talk you up! You can promote yourself all you want, but it's nothing compared to someone else recommending your services. This one can be tricky because of confidentiality issues, but in our opinion it never hurts to ask. Some clients are fine with using their testimonials verbatim. Sometimes it's better to use the quote, taking out any identifying information, and using initials or a description of the athlete instead of their name. It's important that you stay on top of the ethical requirements of your governing association(s) (e.g. APA and AASP), and be sure to get a signed release before using anyone's words, name, or likeness in your marketing materials. We are not attorneys and recommend that you consult an attorney to craft the proper release forms to protect you and your business.

Contact Page

Okay, now they are interested and they like what you have had to say—give them an easy way to contact you. Phone number, e-mail address, e-mail contact form, and office address (if applicable) should go here. It is also good practice to have this on your home page or footer so that people have an easy time finding your contact information.

Those are the basics, and by no means an exhaustive list. You can also use your website to give access to more. Be creative and set yourself apart. Some extras typically can include: calendar of events, products, free resources, member login section, and links to social media (see next section).

Other Helpful Hints

Then there are extras to consider like online security, personalized e-mail, search engine optimization (commonly referred to as SEO), and extra features that you may want to pay for. You can also get a personalized e-mail that goes directly to your website and is typically free when you purchase your domain name. For example, brian@spinw.com or rebecca@ performhappy.com is more professional than brian19304@fakeemailaddress.com. Not only that, but sending out mass e-mailers (see p. 191) is easier and more effective when coming from personalized e-mails.

Once you have created your website, we would love to tell you that you are done, now kick back and wait for those calls and e-mails to start pouring in. However, remember this is a mix of active and passive marketing. You will need to keep content fresh, constantly updating your offerings, blog, events, and testimonials. This will keep giving your passive marketing audience a chance to get to know you, who you are, and what you do. Also, you will want to continually find ways to stay active and point people to your website—you do not want to point them to some out-of-date, stale site. Search engines are always changing their algorithm and what they're looking for, but it's safe to say that today Google is ranking sites higher that are current, active, and optimized for mobile devices.

Let's think about your website as a bridge between your active marketing efforts and your passive marketing. Remember, the website does not take the place of active marketing. Active marketing is going out and doing your work face to face: networking, utilizing your contacts, and talking about your business. After you have made personal contacts, let them know about your site. Put it on your business card, stationery, and other collateral. When you are using active marketing you may not get hired right away, but you want the contact to have a place to go when they need you next month or even a few years down the line. That's where it ties into the passive marketing elements.

For passive marketing, a website is not only helpful to give your active marketing contacts a place to go, it is a great way for people to find you who may have never heard of you or even sport psychology for that matter. Another passive marketing bonus is that you are not limited to the city or state you live in. You have access to the world wide web. For example, I (Brian) live in Oregon, but have worked individually with athletes from as far away as California, Iowa, and Vermont and sold my book all across the U.S. and even in England and other parts of Europe. I (Rebecca) also work with athletes from all over the U.S. and internationally using Skype and FaceTime, as well as doing group workshops live online.

Internet Advertising

When it comes to finding potential clients, it takes either time or money. If you can afford it, advertising on Google and social media can be extremely powerful to speed up your e-mail list growth and drive traffic to your blog or special offer. If you cannot, you will have to focus on posting regularly to your site and social media to slowly build your fan base.

Facebook and Google have sophisticated tools for targeting your ideal client for paid advertising. Groupon and Yelp are two examples of free advertising platforms. When paying for advertising, be sure to track your return on investment (ROI).

Before you place ads, remember your target audience. It's important to consider that, when people are using a search engine like Google, they are actively looking for a solution. What specific problem are you solving? On the other hand, when people come across your ad on Facebook, they are in a more passive state.

Internet advertising is constantly evolving. Before you start spending money, determine who you want to reach and what your objective is. Do you want to drive traffic to your site? Build your e-mail list? Sign people up for free consultations? Host a live event? Sell products? Based on your answers to those questions, you can start to build your ad strategy. If you are getting a good ROI, stick with it. If not, move on to something else.

Social Media

The Pew Research Center (2015) reports that 65% of adults use social networking sites, up from 7% in 2005. Social media is a powerful tool that can allow a consultant to grow his or her name in the field. Twitter, Facebook, Instagram, and LinkedIn are examples of social media sites that professionals in the field are using. Tips for creating a presence and utilizing social media appropriately will be addressed below. While a website and social media platforms will not guarantee that a professional gains clientele, when utilized well these can be important marketing tools to take advantage of.

Considerations

Social media and marketing technologies have already advanced since we started to write this chapter. So ask yourself these questions again: Who is my ideal client? What do they do in their free time? Do they spend time on social media? Which social media platform(s) are they on? Use the answers to these questions to decide which social media platforms to invest time and energy into. Be prepared to change your strategy as your ideal client's attention shifts to other outlets. Whichever social media platform you choose to focus on, we can recommend some best practices to help you make the most of your marketing efforts.

As mentioned previously (but worth noting again), this chapter is being written in 2017. The information in this section is current for today's trends and technology; however, this is sure to evolve and change over time. For example, as we write this, Facebook is the undoubted king of social media, with around 1.5 billion active users; however, my (Brian) 13-year-old son is not on it and I'm not sure if he will be when he's later in his teens or twenties, time will tell. He and his friends, however, are on Instagram (400 million users) and Snapchat (200 million).

As of the time of this writing, Statista (2017) lists the top social media sites by number of active users:

- Facebook—1.96 billion
- YouTube—1 billion
- Instagram—600 million
- Twitter—319 million
- Snapchat—300 million
- Pinterest—150 million
- LinkedIn—106 million

With all these choices, we'll go back to a principle we discussed previously in this chapter: know your audience. As you will see in the section below, different social media sites cater to different populations. When choosing which to use, and the content of your posts, consider your audience. Once you decide which social media platforms will best serve your prospective clients, the next step is to create a business-specific account for each. This allows you to advertise if you choose, and to avoid having personal posts dilute your professional message. That said, here are our thoughts on current social media and the pros and cons of each.

Facebook

According to Wallace (2013), of the 1.5 billion active Facebook users in 2013, over half of them are on the site daily. 25% of Facebook users check their page five times per day, and the average user is on Facebook for an average of 8.3 hours per week.

As you can see from the above stats, Facebook is the largest social media outlet by a considerable margin, so its biggest benefit is the potential number of people you can reach. This is also one of the downsides—with so many users and so many pages, it can become a bit saturated. However, we think having a Facebook page for your business is a no-brainer. Start out with a personal page, and from there you can create a business page. You can then start actively networking through your Facebook friends, then can *passively* network by posting interesting and relevant content, using hashtags (#), mentions (@), and replies. Be consistent and engaging. Offer a mix of information and stories, text, images, and video—both your own content and from other sources that your audience would find interesting. Over time, your goal should be to build the value of your business to the reader. If you like you can also purchase ads, which are fairly inexpensive and you can target specific audiences by age and interests. Not only can you gain likes and followers, but you can link back to your website and give people a way to contact you.

Twitter

According to Rosenstiel, Sonderman, Loker, Ivancin, and Kjarval, writing for The American Press Institute, "Those on Twitter also use the network heavily. About two thirds of Twitter users, 71%, say they use the network several times a day, another 12% daily and 12% several times a week." (2015, para 3).

Twitter is similar to Facebook except that tweets are limited to 140 characters, so you have to be brief (and at times a little clever). This shortness of length of posts is simultaneously the main pro and the main con of Twitter! It is not long enough to get complex and in-depth ideas out there, but it challenges you to get a point out succinctly. So, for example, you can take a quote from one of your writings to catch a reader's eye, and link to your article.

You can build on your passive marketing as people comment on and re-tweet your ideas. You can also re-tweet other people's tweets. Also, like in Facebook, you can purchase ads targeted to specific audiences based on their interests. You might consider a strategic hashtag that you use in all of your social media posts. The bigger your fan base, the more ships go out. This is a great tool for enlarging your sphere of influence and gaining a lucrative following.

Instagram

This is another popular social media platform, especially among younger users. According to Meeker (2015), Instagram is the most important social media outlet for teens. This is a great place to host challenges, do product giveaways, and build a following. What sets Instagram apart from the others is that it is photo-centric, so this one really is not about writing, though you can post photos with words on them, like quotes from famous athletes or even yourself.

Like Facebook and Twitter, you can use hashtags (#), tags (@), and replies to target specific audiences. Many consultants post photos of themselves speaking at events or some variety of sport related photos. You can use *stories* to share short videos with your audience throughout the day. Remember to consider your audience, and keep up with the trends. Consider that in ten years these teenagers will be young adults, and in 20 years they will likely have kids of their own. Be careful to maintain client confidentiality, and follow all current legal requirements before using photos of athletes or teams in social media posts or marketing materials.

LinkedIn

If you are looking to market to middle-aged professionals, LinkedIn is your best bet. According to Shin (2014), LinkedIn usage is especially high among college-educated professionals making $75,000 a year or more.

LinkedIn is similar to Facebook but more professional and business-centric. You can use it to connect with other sport psychology professionals as well as people in complementary fields (e.g. graphic designers, nutritionists, writers/editors, etc.). You can share your blog posts and join in discussions and groups. This is also a good place to market yourself to business performance coaching clients, or to find employment opportunities.

YouTube

This free video sharing website has the second highest number of active users of all social media platforms, with users watching around 6 billion hours of video every month. One common mistake with YouTube marketing is an attempt to make videos that appeal to everyone. The most effective videos are entertaining, informative, and most importantly they speak directly to a particular audience (Passman, 2014). Potential clients do not want to watch a series of sales pitches. Create a balance of information, education, entertainment, and well-placed calls to action. Remember, the client wants to know that you understand their problem. Next, show them that there is a solution. Finally, demonstrate that you are the key to implementing the solution. If you decide to use YouTube as part of your marketing strategy, you again have the choice: Do you have the time and resources to do it yourself, or will you hire someone to help you?

Snapchat

This mobile messaging app is used to share photos, videos, text, and drawings that self-destruct after a few seconds of being viewed. It has become hugely popular in a very short space of time, especially with people age 13–34. According to Edison Research (2016a), Snapchat has more users than Instagram, Twitter, or Pinterest, and it rivals Facebook among ages 12–24. This is a great platform to stay visible to your college-aged fans with new virtual products and incentives. If your ideal client is a high school or college athlete, this might be a good place to focus some marketing efforts.

Pinterest

This is a site that is part social media, part search engine. Pinterest allows people to pin pictures on a virtual bulletin board. These pictures are linked to web articles or shopping sites. It is a marketplace for idea sharing. It allows you to discover and bookmark creative ideas and information. People pin things like recipes, fashion ideas, home decor, landscape design, advice, resources, motivational quotes—you name it, someone is pinning it. If your target market is mothers of youth sport athletes, for example, you might want to share your articles to Pinterest. Edison Research (2016b) reports that 51% of moms use Pinterest.

Even if your ideal audience is not youth sport moms, Pinterest is still a resource worth paying attention to. If you have a blog, use compelling images and pin them. Pinterest drives lots of traffic to many different types of sites, and can help boost traffic to your blog, site, or product.

Live Video

With the added emphasis on video in marketing in 2017, Facebook Live can be a great tool for increasing your following. You can do live mini-trainings, run challenges, and do live question and answer sessions to add value to current or potential clients and get your name out there. You can also broadcast live on YouTube. Google Ads in conjunction with

YouTube videos can help you build your brand, sell a product, and/or gain web traffic. I (Rebecca) have had many people reach out for consultations after they had already watched videos, read articles, and tuned in for live trainings. These offerings can set you apart from others in the field, as well as building familiarity and trust with potential clients.

Best Practices

Whatever your social media platform of choice, there are some best practices we recommend in the following sections.

Be Consistent

Just like your website, the more active you are, and the more consistently you update content, the better. Foley (2015) talks about the rule of repetition in marketing. He says, "any marketing communication is most effective when it is repeatedly brought to the attention of your target market." Foley goes on to explain that repetition builds familiarity, credibility, and the image of stability. Additionally, people are bombarded by distractions in their lives and online. It may take several impressions to make an impact. People need to be reminded that you exist in order to think of you when their performance hits a wall. Although now might not be the right time for your ideal client to contact you, when they decide they want to pursue mental training, you will be the one they turn to because they feel they already know and like you.

Give Useful Information

Remember, your focus should remain on your client. What content do *they* find valuable? Where are you getting the best feedback? Ask your fan base what they like and give them more of it. Do not publish something just because someone else is doing it. Ask your ideal client what they want to read a blog post or article on, then write it. Help them solve their problems and add value for them. That is how you will earn trust and begin building a relationship with your ideal client. Such a relationship will ideally turn into a client or a referral if you have demonstrated your ability to understand their needs and solve their problems. Remember that you can also share useful information that was not created or written by you to add further value.

Communicate Effectively

There are numerous resources available to help you write your marketing copy. Copy is the words you use to get your message across (e.g. the words on your website, ads, blog headlines, e-mails). You can learn to write effectively, or hire someone to do it for you. If you are writing for yourself, here are some ideas to consider: Speak directly to the person who will be hiring you—this may be the client, their parent, coach, athletic department, etc. Use the voice you would use if you were talking to this person face-to-face. Is your ideal customer an adult or a child? Are they well educated? A business professional? Does this person prefer statistics and facts or do they want to hear a joke? Again, it is imperative that you know who your ideal customer is so that you can communicate to him or her effectively.

Call to Action

After you have established that you understand your ideal customer's needs, let them know you have the solution to their problems. This is a place where consultants can get hung up.

Some people in helping professions like ours hesitate to ask for the sale. You may need to practice imagery of a successful call to action to build confidence. Know your offerings, trust that you have what they need, then present it to them.

Consider what we in the sport psychology and mental training fields do for a moment. We help people perform better. We make dreams come true. We make the impossible possible. Really, selling is helping. Unless you sign them up for a session, you cannot help them. There should be a call to action in every blog post and on every page of your website (e.g. "call me to schedule a consultation" or "join the e-mail list"). Social media and search engines direct them there. Once they get there, tell them what to do.

Remember Professionalism

It is possible to invest a lot of time and money building a social media presence and following. Make sure you maintain your professional image by keeping business and professional accounts separate. Check your privacy settings on personal accounts in order to project an image you would like prospective clients to see online.

Writing and Other Forms of Passive Marketing

In this section we will expand on *writing as the expert* and also explore more ways to deliver your content in order to passively market your skills. Creating a website, keeping a blog, and posting on social media all require you to write as the expert. You have to convey ideas about sport psychology to the audience to make it understandable and compelling and motivating.

Blog

As mentioned in the website section, this is a cornerstone of the writing process. Posting regularly to your blog is a way to keep you current and allow people to follow what you are doing. Blogging consistently (e.g. once a week or once a month) is preferred. Also, use your website, newsletter, and social media platforms to distribute your blog articles.

E-mail Newsletter

As we write this, it is not uncommon for consultants to send out a regular e-mail newsletter to their followers. The e-mail newsletter is another way to get your content (blog posts, videos, upcoming events, tips, etc.) to potential clients. One of the pros of an e-mail newsletter is that it is sent out regularly. Even if people don't read it, they see your name once a month. If they do read it, they will see your articles, events and helpful tips. Make sure to use compelling headlines and send relevant, helpful information to increase your e-mail open rates and keep your list warm.

E-mail Autoresponder

When someone opts in to your e-mail list, you can set up a series of e-mails that can send valuable information, resources, and calls to action at pre-determined intervals. A well-crafted autoresponder series can convert someone from a lead to a paying customer and a raving fan. These types of sequences can be set up through e-mail marketing providers such as MailChimp, ConvertKit, or Drip.

Guest Columnist/Blogger for Publications

Consultants are not limited to writing for their own website and social media pages. Think outside the box, *be the expert* and write for others too. Reach out to publications that appeal to your ideal client and write high-quality articles. Whether you are looking to attract performance psychology clients, business clients, youth clients, etc., identify the blogs and publications that these people read, and provide them with quality articles. I (Rebecca) was able to turn two graduate school papers into popular blog posts with a little editing for simplification. As you finish up your schooling, you might want to keep this in mind. You may already have quality content you can pitch to another site.

Sport psychology is an emerging field, and one that people find interesting. Publishers of websites, newspapers, and magazines are always on the lookout for interesting content for their readers. Some benefits are that you get to contribute useful information to people, place yourself as the expert, and broaden your audience. Another benefit is that you can do all this for low cost. If you take out an advertisement, you are paying money and maybe people will look at your ad, maybe they won't. But if you are providing an expert contribution, to a reputable publication, it's likely to be more compelling for the reader.

How do you get into writing for others? Start with your active network – do you know anyone in media? Utilize those contacts and inquire about writing a column. When reaching out to an editor, show them that you are paying attention to the types of content they like to publish. Emphasize the potential benefit to their audience, rather than making it all about you. Send a sample of what you can do (if you already write a blog, you can use that as a resume of sorts). And, as always, figure out who the audience is and write for them.

Interviews

Any time you are featured as an expert interviewee on TV, radio, a podcast, etc., you can expect your web traffic to spike. This is another great way to increase exposure, authority, and make important contacts. Similar to print media, these other media types look for interesting interviews and commentary. Rather than waiting for the hosts or reporters to find you, we recommend you reach out to them as well. I (Rebecca) recommend finding out as much as possible about the journalist before reaching out. Make an impact by showing them that you have done your homework. 64% of writers think it's important to establish a personal connection before pitching to them (Polger, 2014). AASP also has a media list you can sign up for where journalists can search for people in their area. Make an effort to build rapport before you ask them to cover you or your company. Focus your pitch on what's in it for them, and be respectful of their time.

Ethical Guidelines and Considerations

There are a few ethical considerations to be aware of when using a website, e-mail, and social media for marketing purposes. The primary issues to consider are spam laws, confidentiality, the use of testimonials, and proper representation. Keep in mind, we are not attorneys and it is wise to contact an attorney for advice regarding best practices on these matters. Additionally, we are based in the U.S., so make sure you know the laws of your country if you are outside the U.S.

Spam Laws

There are varying ideas of what is okay in the world of e-mail marketing. As of 2016, the Federal Trade Commission (FTC) provides the following compliance guidelines for the use of e-mail for commercial messages, according to the CAN-SPAM Act of 2003: 1) Don't use false or misleading header information, 2) don't use deceptive subject lines, 3) identify the message as an ad, 4) tell recipients where you're located (you are required to include a physical address), 5) tell recipients how to opt-out, 6) honor opt-out requests promptly, 7) monitor what others are doing on your behalf.

E-mail marketing companies like MailChimp often provide links to current guidelines for the ethical use of e-mail to communicate with prospects. Be sure to stay on top of current laws. These are likely to continue to evolve to protect consumers from unsolicited bulk e-mails (a.k.a. spam). Before sending an e-mail marketing campaign, be sure to take necessary precautions to avoid legal repercussions.

Testimonials

One essential part of your professional website is the testimonial section. Before posting anyone's praises on your behalf, ensure that former clients understand and give you full written permission to use their words in your marketing. Especially when working with minors, it is important to have a release form signed by a parent/guardian. In most cases, it is a good practice to protect the client's identity when displaying testimonials. Also, know the current ethical standards set forth by AASP and APA, or your country's governing bodies, in regard to solicitation and use of testimonials.

Photo Use

When using stock photos (or any photos you did not take) for marketing purposes, make sure you have the rights to use them. If you do not have a license to use an image, you put yourself at risk for a lawsuit. When you purchase stock photos, you pay for a usage license. Pay attention to the requirements of the license. For example, some professional photos require a credit to the photographer every time you use the image, even if you purchase a license to use the image commercially. Be aware of your usage rights (e.g. billboards, mass printing or reproduction, resale, one-time use, etc.) to avoid repercussions. Do not simply Google photos; use stock photo websites for your photos (some are free and others require payment).

Representation

Finally, it is important to avoid misrepresentation regarding your professional title. For example, take care not to give the impression that you are a licensed psychologist if you are not, and make sure you are working within your boundaries of not only competence, but also training and qualifications (see Chapter 10 for further discussion on title usage).

Conclusion

Throughout the course of this chapter we have discussed the elements of a passive marketing strategy. This is a broad overview, not intended to replace the advice of a professional marketing strategist or lawyer. Some key themes and considerations have come up frequently in our discussion. First, you will want to consider whether you will invest *time* or *money* into your passive marketing strategy. In many cases, new professionals will choose to dedicate lots of time to designing and maintaining a website, creating content, and building an online presence. Once you have had some success, these might be activities to delegate in order to spend more time on active marketing and client services. Your business plan and budget will help you decide what to do yourself, and what to delegate. Finally, we recommend a combination of active and passive marketing tools to connect with your ideal clients and build your practice.

As technology changes, be sure to change with it. Successful business professionals are constantly evolving and keeping content fresh and up to date. Be consistent and resilient; send ships out every day. Add value to your passive audience and do good work. It is only a matter of time before your ships will return, hopefully full of clients and teams eager to benefit from your services.

A Trainee's Perspective on Marketing Yourself

Dafna Aaronson, M.A., student at JFKU 2014–2016

Dafna is a Mental Skills Coach based in Chicago. She specializes in working with elite athletes, teams, and athletic departments developing teamwork, culture, and communication. Dafna's holistic approach promotes full development as a performer and individual, building awareness, confidence, adaptive thinking, stress-energy management, leadership, attentional control, and imagery. As a mother of two athletes, her philosophy is underscored by an individualized and collaborative style, emphasizing a growth mindset and harnessing passion and joy in the process as critical pillars of success. She currently works for the NY Mets, developing mental skills curricula for players and coaches, and has developed a character analytics model supporting scouting and performance analytics. Her website is www.besportsminded.com, and her Twitter handle is @DafnaAaronson. She can be contacted at daaronson@email.jfku.edu

Delving into the online marketing world was daunting. I was not sure how to balance creating and maintaining a website, Twitter, or Instagram account with school and other priorities. When starting a new practice, we all recognize some form of online marketing (executed well) is better than none. How to build across various dynamic platforms, and engage effectively, was uncharted territory for me.

Recognizing a website will mature with my practice, the initial goal was connecting people visiting the site to my philosophy and, through some initial blog posts and service descriptions, demonstrate professionalism and value. I knew I would have to outsource website development. I asked friends for web designer references, and ultimately used an app that had designers bid on my project. The app "Thumbtack" proved to be the most cost effective method, and with cost in mind I had to prioritize how content was featured. Other unforeseen costs included paying for a domain name and security for the website. The investment fueled my motivation to construct a great website. Costs may exceed your initial budget but, if you are committed, continue being led by passion not despair. Preceding roll out there were several months of testing, reviewing, and revising. Launching the website was exciting, validating, and symbolized my commitment toward achieving my goals. I find the website has served as a great extension to a handshake or brief introduction.

Also relevant was creating content with high SEO value. Search engines will index your website or account more favorably using key phrases, keywords, and links. Writing an "About" or "Bio" page was another area where I had to step outside my comfort zone and highlight past and recent achievements I otherwise would not mention. One way to view the description is a means to connect and relate, not brag. Feature your philosophy and promoting others' work. This means highlighting other professionals', colleagues', athletes', or peoples' (including outside the sports world) work you admire to deliver a great story or message. Maintaining the website offered me the challenge of learning something new. Like cleaning your room—you need to periodically reorganize, de-clutter, and tidy up!

Reflecting back, speaking with other professionals and peers as well as seeking out educational opportunities were keys to framing an online marketing strategy. The JFKU Master's Program and the AASP conference offered many opportunities to learn from and engage with professionals and peers, many of whom navigated similar social media waters. The Master's applied project I did promoted a methodical template for synthesizing marketing streams. Talking through my goals post-graduation with my advisor revealed the next phase in my online marketing strategy would be a Twitter account. Now, I felt outdated. Collectively with classmates and my advisor, I was provided a well-rounded, supportive feedback loop for developing a professional Twitter account. Already having a website encouraged me to shed some introverted tendencies, and begin interacting with the prevalent sport psychology Twitter community. I conducted research to better understand the basics for tweeting, hashtags, and retweeting, and my initial plan structured topics for daily posts according to current and future target markets.

More recently, I created an Instagram account (I also have a business Facebook page, however, that was required as part of creating an Instagram-validated professional account). I continue working out some of the kinks in linking all three. Posting daily can be challenging when cognizant of your followers and their interests. Creating content in advance helped, as has scheduling a time in my calendar to post. Focusing on quality content and linking my network and target market creates pressure to represent myself appropriately and distinctively with each post or blog. The responsibility incentivizes me to be creative and offer people who visit my social media sites something they emotionally connect with and want to share, ultimately building virtual rapport.

Reflective Questions and Activities for You to Consider Before You Proceed

- Who is your ideal client? Spend some time getting clarity on the following questions:

  o What are his/her needs? What is his/her biggest problem? How do you solve it?

  o What social media platforms does he/she frequent?

- What will you invest in your passive marketing strategy? Time, money, or both?
- How can you remain ethical and professional with your marketing plan?

References

Campbell, C. (2002). *The wealthy spirit: Daily affirmations for financial stress reduction.* Naperville, IL: Sourcebooks.

Edison Research. (2016a, April). Americans still prefer Facebook, but Snapchat surges 12–24. Retrieved from www.edisonresearch.com/americans-still-prefer-facebook-snapchat-leads-12-24/

Edison Research. (2016b, May). Moms and Media 2016. Retrieved from www.edisonresearch.com/wp-content/uploads/2016/05/Moms-and-Media-2016-Report.pdf

Foley, M. (2015). *The rule of repetition: How it's crippling your marketing efforts if you're not using it* [Web log post]. Retrieved from www.frugalmarketing.com/dtb/repetitionmktg.shtml

Kralj, M. M. (1994). Understanding your marketing niche. *Consulting Psychology Journal: Practice and Research, 46*(1), 92–93. doi:10.1037/h0092613

Meeker, M. (2015). *2016 Internet trends report.* Retrieved from www.kpcb.com/internet-trends

Passman, A. (2014, May). Making a splash on YouTube takes risk, creativity, planning and luck: To really leverage the video site, putting up a few of the CU's latest commercials is not enough. *Credit Union Journal, 18*(16), 1.

Pew Research Center. (2015). *Social media usage.* Retrieved from www.pewinternet.org/2015/10/08/social-networking-usage-2005-2015/

Polger, O. (2014, November). *Webinar recap: 500 writers and editors on how to pitch.* Retrieved from www.buzzstream.com/blog/how-to-pitch-for-pr.html

Rosenstiel,T., Sonderman, J., Loker, K. Ivancin, M., & Kjarval, N. (2015, Sept 1). *How people use Twitter in general.* Retrieved from www.americanpressinstitute.org/publications/reports/survey-research/how-people-use-twitter-in-general/

Shin, L. (2014, June 26). *How to use LinkedIn: 5 smart steps to career success.* Retrieved from www.forbes.com/sites/laurashin/2014/06/26/how-to-use-linkedin-5-smart-steps-to-career-success/#2a97d2446292

Statista. (2017, April). *Global social media ranking 2017 | Statistic.* Retrieved from www.statista.com/statistics/272014/global-social-networks-ranked-by-number-of-users/

Wallace, D. (2013). *Why every business should use Facebook* [Web log post]. Retrieved from www.searchenginejournal.com/every-business-use-facebook/71281/

Ziglar, Z. (2003). *See you at the top.* Gretna, LA: Pelican Publishing Company.

16 Using Technology in Practice

How Do You Stay Connected?

Trey McCalla and Sean-Kelley Quinn

Technological advancements are rapidly evolving and are changing the way that individuals interact with one another. It continually becomes easier and easier for individuals to communicate, no matter the distance between them. Various innovations have resulted in a global e-society that often expects information at a moment's notice. Applied sport psychology is not impervious to these advancements, and in many ways the field is better off as a result of various innovations. It is now not only possible, but often expected, that clients and professionals can continue to do their work together remotely through the use of video conferencing and other tools, even when the two parties are geographically separated. Connected Consulting is the use of technology for the purpose of applied sport psychology/mental skills consulting. While these innovations are exciting and potentially impactful, practitioners within the field need to ensure they have competence with various technologies and they also need to ensure they consider a bevy of ethical and practical considerations, which will be touched on in this chapter.

Background Information on the Authors

Trey McCalla is a High Performance Mental Skills Specialist. He graduated from JFKU with an M.A. in Sport Psychology and a Graduate Certificate in Sport and Exercise Performance. He is a Certified Consultant through AASP and is currently a Master Resilience Trainer and Performance Expert in the Ready Resilient program for the United States Army. In his private consulting practice, and stemming from his JFKU internship with Red Bull North America, Inc., Trey works with professionals and amateurs (locally and remotely) in action sports—including freestyle skiing and snowboarding, base jumping, and downhill ski racing. He also works in traditional sports arenas with baseball, golf, volleyball, and tennis. He is also a supervisor and adjunct faculty member at JFKU. Trey can be contacted at gmccalla@jfku.edu.

Sean-Kelley Quinn is a Mental Conditioning Consultant with elite experience working with athletes from some of the U.S.'s top performance venues. A graduate of UC Davis in Human Development, Sean also earned his M.A. Degree in Sport Psychology from JFKU. He is a Certified Consultant with AASP and has obtained thousands of hours working with clients throughout the country from diverse backgrounds (in person and remotely), including professionals in baseball, football, basketball, soccer, tennis, and golf, as well as executives from a variety of top corporations. He is currently the Director of Mental Conditioning at Moawad Consulting Group in Scottsdale, Arizona. Sean can be contacted at seankelley.quinn@gmail.com.

Our Connected World

In 1929, Frigyes Karinthy proposed a unique hypothesis that any two individuals, anywhere in the world, could be connected through at most five other acquaintances (Wikipedia, 2016). John Guare then wrote a play on the basis of Frigyes' hypothesis; this concept became a worldwide phenomenon commonly known as *six degrees of separation* and has been a topic of great intrigue among researchers and parlor-game enthusiasts alike. What is of particular interest to us though is that the world of *six degrees of separation* has now been reduced to nearly "*three and a half degrees of separation*" (Edunov, Diuk, Filiz, Bhagat, & Burke, 2016). The explanation is simple—we now live in a technological world with a vastly greater number of ways to be connected.

The ways we can stay connected span across different mediums and different devices. The creation of the Internet opened a veritable Pandora's box for supplying access to information and different ways in which to access that information. With information comes creation, and with creation comes innovation. The way we share information today has changed dramatically from decades past as it continues to develop at a wondrous and expansive rate. Think back 15 years to what type of devices you, your friends, or your family had, and how those devices were connected. For accessing the Internet, you had to be hard-wired in, and dial-up was a popular way in which to connect. Cell phones were starting to become more available, but were not commonplace; people were still using pagers as a way to learn that someone wanted to get in touch with them. Times have changed, and today accessibility to the Internet and cell phones are widespread.

It is estimated that, as of February 2017, there are just under 3.6 billion Internet users worldwide, which is nearly half of the world's population (Internet Live Stats, 2017). How an Internet user is defined by Internet Live Stats is an "individual who can access the Internet, via computer or mobile device, within the home where the individual lives." The number of users in specific countries certainly varies based on socioeconomic and other factors but, to give you a small understanding of some specific statistics, 88.5% of the United States population is a connected Internet user, and in the United Kingdom is it nearly 93% of the population, with the largest increase in the world during the past year in India with a growth of 30.5% of its population (Internet Live Stats, 2017).

While the statistics regarding Internet users are monumental, cell phone users have an even larger outreach. Statista (2017) estimates that, in 2017, there are 4.77 billion cell phone users worldwide. Anderson (2015) of the Pew Research Center found that, in 2015, of the cell phone users in the United States, 92 % of adult Americans owned a cell phone, with 68% owning a smartphone, and in the age range from 18–29 an astounding 98% owned cell phones, with 86% owning a smartphone. Yet cell phones are not the only way to stay connected with people. As we know, computers have always been a way to stay connected, and with recent technological advancements computers have the capacity to connect with people in the same way a cell phone does. Tablets, a device developed more recently, are another way of connecting with those near and far. Again, the Pew Research Center (Anderson, 2015) found that, in 2015, in the United States, 73% of all Americans owned a computer and 45% owned a tablet, and in the age range of 18–29 78% owned a computer and 50% owned a tablet.

While the statistics above are impressive, what is their significance for us in sport psychology? We have become a world in which having the ability to be connected is of vital importance, whether for professional or personal purposes. Yet this idea should come as no surprise. The need to stay connected has been around for quite some time, just not in the same capacity as today. Teleconference calls were the main platform in the past for businesses to connect a large group of people that reside in various locations. While teleconferencing is still a widely-used tool among businesses, there are now various options for how businesses choose to teleconference. The use of videoconferencing is becoming more commonplace as the preferred way to connect. Videoconferencing allows a more intimate interaction with those members that are not centrally located because they not only hear each other, but see each other as well.

The reason this idea of using technology in applied sport psychology becomes important is because, as you enter into the field, you will need to be available to your clients and technology is the way to be available. Connectivity is availability. Clients will travel and you will travel. Having common ground on using technology as a way to keep connected will not only allow for you and your clients to have a strong relationship, but for you to have the ability to grow and expand your consulting practice.

How Does Consulting Through Technology Work?

In October 2007, Habersoth, Parr, Bradley, Morgan-Fleming, and Gee (2008) entered the keyword "counseling" into Google and came back with results of over 66 million hits. We replicated this process in February 2017 and the results came back with 170 million hits! Though what we do in our profession is not specifically counseling, this demonstrates the growing interest in or need for seeking out helping professions, which is what we do for our clients in their quest for high performance. And with that many hits from a general Google search, there is a large audience we can reach.

When we talk about doing applied sport psychology through technology, there are many terms often discussed such as web-based therapy, e-therapy, cybertherapy, computer-mediated interventions, online therapy (or counseling), and remote consulting (Barak, Klein, & Proudfoot, 2009). As you can see, a few of the terms are closely related, while others speak to an entirely different type of work. For the purpose of this chapter and perhaps future use in the field, we have decided to coin the term *Connected Consulting* to speak to the use of technology for the purpose of applied sport psychology/mental skills consulting. We feel the aforementioned terms do not fully encompass the outreach technology has, and Connected Consulting is a double meaning for 1) being connected to the client via technology but also 2) on a more personal level, of being there with the client, in the trenches, as best you can, even when not with them in the same room.

That being said, what exactly does Connected Consulting mean? Connected Consulting helps to supplement face-to-face (FTF) consulting by providing increased access on the basis of necessity or convenience through cognitive, affective, behavioral, or systematic intervention strategies, that address wellness, personal growth, or career development (National Board for Certified Counselors [NBCC], 2005). This allows for a broadening of the scope and diversity of opportunities for approaching and reaching out to different clientele, and treating of diverse problems (Barak et al., 2009). When engaging in Connected Consulting, it is vital to understand how the interactions can work. The NBCC (2005) discusses how the interactions can be synchronous or asynchronous, with "synchronous interaction occur[ring] with little or no time gap in between the responses of the [consultant] or the client . . . [and] asynchronous interaction occur[ring] with a gap in time between responses of the [consultant] and the client" (p. 2).

In theory, the idea of Connected Consulting is a utopian practice for applied sport psychology. You have an ability to reach a large audience to supplement standard FTF consulting and can use creative strategies to improve health and performance. Why would someone *not* want to include such services in their consulting? A practitioner might be hesitant because there are many intricacies to using technology for Connected Consulting. As the AASP ethical guidelines state,

AASP members should be sensitive to the needs and interests of their client(s) and should only make the decision to incorporate specific forms of technology in their professional practice with the consent of their client(s), and only once the client fully understands the strengths and weaknesses pertaining to the specific medium of [contact].

(Association of Applied Sport Psychology [AASP], 2011, section 26, b).

Thus, it is vital to clarify with your clients whether or not they have an openness to Connected Consulting if it is a service you ultimately wish to provide in your consulting. You may find some clients have no interest in using Connected Consulting even if you do offer it, but you will discover their answer through your intentional questioning as you discuss working with the client.

Types of Connected Consulting

When discussing the different types of Connected Consulting, it is important to understand the various mediums of communication that can be based on what is read in text, what is heard from audio, or what is seen and heard in video (NBCC, 2005). What follows is a brief summary of the various types of Connected Consulting (some of which will probably be very familiar to you) and then we are going to illustrate ways to engage in Connected Consulting in your practice.

Email, Web Pages and Blogging

Starting with the most common medium of Connected Consulting, email has been a heavily used source to maintain contact when there is distance between the practitioner and client. As the Internet continued to flourish, other mediums began to take hold. Web pages are a source that can be considered part of Connected Consulting. While not connecting directly with one client, information described through a web page can initiate a consulting relationship in which a potential client learns some information and can reach out for continued support. A prime example of such is blogging or written contributions. Whether it is written specifically for your personal web page or a contribution piece for a company, you are able to instill knowledge and skills to a wide audience with your words. Along the lines of web-based outreach, a newer developed entity is cloud sharing services. It involves the ability to provide your clients accessibility to tools such as worksheets, journals, etc. that you may not be able to supply at a moment's notice. Dropbox, Inc. is an example of such a service where you can store these tools and share a link with the client to access and update as needed or suggested.

Social Media

Use of social media is newer, but still a well-known method of keeping connected. Social media, a primary cause in the reduction of the degrees of separation, reaches a vast audience and, much like written contributions, you can dictate a message to deliver to your audience. Common uses are Twitter and Facebook, but there are many other avenues to pursue (see Chapter 15 in this book for more information on how to utilize social media). In particular, using podcasts has blossomed as a way to share clients' stories (obviously with their approval) and to express through audio what you may not be able to express in written words.

Instant Messaging Services

Instant messaging services, such as AOL Instant Messenger and Facebook Messenger, are another way to connect with your clients. This form of communication is more synchronous (real-time) than email. The ability to write back and forth with near immediate responses allows for you to be able to, in theory, have a consultation session anywhere, anytime. These chat services (as well as texting) can be used on an individual basis one-on-one, or also as a group, to bring together a larger audience to discuss a topic or idea.

Phone Calls and Texting

Talking on the phone has continued to be a valuable way of staying connected. Whether it be a cell phone or landline (less common in personal use), this provides an opportunity to speak directly and synchronously to your client when necessary. Voicemail can be set up to make sure that, if you are unavailable, a message can still be delivered. With cell phone use though, you can take connecting one step further—text messaging. With immediacy of contact and ease of use, text messaging provides unique opportunities for more frequent, spontaneous, and casual interactions with your clients; a connected presence (Zizzi & Schmid, 2012). Text messaging continues to develop as applications for cell phone devices and use of emojis has become prevalent, for example, in the Whatsapp application. Smiley faces and thumbs up can convey simply in one image what would normally require the typing of multiple words. They can, however, also be easily misinterpreted.

Videoconferencing

Finally, as mentioned above, videoconferencing has been utilized in the business world for some time. That idea is the same with sport psychology and mental skills consulting. There are a variety of video services you can use to hold a session with a client or group, with Skype, Zoom, and FaceTime being primary applications. This style of service differs from all others by giving the closest representation to FTF consulting, because the video allows to you to see the client(s).

Overall, it is imperative that, as you explore Connected Consulting, you consider the options available and what fits best in your practice. By no means is there a requirement as to which options you should have, but make sure to give yourself a fighting chance to connect using various means. Each option offers different ways to connect with clients (actual or potential) and you will want to reflect on and understand the significance it can have on your outreach to those clients and how you will ultimately connect with them.

Effectiveness of Connected Consulting

While there is not a plethora of research on the effectiveness of Connected Consulting in the applied sport psychology world, there is a steady amount stemming from the counseling field. The research shows that, whether the counseling interventions are for smoking cessation (Schneider, Schwartz, & Fast, 1995), anxiety (Cohen & Kerr, 1998), bulimia nervosa (Mitchell, et al., 2008), other various treatment groups (Day & Schneider, 2002), or session impact and alliance between a therapist and client (Reynolds, Stiles, & Grohol, 2006), the consensus is that the idea of Connected Consulting shows equal, if not greater, results in overall success outcome and client participation than FTF consulting. We could therefore infer that the same might be true for sport psychology/mental skills applied work.

Finn and Barak (2010) reported that 74% of surveyed counselors were satisfied with their experience in their connected counseling services. Yet they discussed that, between

FTF and connected counseling, 90% of those counselors do not work online with clients they have previously seen FTF, 93% did not work with clients online and FTF at the same time, and 93% did not see FTF clients that they have previously seen online. The numbers are alarming because of not only a strong amount of evidence showing the success of using Connected Consulting, but counselors refusing to utilize both approaches—seeing it as one or the other. Barak et al. (2009) discuss that many of the studies show that close, empathetic, warm, and allied relationships can be formed through the various uses of technology. The NBCC (2005) expands on barriers such as being far from service provision, geographic separation of a couple, or limited physical mobility as a result of a disability, all broken down through the use of Connected Consulting. Finally, additional advantages include having more time to think, the power balance seeming more equal between the consultant and client, and clients being more focused and expressive (Bambling, King, Reid, & Wegner, 2008). As the research continues to emerge regarding Connected Consulting, it illustrates how valuable this approach can be in your own practice.

Challenges to Connected Consulting

With how effective Connected Consulting can be, it is not without its own challenges. These challenges can stem from different sources including self-knowledge, access to and use of technology, and ethical considerations. Habersoth et al. (2008) discovered a list of common concerns in utilizing Connected Consulting, ranging from technological barriers, counseling without verbal and visual cues, clinical concerns, time and content issues, and theoretical approaches. While the concerns above may not be present in each medium of connection, they are important to review and to understand how you can counter any challenges you are presented with. Some are addressed in the next section, and some are addressed in the section further below titled "Beginning a Connected Consulting relationship."

Technological Barriers

In relation to technological barriers, this is a multi-dimensional challenge. Firstly, it begins with whether or not you or your client have the means and the ability to use the technological tools. Perhaps a client does not have a cell phone, or you do not have a working computer. Situations can be infinite, but each person must have the ability (skills) and the means (funds) to connect. Second, once connected, you must have basic technological competencies to troubleshoot software and hardware problems (Habersoth et al., 2008). This idea is further annotated in the AASP ethical guidelines: "AASP members should only incorporate the various forms of technology in their professional and scientific work in which they have appropriate technical and practical competencies, and when such technology does not subject another party to harm or discomfort" (AASP, 2011, section 26, a). Adding to that challenge, you also must be patient and understanding if you encounter a client who is unfamiliar with certain technologies. A third and final challenge is having a backup plan in case your primary medium of connecting does not work. Cell phones die. Internet connection can be lost. Best practice is to discuss with your client ahead of time what the best way to connect is, but also to establish how to reconnect if a technical snafu occurs.

Using Counseling Skills Without Seeing Body Language

We all know and have learned that body language is paramount in communication; it is not what someone says but how they say it. This is something that can easily be lost depending on which option you utilize to connect with your client. Habersoth et al. (2008) comment on how, through online chat, losing access to clients' vocal tones, body language, or eye contact created a sense of loss of control. These important elements were countered by attempting to visualize the client, using symbols to bracket affect, and being aware that what is written may be perceived as literal by the client; so carefully constructing statements to avoid as much ambiguity as possible that the client can use to fuel any self-fulfilling prophecies (Anthony & Nagel, 2010; Habersoth et al., 2008).

The asynchronous timing that can occur between responses in a connected session using technologies such as email, texting and even faster connections using Skype or FaceTime can have its challenges, but also its advantages. At times, the time lag between responses can significantly slow the pace of a session (Habersoth et al., 2008). The content you cover over the course of 50 minutes may be covered in less time in a FTF or more synchronous connection. Yet, that lapse can be utilized to help build your counseling skills, as noted by Habersoth et al. (2008):

> I think it really helps me to make sure I'm reflecting or summarizing rather than going straight into a question. . . . It just seems like when you're face-to-face you're doing five things at once. You're attending, you're listening, you're processing yourself, and trying to think about what direction you want to go. Here, all you have to do is think about what directions you want to go, and just kind of process it. And so I find that you're better able to focus on that.
>
> (pp. 466–467)

Due to how the response timing can vary between an immediate, synchronous approach and an asynchronous approach, this will influence users' time to craft responses (Zizzi & Schmid, 2012). You must have your own filter about how responses are being formulated, not necessarily from yourself, but from your client as well.

Ethical Considerations

As we have discussed some of the ways to connect and various strengths and weaknesses of Connected Consulting, there are a few other ethical and moral considerations to take into account. The realm of Connected Consulting is different from that of FTF consulting. It is essential to make a full commitment to knowing oneself thoroughly and being able to recognize dynamics that come into play as communication with others without a bodily presence takes place (Anthony & Nagel, 2010). Anthony and Nagel (2010) expand further by explaining that, while you are trained in the ability to put yourself into someone else's shoes, and are able to do so through typed text, effectively, trusting the empathy felt for the client, and without diminishing their sense of potentially being alone, this is a skill that takes time and training to develop.

Hanley (2006) found that professionals raised the issues of contracting, confidentiality, and informed consent as concerns about Connected Consulting. Since all of these aspects must be considered when establishing a FTF consulting relationship as well, perhaps further steps need to be made clearer or approached with more caution when working in a Connected Consulting relationship.

The NBCC (2005) outlines some specific steps as to what can be done to protect the aforementioned concerns, stating:

- In situations where it is difficult to verify the identity of the client, steps are taken to address impostor concerns, such as by using code words or numbers.

- As part of the orientation process, the consultant collaborates with the client to identify a crisis intervention, if needed. This is typically covered in the informed consent process of referrals or an emergency contact (i.e. by calling 911).
- Consultants must follow appropriate procedures regarding the release of information for sharing client information with other electronic sources.
- The consultant informs the client of encryption methods being used to help ensure the security of client/consultant/supervisor communications. Encryption should be used whenever possible. If encryption is not made available to clients, clients must be informed of the potential hazards of unsecured communication.

AASP guidelines (AASP, 2011) further impress upon its members the need to take reasonable precautions to verify the privacy and confidentiality of electronic communications in their professional work.

Depending on your training, qualifications, and the work you plan on beginning with your client in your Connected Consulting relationship, you may have one more consideration to take note of—licensure. If you happen to be someone who is licensed to work in counseling, you must look into what your state and the client's state licensure rules are, for example, whether the counseling is considered to be taking place in your state or the client's (NBCC, 2016). The reason is that the client is viewed as traveling the information superhighway, like a client driving an interstate highway, and the Internet is not a free city in the sky where no standards apply (Midkiff & Joseph Wyatt, 2008). You should also consider the ethical implications of doing clinical/counseling work via such technologies and whether it is viable.

Before Beginning a Connected Consulting Relationship

Before you begin a Connected Consulting relationship, here are some questions to consider about whether it is a good fit for your style of consulting and training background.

How to Handle the Increased Connectivity You May Achieve with Connected Consulting

While there are many ethical and legal considerations to consider, and additional steps to protect client confidentiality through Connected Consulting, it gives you and your clients a way to stay current with success, challenges, failures, and changes the client experiences. Yet it can be quite daunting with the various ways you can be contacted by a client and how and what to respond to all the outreach. What this connected world creates is where you, the consultant, can become a *perfect parent* in some ways—where you are available 24 hours a day, seven days a week, for eternity. If this breaks down it can be unbearable for the client and can be likened to being let down by a parent (Anthony & Nagel, 2010).

By establishing clear guidelines and boundaries during the informed consent process, the client and yourself can distinguish appropriate communication windows with expected response times which don't make you appear that you do not want to reply or do not care, as well as determine to what extent your client desires to be accessible and with what degree of volume to be contacted (Zizzi & Schmid, 2012). Without realizing it, you can be perceived as a crutch or rescuer, and any subsequent feelings of abandonment, betrayal, or distress might lead the client to question your trusting and caring qualities (Zizzi & Schmid, 2012).

Text messaging is a simple example of where you can determine with your client how frequently communication can be used and for what purpose. Ways in which you can use

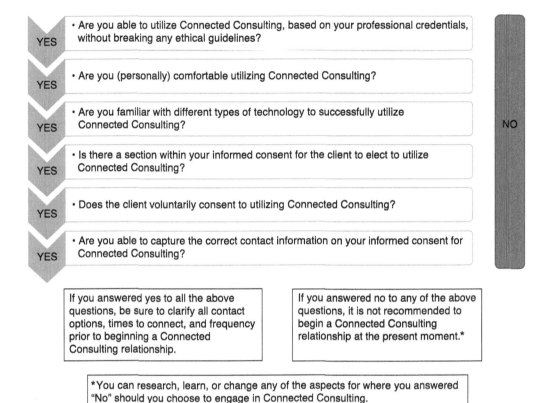

Figure 16.1 Determining whether to begin a Connected Consulting relationship

texting in your consulting include: reminders of an upcoming session, reminders of behavioral goals, self-affirmations or brief pre-competition messages that emphasize elements of previous sessions, post-competition debriefing such as congratulations, or to provide social support (Zizzi & Schmid, 2012). This list of ways are just examples and how text messaging is used can constantly be molded to benefit the client and should be discussed every so often. Yet a question that is imperative for you to consider is based on how frequently you text message, i.e. do you charge the client for your work via texts? As referenced earlier in the chapter, make sure you know your expectations for yourself and begin to draw out your limitations for your client relationship.

Conclusion

There are certainly costs and benefits to having a more Connected Consulting relationship with your clients and it is worth considering whether or not it is something you wish to use in your practice every time you consult (see figure 16.1). However, the increased use of non-traditional methods of communicating is hard to deny, and embracing them would seem fruitful, especially if working with younger generations of performers.

Zizzi and Perna (2002) discovered that electronic communication between consultant and client was preferred over traditional methods, yet the most common barrier for 87% of participants was a perceived lack of time to engage in consulting services. This is a barrier that to this day we continue to fight. Connected Consulting gives a resolution to this barrier by offering different ways to communicate that can be more time efficient.

Yet in order to help accommodate clients with the use of Connected Consulting, we must understand how to implement it in its fullest capacity. We have outlined in this chapter what Connected Consulting is and the different ways to engage in it, but it is not exhaustive. And as it is not exhaustive, the most critical piece is to familiarize yourself with what options are available to you. Research what is out there and then become familiar with a program by using it in a non-consulting capacity, with family or friends, until you become comfortable. Then, continue to gather information and ask questions from other professionals who are using similar services themselves. From that point on, you will have strong knowledge of the nuances that come with setting yourself up for the success of being there for your clients when it is physically impossible to do so.

We again must always keep in mind the ultimate purpose of applied sport psychology work; as consultants, we are merely an intermediary for our clients to build self-awareness and self-regulation, and to become self-sufficient in overcoming their challenges and achieving their performance goals. With the growing popularity of virtual and augmented reality, perhaps one day we will be sitting in the "same" location as our client, in a FTF scenario, but the reality being that we could be half a world away. There is no telling where Connected Consulting will take us and it is hardly realistic to think there will not be newer technology introduced to aid in our endeavor to stay connected.

A Trainee's Perspective on Connected Consulting

Tammara Bode, M.A., student at JFKU 2013–2017

Tammara is working full-time as a consultant with competitive gymnasts at Seattle Gymnastics Academy through her private practice in the Pacific Northwest. She works primarily with fear and performance anxiety for athletes in sports including gymnastics, rock climbing, BMX, and diving. She can be contacted at tbode@email.jfku.edu.

During my time as a student, I became very familiar and comfortable with different video-conferencing services such as Google Hangout, FaceTime, and Skype. Currently, as a practitioner, while meeting with clients face-to-face is important, I need to regularly connect with 17 different teams and individual athletes as they travel to different competitions. Without this technology and the possibility of Connected Consulting, it would be impossible to attend to and check in with the teams because they often compete during the same time frame in different locations. As I primarily work with youth athletes, it can be difficult to navigate tight daily time constraints with school, long practices, and homework. This is a common issue that can present itself in all domains and ages of sport. An effective way that I have discovered (to overcome time constraints) is to do a mini-session with athletes as they are driven to and from school using a tablet and video conferencing. For many athletes this provides that boost of confidence or reinforcement of the mental skills technique they need to have a successful practice that day.

One area of technology to explore more is texting (as indicated earlier in the chapter). I have become more conservative with texting in my private practice than as a student. During my Master's program, I did not have any challenges texting with my clients directly as they were all adults and able to give their own consent for using this medium. Currently, with my youth athletes, I will text the coaches and parents to set up the appointments. With youth athletes, texting directly is based on my comfort level and I make sure to set limitations and boundaries to the amount and timing of texting through the informed consent which helps to negate any ambiguity with what is appropriate for texting as part of consulting.

Reflective Questions and Activities for You to Consider Before You Proceed

- What technology are you using today that you can incorporate into your professional life?
- How would you do this?
- What would be your own personal challenges using the technology of today?
- How are you continuing your personal learning with new and changing technology?
- What backup plans can you establish in case your primary technology fails?
- What are your expectations of when and how to communicate with your clients?
- Regarding ethical and professional considerations, what considerations should you take into account with clients when being more connected?

References

AASP. (2011). Ethics code: AASP principles and standards. Retrieved from www.appliedsportpsych.org/about/ethics/ethics-code

Anderson, M. (2015, October). *Technology device ownership: 2015*. Retrieved from www.pewinternet.org/2015/10/29/technology-device-ownership-2015/

Anthony, K., & Nagel, D. M. (2010). *Therapy online: A practical guide.* London, UK: SAGE.

Bambling, M., King, R., Reid, W., & Wegner, K. (2008). Online counselling: The experience of counsellors providing synchronous single-session counselling to young people. *Counselling & Psychotherapy Research, 8*(2), 110–116. doi:10.1080/14733140802055011

Barak, A., Klein, B., & Proudfoot, J. G. (2009). Defining internet-supported therapeutic interventions. *Annals of Behavioral Science, 38*(1), 4–17. doi: 10.1007/s12160-009-9130-7

Cohen, G., & Kerr, B. (1998). Computer-mediated counseling: An empirical study of a new mental health treatment. *Computers in Human Services, 15*(4), 13–26. doi: 10.1300/J407v15n04_02

Day, S. X., & Schneider, P. L. (2002). Psychotherapy using distance technology: A comparison of face-to-face, video and audio treatment. *Journal of Counselling Psychology, 49*(4), 499–503. doi: 10.1037/0022-0167.49.4.499

Edunov, S., Diuk, C., Filiz, I. O., Bhagat, S., & Burke, M. (2016, February). *Three and a half degrees of separation*. Retrieved from https://research.facebook.com/blog/three-and-a-half-degrees-of-separation/

Finn, J., & Barak, A. (2010). A descriptive study of e-counsellor attitudes, ethics, and practice. *Counselling and Psychotherapy Research, 10*(4), 268–277. doi: 10.1080/14733140903380847

Habersoth, S., Parr, G., Bradley, L., Morgan-Fleming, B., & Gee, R. (2008). Facilitating online counseling: Perspectives from counselors in training. *Journal of Counseling & Development, 86*(4), 460–470. doi: 10.1002/j.1556-6678.2008.tb00534.x

Hanley, T. (2006). Developing youth-friendly online counselling services in the United Kingdom: A small scale investigation into the views of practitioners. *Counselling & Psychotherapy Research, 6*(3), 182–185. doi:10.1080/14733140600857535

Internet Live Stats. (2017, February). *Internet users*. Retrieved from www.internetlivestats.com/internet-users/

Midkiff, D. M., & Joseph Wyatt, W. (2008). Ethical issues in the provision of online mental health services. *Journal of Technology in Human Services, 26*(2–4), 310–332. doi: 10.1080/15228830802096994

Mitchell, J. E., Crosby, R. D., Wonderlich, S. A., Crow, S., Lancaster, K., Simonich, H., . . . Myers, T. C. (2008). A randomized trial comparing the efficacy of cognitive-behavioral therapy for bulimia nervosa delivered via telemedicine versus face-to-face. *Behaviour Research and Therapy, 46*(5), 581–592. doi:10.1016/j.brat.2008.02.004

National Board for Certified Counselors [NBCC]. (2005). *The practice of internet counseling.* Retrieved from www.nbcc.org/assets/ethics/internetcounseling.pdf

National Board for Certified Counselors [NBCC]. (2016). *National board for certified counselors (NBCC) policy regarding the provision of distance professional services.* Retrieved from www.nbcc.org/Assets/Ethics/NBCCPolicyRegardingPracticeofDistanceCounselingBoard.pdf

Reynolds Jr., D. A. J., Stiles, W. B., & Grohol, J. M. (2006). An investigation of session impact and alliance in Internet based psychotherapy: Preliminary results. *Counselling & Psychotherapy Research, 6*(3), 164–168. doi:10.1080/14733140600853617

Schneider, S. J., Schwartz, M. D., & Fast, J. (1995). Computerized, telephone-based health promotion: 1. Smoking cessation program. *Computers in Human Behavior, 11*(1), 135–148. doi: 10.1016/0747-5632(94)00027-F

Statista. (2017, February). *Number of mobile phone users worldwide from 2013 to 2019 (in billions).* Retrieved from www.statista.com/statistics/274774/forecast-of-mobile-phone-users-worldwide/

Wikipedia. (2016, May 21). *Frigyes Karinthy.* Retrieved from https://en.wikipedia.org/wiki/Frigyes_Karinthy

Zizzi, S. J., & Perna, F. M. (2002). Integrating web pages and e-mail into sport psychology consultations. *The Sport Psychologist, 16*(4), 416–431.

Zizzi, S., & Schmid, O. (2012). Reach out and text someone: The creative and effective use of text messaging in sport performance consultations. In R. Schinke (Ed.), *Athletic insight's writings in sport psychology* (pp. 317–327). Hauppauge, NY: Nova Science Publishers.

17 Continuing Education

There's Still More to Learn?

Brad Baumgardner and Katie Irwin

Post-training continuing education (CE) takes the form of formal and informal experiences. Formal experiences include attending workshops, seminars, conferences, and CE courses. Informal experiences include reading journal articles, books, learning from peer consultations, and contributing to discussion groups in the field. Continuing education is vital to a successful career and should include professional growth. This will occur when, for example, the need arises to learn a new sport culture, i.e. when asked to work with a team from a sport one knows little about. Taking the perspective that learning continues after school ends is key to continuing to develop oneself and one's practice. This chapter will address important resources to consult when leaving the relative security of the training environment and moving into the professional world of applied sport psychology.

Background Information on the Authors

Brad Baumgardner received his Master's Degree in Sport Psychology from JFKU. He is an AASP certified consultant and has presented at multiple conferences. Currently, he is working with the United States Army, teaching performance enhancement, resilience, team building, and academic performance to soldiers and Army Civilians. He also has a private practice where he works with athletes to help them meet their performance goals (www.mentalcomponent.com). Brad can be reached at Bbaumgardner@jfku.edu.

 Katie Irwin received her Master's Degree in Sport Psychology from JFKU. Currently, she is working with the United States Army, teaching performance enhancement, resilience, team building, and academic performance to soldiers and Army Civilians. She has worked in applied sport psychology for the last five years and maintains a private practice consulting with athletes (www.katieirwin.com). Katie can be reached at Kirwin@jfku.edu.

Whether you are a current student, a recent graduate, or a professional in the field, continued/continuing education (CE) is critical to success. Sport psychology is a relatively young field within psychology and researchers and consultants are continually advancing the knowledge and understanding of the discipline. Regardless of the field that a practitioner is in, motivation for professional growth is a key factor in the success of that individual. To experience professional growth, CE is a must. Pulling from the AASP Code of Ethics, those in the field must "maintain knowledge related to the services they render, and they recognize the need for ongoing education" (AASP, 2011, paragraph 8). Those who are AASP members must abide by this practice. For those who are not AASP members, we suggest that CE is a best practice for competent professionals. CE comes in many shapes and forms, and it is up to the individual to seek out what is appropriate for them. We will go into more detail about these different experiences (formal and informal CE options) below.

As you begin exploring the variety of options when it comes to CE, you first want to be aware of any special requirements that are needed for the certifications or licenses that you may possess. For example, if you are a certified consultant through AASP, you must "participate (by attending or conducting) in at least one continuing education workshop or course during each 5-year recertification cycle" and that workshop or course must be "comparable in depth or intensity to 6 hours of AASP pre-conference continuing education workshops" (Recertification, 2016, paragraph 6). If you are a licensed sport psychologist, the number of continuing education units varies by state. In California, for example, psychologists need "36 hours of Continuing Education (CE)" for each 2-year renewal period and, of those 36 hours, "a minimum of 25% (9 hours) must be 'live'" (Continuing Education Information, 2016, paragraph 1). Be sure to know your requirements depending on your title and where you are located.

Formal CE Options

When exploring formal opportunities, there are many different options to consider. The first experience we will discuss is attending conferences. Attending conferences is a great strategy for professional development. A conference is a formal meeting that is created to discuss various topics of a certain field. Sport psychology conferences are offered regionally, nationally, and internationally. Through AASP, for example, there are several regional conferences and one national conference offered each year. The national conference's location varies due to a three-year geographical rotation. Looking at other relevant professional organizations, other conferences include: the annual APA convention, the North American Society for Psychology of Sport and Physical Activity's annual meeting, BASES's Exercise and Sport Science Conference, National University's Center for Performance Psychology, ISSP's Sport Psychology Congress, and the International Convention on Science, Education and Medicine in Sport. Not only should one consider attending sport-psychology-specific conferences, but potentially think outside of the box as well. For example, it may be of interest for a professional to attend conferences geared toward coaches, specific sports, or other areas within psychology.

Conferences can vary quite drastically. For example, the size of a conference can go from just a handful of people to hundreds if not thousands in attendance. Often when you first arrive at a conference and check in, you receive your name tag and information regarding the conference. One of the things you will receive is a program guide with details regarding all of the sessions at the conference. You can also often acquire a copy of the program online before the conference. Before each day, read the title and the summary for each presentation, highlighting and noting the ones that seem most interesting to you. If more than one session at the same time is of interest to you, note the order in which they seem interesting and go to the first one. If after 15 minutes you do not feel like you are getting anything out of it, feel free to leave, quietly, and go to your second choice.

As you attend more conferences, you may begin to find that you have a particular type of presentation style that you prefer. Many conferences offer some combination, or all, of the following: symposia, workshops, lectures, posters, and panels. Symposia generally have three to five individuals speaking on different aspects with one underlying theme. One of the benefits of attending a symposium is that you can gain a greater understanding of that particular topic. Workshops are geared toward learning new approaches, techniques, or skills. They provide an opportunity to get hands-on experience under the leadership of the workshop presenters. This is a great place to pick up some new practical skills. Lectures can vary in length, from 10 minutes to an hour, and are focused on the research of the presenter(s). Often, several lectures are placed together under a common topic, although the presenters are not connected to each other as they are in a symposium; that is, the speakers in a symposium submit their proposal together, while grouped lectures are often assigned by the conference organizers. Panels consist of several members that are willing to share their experiences within a certain topic, and are typically set up in a Q&A format. This is a great opportunity to ask and get answers from practitioners with years of experience. Posters allow the opportunity to see what research is currently being done from around the field. In a poster session, presenters have created a large poster to present their research in a visual manner. A collection of posters will be in one given location of the conference and the presenter will stand next to their poster. Attendees of the conference will then browse through the posters and potentially discuss the work with the presenter.

A key part of attending a conference is meeting new people and building professional networks. Current students (undergraduate or graduate) may use the conference as an opportunity to help with their future in the field and to explore areas of study they are interested in. Professionals, both new and seasoned, can use the conference as an opportunity to build their connections and create a network. If you are attending a conference where you know some of the attendees, you might feel more comfortable spending time with the people you know. However, attending a conference is a perfect time to get out of your comfort zone and hear about the great work other people are doing. Do not be afraid to talk to people and ask questions at conferences. You will have the opportunity to meet individuals from around the field—make the most of it. Be sure to bring along a handful of business cards with your contact information to share with your new connections and do not forget to get the contact information of those you meet as well.

It is also important to remember to follow up with the people that you met at the conference. You will make many new connections and it is easy to lose contact with them if you do not immediately reach out. Building these relationships can become quite helpful in the future if you need to refer a client to another professional in a different geographical location, for potential employment opportunities, or even just to have a colleague with a different perspective on how to approach your work.

Another important point to consider is contributing something to the conference that you are planning on attending. More than likely by the time you have finished your degree, you have created some work that is of interest to others in this field. Some ideas that you may want to consider are any research that you have done, a project that you have completed, or even work that you have done with a particular population. This is a great opportunity to share with the sport psychology community what you have been working on as well as meet others who might be interested in the same topic. If you are planning on presenting your work with a particular team, be sure they have given you permission to disclose their identity if you are sharing information about them at a conference.

Along with attending conferences, one should also consider attending a workshop, a seminar, or even a webinar. These may be offered while attending a conference, but can also be offered separately throughout the year in various locations by various professional organizations/entities. Most workshops, seminars, and webinars come with an additional fee. These courses cover a broad range of topics instructed by professionals in the field. To find a list of available courses, you can check out online sites such as the AASP website.

Another formal option would be to take CE courses. Most psychologists and mental health professionals are required to take CE classes, and many universities offer classes that meet these requirements. Before signing up for one of these classes, it would serve you well to read about the course to make sure that it is relevant to you.

Informal CE Options

There are several inexpensive and easy ways to stay informed and current. One way to stay current with topics in the field is to join an email listserv. Two of the most used listservs in sport psychology in the U.S. are run by Dr. Michael Sachs at Temple University and APA Division 47. These two listservs allow individuals to post areas of research or information about relevant conferences or workshops, ask questions in relation to consulting, look for local referrals, and also discuss ethical issues. You will find that the users on these two listservs offer a range of insights to the various topics.

If you are planning to join an email listserv, it is important to know some of the formal and informal rules of the community. The APA Division 47 has a set of four formal rules, ranging from not using the email list for illegal purposes to not using it for "commercial" purposes (Division 47 Email List, 2016). One of the most important informal rules is to be very careful when you choose to reply to a post. Before replying, asking yourself is this something that only the original poster should receive, or is it something the whole group should receive? Then double and even triple check that you are sending it to the correct recipient before hitting send. Often times it is much more beneficial to just send the response to the original poster and then let them compile what they have received and send them all out in one email. This can dramatically reduce the amount of emails that the entire listserv is receiving. If you just want to thank someone for their contribution it is best to send it only to them. If you are planning on posting to the entire listserv, some points to consider are to make sure your email has a signature that includes your name, title, affiliation, and email address, and ensure your subject line is short and specific while the body of the email only contains the most important information. Since the listservs can be quite active, resulting in multiple emails a day, you might want to consider creating a second email address to receive them, or utilize your email's filter functions. Listservs are a great way to get the perspective of many different individuals from across the country or even worldwide. Some additional uses of a listserv can be when you are looking for research participants, or when you need to refer a client to a professional who specializes in a particular topic or is located in a certain region.

Peer Groups

While you are in graduate school, you have peers and professors to discuss clients, theories, and ethical dilemmas with, and to bounce ideas off. Once you have graduated, you may no longer have that level of built-in support readily available to you. To help with this, consider forming a peer group to utilize post-graduation. A peer group can be a small group of other sport psychology practitioners coming from either research, performance enhancement, or clinical backgrounds who meet regularly to support, provide feedback, and give each other advice. Rhodius and Sugarman (2014) suggest that a peer group is a great place to discuss ethical dilemmas and marketing ideas, network, share resources, find referral sources, and share recent experiences with clients to get different opinions on the best approach to take. There are many benefits to having a peer group, including professional development opportunities, building further motivation around your work, and creating camaraderie and support (Rhodius & Sugarman, 2014). When forming a peer group, you want to take a few things into consideration. Do you want to join an established peer group or begin a group of your own? If you are joining an already-established group, you may want to ask how long they have been established and how they feel about a new member joining the group. Some other considerations before joining a peer group include the size of the group, whether they meet online or in person, how available the individuals in the group are, and how much everyone participates.

If you are creating your own group, you will need to consider who you want to have as members in the group. Peer groups can consist of former students from your cohort, professionals who have been in the field for some time, recent graduates from other schools, or whoever else you see fit. Also, how many people would you want to have in the group? With too few members, will this meet the needs of the group? With too many, will people's voices be heard? Also, consider how often you want to meet, what it is that you want to discuss within each meeting, and what the guidelines are of being in the group. Some ideas to guide the discussions are marketing oneself, challenging clients/parents/coaches, self-care, and professional development. An ethical consideration to be aware of is maintaining client confidentiality when discussing any work you may be doing. If you are discussing a client's challenge with a peer group, be sure to not discuss any information that may give away your client's identity. One area to be mindful of is not letting one member of the group dominate the discussions, have the focus be solely on problem solving for their practice, or complain the whole time. When considering joining or starting a peer group, location also comes into play. If you live in an area where there are a lot of consultants, it will probably be more feasible to meet with a group in person. However, do not feel pressured to join a group if it does not meet your needs. If you are not near other consultants, then you may have to think about meeting with peer groups remotely.

Special Interest Groups

Another way to stay connected with others who are interested in the same topics as you is to join a special interest group (SIG) through any number of professional organizations. SIGs can revolve around many different topics, from specific sports to more general sport psychology topics. The goals of SIGs are to promote professional growth and increase interest in a particular topic (AASP Special Interest Groups, 2016). Many SIG members build relationships at conferences and then continue to interact throughout the year via email or group meetings. One way to join a SIG through AASP is to go to http://www.appliedsportpsych.org/about/special-interest-groups/ and contact the SIG Coordinator for the group you are interested in.

Other Informal Options

Another strong source for information is books and journals. To help guide you in the right direction, APA Division 47 has a great list of books and journals to get you started (http://www.apadivisions.org/division-47/about/resources/books-journals.aspx). The AASP website has additional resources as well (http://www.appliedsportpsych.org/resource-center/professional-resources-for-sport-and-exercise-psychology/). When considering which books to read, consider also checking out autobiographies and biographies of athletes and coaches, along with topics that are of interest to you. As you are reading these books, consider joining a book club with other consultants (or your peer group if you have one established). Once you have all finished your book of choice, you can have discussions geared toward how you can apply this information to your practice.

Read often and read from a variety of sources. Think outside of the box when it comes to what you are reading. You are not just limited to topics about sports or athletes. Consider other fields of performance (e.g. exercise, military, music, the performing arts, and business). Also, as you read, break it up into manageable chunks. You do not necessarily need to knock out an entire journal in one sitting. Maybe once you receive a new journal in the mail, read an article a day for that week.

Another way to approach your continued professional development is to ask yourself if there is a particular area you want to have a greater understanding in. Keeping this question in mind could potentially help direct where to devote your time and energy in continuing education. For example, if you want to work with a particular sport, say soccer, it would serve you well to invest your time with the sport. One could do additional readings in the sport, watch or attend various levels of soccer matches, seek out information about team sports, attend soccer coach conferences, and talk to current and former players. Keep in mind you do not need to be an expert in this sport but it would help to know some of the basic rules. Prior to working with the military, both of us had minimal knowledge of what working with that population would be like. We read countless articles on the use of sport psychology with the military, shadowed other professionals in the field, observed the soldiers in their given environments, and were not afraid to ask questions when we did not understand something. Even with our three-plus years of experience working with the military, we continue to gather additional information for working with this unique population.

To further your ongoing development, be open to new experiences. If you come across areas that interest you, see if there are ways you can bridge the gap with sport psychology. For instance, if you are interested in mindfulness, take a class and learn more about it. Another idea that you may not have covered in graduate school is hypnosis. This is not a Vegas-show version of hypnosis where you end up swinging a pocket watch in front of an individual until you can make them meow like a cat, but rather hypnosis or hypnotherapy can help individuals relax and even enhance their imagery experience. Another time to be open to new experiences is when clients tell you that they use a specific method to relax or prepare for a performance. An example of a new experience was when an athlete I (Brad) worked with liked to use a sensory deprivation tank to relax before competitions. Before his next session, I decided to give it a try so I knew how to include it in our work together.

Choosing the Right CE Options to Pursue

When considering what CE opportunities to pursue, there are additional considerations the trainee should make. Experiences can cost money, especially when it comes to formal experiences. The various conferences, workshops, and seminars come at a fee. Some of these fees, such as conference fees, are quite high and other expenses are often needed such as travel, lodging, and food; all together it can become quite expensive. CE courses also traditionally come with a fee as well. Be sure to identify what you will receive from this course after participating and ensure it meets the needs of what you are looking for. Also keep in mind that there are free courses as well, so be sure to look for those. We recommend staggering your attendance at these various conferences and seminars if you need to keep your budget in mind. Along with the formal experience costs, the informal experience prices can add up as well. Books, journals, and sporting events all come at a cost. Perhaps consider borrowing books from a colleague or a member in your peer group. If you are unable to borrow a book, consider buying books from a used-book store or getting them from the library. Ultimately, consider what the value is of the purchase when making the decision.

Along with money, you also need to consider the time commitment needed for these various experiences, both formal and informal. One way to help with the consideration of time is the idea of value. Do you have to take time off work to attend a conference or seminar? What is the time commitment for the class or workshop? The value of the experience should outweigh the cost. It would not make sense to put yourself in the hole if it does not pan out. Consider not only the price of the professional development but also the lost time of working with clients.

Conclusion

CE can seem like a daunting component of being a professional. To help make this more manageable, create a game plan of what you want to do. For some formal experiences you may have to reserve time on your calendar well in advance, while other experiences may be able to be planned out quarterly or monthly. Utilize your understanding of setting challenging yet realistic goals and set some for yourself. Set goals for how many listserv email threads you will follow/interact with, how many seminars/webinars you want to attend in a year, etc. With a solid game plan, you will have manageable things you can work on daily, weekly, and/or monthly. By planning and implementing CE, you will be on the path to being a stronger, more competent professional in the field.

A Trainee Perspective on Continuing Education

James Branham, M.A., M.B.A., student at JFKU 2011–2015

James currently lives in Lawton, Oklahoma, and is a Master-Resilience Trainer and Performance Expert for the Army Resilience Directorate at the Department of Defense and U.S. Army. He has developed leadership and team building programs for junior and senior enlisted leaders at Fort Sill to support the performance enhancement of the soldiers in Basic Combat Training and Advanced Individual Training at the U.S. Army's Fires Center of Excellence. He will continue to work with the U.S. Army as a MRT-PE and support the resilience and performance enhancement programs available to the soldiers and their families. He is finishing a Master's Degree in Sports Performance, to better understand how to bridge the gap between Sport Psychology and Sports Performance for coaches and leaders within the sport and fitness industry. James can be reached at jlbranham@ miperformance.com.

As I started my education in sport psychology, I made it my goal to attend the AASP National Conference and one regional conference every year. Doing so gave me access to experts in the field of sport psychology that I would not otherwise have had the opportunity to hear. In 2015, I attended a workshop on branding for sport psychology professionals where Dr. Jim Taylor discussed the importance of knowing my unique value proposition and developing my own performance model for what it means to be a successful sport psychology professional. Organizing my ideas and thoughts about how to best help clients optimize performance and achieve their goals helped me to better structure my consulting process. Early in my internship experiences I often felt like I was too rigid. I would enter a session with an idea of what we were going to cover, and I rarely veered off that plan. Putting together my performance model helped me to identify that meeting my clients' needs was one of my foremost goals, and that to do so I needed to be more flexible. With this in mind, in my later internships I made sure to involve my clients more in deciding which strategies to teach and also be open to pivoting when necessary.

CE is an ongoing experience for me. I am still and always will be in the process of becoming a better consultant. As a student it is not an easy process to balance the coursework and internships with additional reading and traveling for conferences. As a young professional, I face similar challenges. However, without a structure and process to further my own knowledge I cannot be the sport psychology professional I hope to be for my clients. By leveraging the experience of others, and the support provided by my peers, I can continue to grow and improve.

Reflective Questions and Activities for You to Consider Before You Proceed

- What formal CE options are available to me?
- What informal CE options are available to me?

Once you find CE options, consider the following:

- What is the added value of pursuing this CE experience?
- How will I grow/improve as a consultant with this information?
- What resources can I utilize to maximize my CE experience?
- What prevents me from getting the most out of the CE process?
- What are some of the potential obstacles that prevent me from completing CE?

References

AASP. (2011). *Ethics code: AASP ethical principles and standards*. Retrieved from www.appliedsportpsych.org/about/ethics/ethics-code/

AASP Special Interest Groups. (2016). Retrieved from www.appliedsportpsych.org/about/special-interest-groups/

Continuing Education Information. (2016). Retrieved from www.psychology.ca.gov/licensees/ce_faqs.shtml

Division 47 *Email List*. (2016). Retrieved from www.apadivisions.org/division-47/about/email/index.aspx

Recertification. (2016). Retrieved from www.appliedsportpsych.org/certified-consultants/recertification/

Rhodius, A., & Sugarman, K. (2014). Peer consultations with colleagues: The significance of gaining support and avoiding the "Lone Ranger trap." In J. G. Cremades & L. S. Tashman (Eds.), *Becoming a sport, exercise, and performance psychology professional: A global perspective*, (pp. 331–338). New York, NY: Psychology Press.

Index